COUNTERFEIT MIRACLES

COUNTERFEIT MIRACLES

BENJAMIN B. WARFIELD

THE BANNER OF TRUTH TRUST

THE BANNER OF TRUTH TRUST
3 Murrayfield Road, Edinburgh EH12 6EL
PO Box 621, Carlisle, Pennsylvania 17013, USA

*

First published 1918
First Banner of Truth Trust edition 1972
Reprinted 1976
Reprinted 1983
ISBN 0 85151 166 X

*

Printed in Great Britain by
McCorquodale (Scotland) Ltd., Glasgow

THIS VOLUME CONTAINS

THE THOMAS SMYTH LECTURES FOR 1917–1918

DELIVERED AT THE

COLUMBIA THEOLOGICAL SEMINARY

COLUMBIA, SOUTH CAROLINA

OCTOBER 4–10, 1917

IT IS DEDICATED TO

THE BOARD OF DIRECTORS AND THE FACULTY
OF COLUMBIA THEOLOGICAL SEMINARY

IN APPRECIATION OF
THEIR INVITATION TO DELIVER THE LECTURES
AND IN PLEASANT RECOLLECTION OF
THEIR MANY COURTESIES

CONTENTS

THE CESSATION OF THE CHARISMATA

THE CESSATION OF THE CHARISMATA

WHEN our Lord came down to earth He drew heaven with Him. The signs which accompanied His ministry were but the trailing clouds of glory which He brought from heaven, which is His home. The number of the miracles which He wrought may easily be underrated. It has been said that in effect He banished disease and death from Palestine for the three years of His ministry. If this is exaggeration it is pardonable exaggeration. Wherever He went, He brought a blessing:

> One hem but of the garment that He wore
> Could medicine whole countries of their pain;
> One touch of that pale hand could life restore.

We ordinarily greatly underestimate His beneficent activity as He went about, as Luke says, doing good.[1]*

His own divine power by which He began to found His church He continued in the Apostles whom He had chosen to complete this great work. They transmitted it in turn, as part of their own miracle-working and the crowning sign of their divine commission, to others, in the form of what the New Testament calls spiritual gifts[2] in the sense of extraordinary capacities produced in the early Christian communities by direct gift of the Holy Spirit.

The number and variety of these spiritual gifts were considerable. Even Paul's enumerations, the fullest of which occurs in the twelfth chapter of I Corinthians, can hardly be read as exhaustive scientific catalogues. The name which is commonly applied to them[3] is broad enough to embrace what may be called both the ordinary and the

* For all references see corresponding numbers at the end of the volume.

3

specifically extraordinary gifts of the Spirit; both those, that is, which were distinctively gracious, and those which were distinctly miraculous. In fact, in the classical passage which treats of them (I Cor. 12–14) both classes are brought together under this name. The non-miraculous, gracious gifts are, indeed, in this passage given the preference and called " the greatest gifts"; and the search after them is represented as "the more excellent way"; the longing for the highest of them—faith, hope, and love— being the most excellent way of all. Among the miraculous gifts themselves, a like distinction is made in favor of "prophecy" (that is, the gift of exhortation and teaching), and, in general, in favor of those by which the body of Christ is edified.

The diffusion of these miraculous gifts is, perhaps, quite generally underestimated. One of the valuable features of the passage, I Cor. 12–14, consists in the picture given in it of Christian worship in the Apostolic age (14 : 26 ff.).[4] "What is it, then, brethren?" the Apostle asks. "When ye come together, each one hath a psalm, hath a teaching, hath a revelation, hath a tongue, hath an interpretation. Let all things be done unto edifying. If any man speaketh in a tongue, let it be by two or at the most three, and that in turn; and let one interpret: but if there be no interpreter, let him keep silence in the church; and let him speak to himself, and to God. And let the prophets speak by two or three, and let the others discern. But if a revelation be made to another sitting by, let the first keep silence. For ye all can prophesy one by one, that all may learn, and all may be comforted; and the spirits of the prophets are subject to the prophets; for God is not a God of confusion, but of peace." This, it is to be observed, was the ordinary church worship at Corinth in the Apostles' day. It is analogous in form to the freedom of our modern prayer-meeting services. What chiefly distinguishes it from them is that those who took part in it might often have a mirac-

ulous gift to exercise, "a revelation, a tongue, an interpretation," as well as "a psalm or a teaching." There is
no reason to believe that the infant congregation at Corinth was singular in this. The Apostle does not write as
if he were describing a marvellous state of affairs peculiar
to that church. He even makes the transition to the next
item of his advice in the significant words, "as in all the
churches of the saints." And the hints in the rest of his
letters and in the Book of Acts require us, accordingly, to
look upon this beautiful picture of Christian worship as
one which would be true to life for any of the numerous
congregations planted by the Apostles in the length and
breadth of the world visited and preached to by them.

The argument may be extended to those items of the
fuller list, given in I Cor. 12, which found less occasion for
their exhibition in the formal meetings for worship, but
belonged more to life outside the meeting-room. That
enumeration includes among the extraordinary items, you
will remember, gifts of healings, workings of miracles,
prophecy, discernings of spirits, kinds of tongues, the interpretation of tongues—all of which, appropriate to the worshipping assembly, are repeated in I Cor. 14 : 26 ff. We
are justified in considering it characteristic of the Apostolic
churches that such miraculous gifts should be displayed in
them. The exception would be, not a church with, but a
church without, such gifts. Everywhere, the Apostolic
Church was marked out as itself a gift from God, by showing forth the possession of the Spirit in appropriate works
of the Spirit—miracles of healing and miracles of power,
miracles of knowledge, whether in the form of prophecy
or of the discerning of spirits, miracles of speech, whether
of the gift of tongues or of their interpretation. The
Apostolic Church was characteristically a miracle-working
church.[5]

How long did this state of things continue? It was
the characterizing peculiarity of specifically the Apostolic

Church, and it belonged therefore exclusively to the Apostolic age—although no doubt this designation may be taken with some latitude. These gifts were not the possession of the primitive Christian as such;[6] nor for that matter of the Apostolic Church or the Apostolic age for themselves; they were distinctively the authentication of the Apostles. They were part of the credentials of the Apostles as the authoritative agents of God in founding the church. Their function thus confined them to distinctively the Apostolic Church, and they necessarily passed away with it.[7] Of this we may make sure on the ground both of principle and of fact; that is to say both under the guidance of the New Testament teaching as to their origin and nature, and on the credit of the testimony of later ages as to their cessation. But I shall not stop at this point to adduce the proof of this. It will be sufficiently intimated in the criticism which I purpose to make of certain opposing opinions which have been current among students of the subject. My design is to state and examine the chief views which have been held favorable to the continuance of the charismata beyond the Apostolic age. In the process of this examination occasion will offer for noting whatever is needful to convince us that the possession of the charismata was confined to the Apostolic age.

The theologians of the post-Reformation era, a very clear-headed body of men, taught with great distinctness that the charismata ceased with the Apostolic age. But this teaching gradually gave way, pretty generally throughout the Protestant churches, but especially in England, to the view that they continued for a while in the post-Apostolic period, and only slowly died out like a light fading by increasing distance from its source.[8] The period most commonly set for their continuance is three centuries; the date of their cessation is ordinarily said to have been about the time of Constantine. This, as early as the opening of the eighteenth century, had become the leading opinion, at least among theologians of the Anglican school, as Conyers Middleton, writing in the middle of that century, advises us. "The most prevailing opinion," he says in his *Introductory Discourse* to a famous book to be more fully described by and by, "is that they subsisted through the first three centuries, and then ceased in the beginning of the fourth, or as soon as Christianity came to be established by the civil power. This, I say, seems to be the most prevailing notion at this day among the generality of the Protestants, who think it reasonable to imagine that miracles should then cease, when the end of them was obtained and the church no longer in want of them; being now delivered from all danger, and secure of success, under the protection of the greatest power on earth." [9]

Middleton supports this statement with instances which bring out so clearly the essential elements of the opinion that they may profitably be quoted here. Archbishop John Tillotson represents "that on the first planting of the Christian religion in the world, God was pleased to accompany it with a miraculous power; but after it was planted, that power ceased, and God left it to be maintained by ordinary ways." So, Nathaniel Marshall wrote, "that there are successive evidences of them, which speak full and home to this point, from the beginning down to the age of Constantine, in whose time, when Christianity had acquired the support of human powers, those extraordinary assistances were discontinued." Others, sharing the same general point of view, would postpone a little the date of entire cessation. Thus the elder Henry Dodwell supposes true miracles to have generally ceased with the conversion of the Roman Empire, yet admits some special miracles, which seem to him to be exceptionally well attested, up to the close of the fourth century. Daniel Waterland, in the body of his treatise on the *Trinity*, speaks of miracles as continuing through the first three centuries at least, and in the Addenda extends this through the fourth. John

Chapman's mode of statement is "that though the establishment of Christianity by the civil power abated the necessity of miracles, and occasioned a visible decrease of
them, yet, after that revolution, there were instances of
them still, as public, as clear, as well-attested as any in the
earlier ages." He extends these instances not only through
the fourth century but also through the fifth—which, he
says, "had also its portion, though smaller than the fourth."
William Whiston, looking upon the charismata less as the
divine means of extending the church than as the signs of
the divine favor on the church in its pure beginnings, sets
the date of their cessation at A. D. 381, which marks the
triumph of Athanasianism; that being to him, as an Arian,
the final victory of error in the church—which naturally
put a stop to such manifestations of God's favor. It is a
similar idea from his own point of view which is given expression by John Wesley in one of his not always consistent
declarations on the subject. He supposes that miracles
stopped when the empire became Christian, because then,
"a general corruption both of faith and morals infected the
church—which by that revolution, as St. Jerome says, lost
as much of its virtue as it had gained of wealth and
power." [10] These slight extensions of the time during
which the miracles are supposed to persist, do not essentially alter the general view, though they have their significance—a very important significance which Middleton
was not slow to perceive, and to which we shall revert
later.

The general view itself has lost none of its popularity
with the lapse of time. It became more, rather than less,
wide-spread with the passage of the eighteenth into the
nineteenth century, and it remains very usual still. I need
not occupy your time with the citation of numerous more
recent expressions of it. It may suffice to adduce so popular a historian as Gerhard Uhlhorn who, in his useful book
on *The Conflict of Christianity with Heathenism*,[11] declares

explicitly that "witnesses who are above suspicion leave no room for doubt that the miraculous powers of the Apostolic age continued to operate at least into the third century." A somewhat special turn is given to the same general idea by another historian of the highest standing—Bishop Mandel Creighton. "The Apostles," he tells us,[12] "were endowed with extraordinary powers, necessary for the establishment of the church, but not necessary for its permanent maintenance. These powers were exercised for healing the sick and for conveying special gifts of the Holy Spirit; sometimes, but rarely, they were used for punishment. . . . These special powers were committed to the church as a means of teaching it the abiding presence of God. They were withdrawn when they had served their purpose of indicating the duties to be permanently performed. To 'gifts of tongues' succeeded orderly human teaching; to 'gifts of healing' succeeded healing by educated human skill; to supernatural punishment succeeded discipline by orderly human agency."

This, then, is the theory: that, miracles having been given for the purpose of founding the church, they continued so long as they were needed for that purpose; growing gradually fewer as they were less needed, and ceasing altogether when the church having, so to speak, been firmly put upon its feet, was able to stand on its own legs. There is much that is attractive in this theory and much that is plausible: so much that is both attractive and plausible that it has won the suffrages of these historians and scholars though it contradicts the whole drift of the evidence of the facts, and the entire weight of probability as well. For it is only simple truth to say that both the ascertained facts and the precedent presumptions array themselves in opposition to this construction of the history of the charismata in the church.

The facts are not in accordance with it. The view requires us to believe that the rich manifestations of spiritual gifts present in the Apostolic Church, gradually grew less through the succeeding centuries until they finally dwindled away by the end of the third century or a little later. Whereas the direct evidence for miracle-working in the church is actually of precisely the contrary tenor. There is little or no evidence at all for miracle-working during the first fifty years of the post-Apostolic church; it is slight and unimportant for the next fifty years; it grows more abundant during the next century (the third); and it becomes abundant and precise only in the fourth century, to increase still further in the fifth and beyond. Thus, if the evidence is worth anything at all, instead of a regularly progressing decrease, there was a steadily growing increase of miracle-working from the beginning on. This is doubtless the meaning of the inability of certain of the scholars whom we have quoted, after having allowed that the Apostolic miracles continued through the first three centuries, to stop there; there is a much greater abundance and precision of evidence, such as it is, for miracles in the fourth and the succeeding centuries, than for the preceding ones.

The matter is of sufficient interest to warrant the statement of the facts as to the evidence somewhat more in detail. The writings of the so-called Apostolic Fathers contain no clear and certain allusions to miracle-working or to the exercise of the charismatic gifts, contemporaneously with themselves.[13] These writers inculcate the elements of Christian living in a spirit so simple and sober as to be worthy of their place as the immediate followers of the Apostles. Their anxiety with reference to themselves seems to be lest they should be esteemed overmuch and confounded in their pretensions with the Apostles, rather than to press claims to station, dignity, or powers similar to theirs.[14] So characteristic is this sobriety of attitude of their age, that the occurrence of accounts of miracles in the letter of the church of Smyrna narrating the story of the martyrdom of Polycarp is a recognized difficulty in the way

of admitting the genuineness of that letter.[15] Polycarp
was martyred in 155 A. D.   Already by that date, we meet
with the beginnings of general assertions of the presence of
miraculous powers in the church.   These occur in some
passages of the writings of Justin Martyr.   The exact nature of Justin's testimony is summed up by Bishop John
Kaye as follows:[16]   "Living so nearly as Justin did to the
Apostolic age, it will naturally be asked whether, among
other causes of the diffusion of Christianity, he specifies
the exercise of miraculous powers by the Christians.   He
says in general terms that such powers subsisted in the
church (*Dial.*, pp. 254 ff.)—that Christians were endowed
with the gift of prophecy (*Dial.*, p. 308 B, see also p. 315 B)
—and in an enumeration of supernatural gifts conferred
on Christians, he mentions that of healing (*Dial.*, p. 258 A).
We have seen also, in a former chapter, that he ascribes
to Christians the power of exorcising demons (chap. VIII).
But he produces no particular instance of an exercise of
miraculous power, and therefore affords us no opportunity
of applying those tests by which the credibility of miracles
must be tried."   And then the bishop adds, by way of
quickening our sense of the meaning of these facts: "Had
it only been generally stated by the Evangelists that Christ
performed miracles, and had no particular miracle been recorded, how much less satisfactory would the Gospel narratives have appeared! how greatly their evidence in support of our Saviour's divine mission been diminished!"

This beginning of testimony is followed up to precisely
the same effect by Irenæus, except that Irenæus speaks
somewhat more explicitly, and adds a mention of two new
classes of miracles—those of speaking with tongues and of
raising the dead, to both of which varieties he is the sole
witness during these centuries, and of the latter of which
at least he manages so to speak as to suggest that he is
not testifying to anything he had himself witnessed.[17]
Irenæus's contemporary, indeed, Theophilus of Antioch,

while, like Irenæus, speaking of the exorcism of demons as a standing Christian miracle, when challenged by Autolycus to produce but one dead man who had been raised to life, discovers by his reply that there was none to produce; and "no instance of this miracle was ever produced in the first three centuries." [18] For the rest, we say, Irenæus's witness is wholly similar to Justin's. He speaks altogether generally, adducing no specific cases, but ascribing miracle-working to "all who were truly disciples of Jesus," each according to the gift he had received, and enumerating especially gifts of exorcism, prediction, healing, raising the dead, speaking with tongues, insight into secrets, and expounding the Scriptures (*Cont. Hær.*, II, lvi, lvii; V, vi).[19] Tertullian in like manner speaks of exorcisms, and adduces one case of a prophetically gifted woman (*Apol.*, xxviii; *De Anima*, ix); and Minucius Felix speaks of exorcism (*Oct.*, xxvi).[20] Origen professes to have been an eye-witness of many instances of exorcism, healing, and prophecy, although he refuses to record the details lest he should rouse the laughter of the unbeliever (*Cont. Cels.*, I, ii; III, xxiv; VII, iv, lxvii). Cyprian speaks of gifts of visions and exorcisms. And so we pass on to the fourth century in an ever-increasing stream, but without a single writer having claimed himself to have wrought a miracle of any kind or having ascribed miracle-working to any known name in the church, and without a single instance having been recorded in detail. The contrast of this with the testimony of the fourth century is very great. There we have the greatest writers recording instances witnessed by themselves with the greatest circumstantiality. The miracles of the first three centuries, however, if accepted at all, must be accepted on the general assertion that such things occurred— a general assertion which itself is wholly lacking until the middle of the second century and which, when it does appear, concerns chiefly prophecy and healings, including especially exorcisms,[21] which we can scarcely be wrong in supposing precisely the classes of marvels with respect to which excitement most easily blinds the judgment and insufficiently grounded rumors most readily grow up.[22]

We are no doubt startled to find Irenæus, in the midst of delivering what is apparently merely a conventional testimony to the occurrence of these minor things, suddenly adding his witness to the occurrence also of the tremendous miracle of raising the dead. The importance of this phenomenon may be thought to require that we should give a little closer scrutiny to it, and this the more because of the mocking comment which Gibbon has founded on it. "But the miraculous cure of diseases of the most inveterate or even preternatural kind," says he,[23] "can no longer occasion any surprise when we recollect that in the days of Irenæus, about the end of the second century, the resurrection of the dead was very far from being esteemed an uncommon event; that the miracle was frequently performed on necessary occasions, by great fasting and the joint supplication of the church of the place; and that the persons thus restored by their prayers had lived afterward among them many years. At such a period, when faith could boast of so many wonderful victories over death, it seems difficult to account for the scepticism of those philosophers who still rejected and derided the doctrine of the resurrection. A noble Grecian had rested on this important ground the whole controversy, and promised Theophilus, bishop of Antioch, that, if he could be gratified by the sight of a single person who had been actually raised from the dead, he would immediately embrace the Christian religion. It is somewhat remarkable that the prelate of the first Eastern church, however anxious for the conversion of his friend, thought proper to decline this fair and reasonable challenge."

The true character of Gibbon's satirical remarks is already apparent from the circumstances to which we have already alluded, that Irenæus alone of all the writers of this

period speaks of raisings of the dead at all, and that he
speaks of them after a fashion which suggests that he has
in mind not contemporary but past instances—doubtless
those recorded in the narratives of the New Testament.[24]
Eusebius does no doubt narrate what he calls "a wonderful story," told by Papias on the authority of the daughters of Philip, whom Papias knew. "For," says Eusebius,
"he relates that in his time," that is to say in Philip's time,
"one rose from the dead." [25]   This resuscitation, however,
it will be observed, belongs to the Apostolic, not the post-
Apostolic times, and it is so spoken of as to suggest that it
was thought very wonderful both by Eusebius and by Papias.   It is very clear that Eusebius was not familiar with
raisings from the dead in his own day, and also that Papias
was not familiar with them in his day;[26] and it is equally
clear that Eusebius did not know of numerous instances
of such a transaction having been recorded as occurring in
the course of the early history of the church, which history
he was in the act of transcribing.[27]   One would think that
this would carry with it the implication that Eusebius did
not understand Irenæus to assert their frequent, or even
occasional, or even singular, occurrence in his time.   Nevertheless when he comes to cite Irenæus's witness to the continuance "to his time in some of the churches"—so he
cautiously expresses himself—"of manifestations of divine
and miraculous power," he quotes his words here after a
fashion which seems to imply that he understood him to
testify to the occurrence in his own time of raisings from
the dead.[28]

It is an understatement to say that Irenæus's contemporaries were unaware that the dead were being raised in
their day.   What they say amounts to testimony that they
were not being raised.   This is true not only of the manner
in which Theophilus of Antioch parries the demands of
Autolycus,[29] but equally of the manner in which Tertullian
reverts to the matter.   He is engaged specifically in con-

trasting the Apostles with their "companions," that is, their immediate successors in the church, with a view to rebuking the deference which was being paid to the *Shepherd* of Hermas. Among the contrasts which obtained between them, he says that the Apostles possessed spiritual powers peculiar to themselves, that is to say, not shared by their successors. He illustrates this, among other things, by declaring, "For they raised the dead."[30] It would be strange indeed if Irenæus has nevertheless represented raisings from the dead to have been a common occurrence precisely in the church of Theophilus and Tertullian.

A scrutiny of his language makes it plain enough that he has not done so. In the passages cited [31] Irenæus is contrasting the miracles performed by Christians with the poor magical wonders to which alone the heretics he is engaged in refuting can appeal. In doing this he has in mind the whole miraculous attestation of Christianity, and not merely the particular miracles which could be witnessed in his own day. If we will read him carefully we shall observe that, as he runs along in his enumeration of the Christian marvels, "there is a sudden and unexpected change of tense when he begins to speak of this greatest of miracles" —raising from the dead. "Healing, exorcism, and prophecy—these he asserts are matters of present experience; but he never says that of resurrection from the dead. 'It often happened,' *i. e.*, in the past; 'they were raised up,' *i. e.*, again at some time gone by. The use of the past tense here, and here alone, implies, we may say, that Irenæus had not witnessed an example with his own eyes, or at least that such occurrences were not usual when he was writing. So, when he states, 'Even the dead were raised and abode with us many years'—it does not appear that he means anything more than this—that such events happened within living memory." In these last remarks we have been quoting J. H. Bernard, and we find ourselves fully in accord with his conclusion.[32] "The inference from the whole passage," says he, "is, we believe, that these major miracles no longer happened—an inference which is corroborated by all the testimony we have got."

When we come to think of it, it is rather surprising that the Christians had no raisings from the dead to point to through all these years. The fact is striking testimony to the marked sobriety of their spirit. The heathen had them in plenty.[33] In an age so innocent of real medical knowledge, and filled to the brim and overflowing with superstition, apparent death and resuscitation were frequent, and they played a rôle of importance in the Greek prophet and philosopher legends of the time.[34] A famous instance occurs in Philostratus's *Life of Apollonius of Tyana*, which, from a certain resemblance between it and the narrative of the raising of the widow of Nain's son, used to be thought an imitation of that passage.[35] Things are better understood now, and it is universally recognized that we have in this beautiful story neither an imitation of the New Testament nor a polemic against it, but a simple product of the aretalogy of the day. Otto Weinreich has brought together the cases of raising from the dead which occur in this literature, in the first excursus to his treatise on *Ancient Miracles of Healing*.[36] He thus enables us to observe at a glance the large place they take in it. It is noticeable that they were not esteemed a very great thing. In the instance just alluded to, the introduction of a resuscitation into Philostratus's *Life of Apollonius* is accompanied by an intimation that it may possibly be susceptible of a natural explanation. Philostratus does not desire to make the glory of his hero depend on a thing which even a common magician could do, but rather rests it on those greater miracles which intimate the divine nature of the man.[37]

You probably would like to have the account which Philostratus gives of this miracle before you. "Here too," he writes,[38] "is a miracle which Apollonius worked: A girl had died just in the hour of her marriage, and the bridegroom was following her bier lamenting, as was natural, his marriage left unfulfilled; and the whole of Rome was mourning with him, for the maiden belonged to a consular family. Apollonius, then, witnessing their grief, said: 'Put down the bier, for I will stay the tears that you are shedding for this maiden.' And withal he asked what was her name. The crowd accordingly thought he was about to deliver such an oration as is commonly delivered as much to grace the funeral as to stir up lamentation; but he did nothing of the kind, but merely touching her and whispering in secret some spell over her, at once woke up the maiden from her seeming death; and the girl spoke out loud and returned to her father's house; just as Alkestis did when she was brought back to life by Herakles. And the relations of the maiden wanted to present him with one hundred and fifty thousand sesterces, but he said that he would freely present the money to the young lady by way of a dowry. Now, whether he detected some spark of life in her, which those who were nursing her had not discovered—for it is said that, although it was raining at the time, a vapor went up from her face—or whether life was really extinct, and he restored it by the warmth of his touch, is a mysterious problem which neither I myself nor those who were present could decide."

We are naturally led at this point to introduce a further remark which has its importance for the understanding of the facts of the testimony. All that has been heretofore said concerns the church writers, properly so-called, the literary remains of the church considered as the body of right-believing Christians. Alongside of this literature, however, there existed a flourishing growth of apocryphal writings—Acts of Apostles and the like—springing up in the fertile soil of Ebionitish and Gnostic heresy, the most respectable example of which is furnished by the Clementina. In these anonymous, or more usually pseudonymous, writings, there is no dearth of miraculous story, from what-

ever age they come. Later, these wild and miracle-laden
documents were taken over into the Catholic church, usually after a certain amount of reworking by which they
were cleansed to a greater or less—usually less—extent of
their heresies, but not in the least bit of their apocryphal
miracle-stories. Indeed, by the relative elimination of
their heresies in the Catholic reworking, their *teratologia*—
as the pedants call their miracle-mongering—was made
even more the prominent feature of these documents, and
more exclusively the sole purpose of their narrative.[39] It
is from these apocryphal miracle-stories and not from the
miracles of the New Testament, that the luxuriant growth
of the miraculous stories of later ecclesiastical writings draw
their descent. And this is as much as to say that their
ultimate parentage must be traced to those heathen wonder-tales to which we have just had occasion to allude.

For the literary form exemplified in the *Wanderings of the
Apostles* was not an innovation of the Christian heretics,
but had already enjoyed a vast popularity in the heathen
romances which swarmed under the empire, and the best
known names of which are Antonius Diogenes's *Incredible
Tales of Beyond Thule*, Jamblicus's *Babylonian Tales*, the
Ephesian Stories of the later Xenophon, the *Ethiopians* of
Heliodorus, the romances of Achiles Tatius and of Chari-
ton, not to mention the *Metamorphoses* of Apuleius.[40] R.
Reitzenstein no doubt insists that we shall draw into a
somewhat narrower category and no longer speak of these
wonder-tales with which we have here especially to do,
broadly, as romances. He wishes to retain that term to
describe a highly artistic literary form which, developing
out of the historical monograph, was strictly governed by
technical laws of composition derived ultimately from the
drama. With the romance in this narrow sense, the collections of marvellous stories loosely strung together in the
wonder-tales have but a distant relationship. We must
not confuse, Reitzenstein counsels us, two kinds of fiction,

which were sharply distinguished in ancient æsthetics, πλάσμα and ψεῦδος,[41] or mix up two literary forms which were quite distinct in their whole technic and style— merely because they were born together and grew up side by side. The romance plays on every string of human emotion; the wonder-tale—*aretalogy* is the name which Reitzenstein gives to this literary form—strikes but one note, and has as its single end to arouse astonishment.[42] It represented in the ancient world, though in an immensely more serious vein, our modern *Gulliver's Travels* or *Adventures of Baron Munchausen*, which in fact are parodies of it, like their inimitable forerunners with which Lucian has delighted the centuries. It will be readily understood that the wonder-tale—the motives of the travelling prophet or philosopher having been fairly worked out—should eagerly seize on the new material offered it by Christianity. But as Von Dobschütz remarks,[43] the matter did not end by its seizing on Christianity. Christianity turned the tables on it and seized on it, and produced out of it the mission aretalogy which we know in general as the Apocryphal Acts of the Apostles.

With its passage thus into Christian hands this literary form lost none of its marvel-mongery—to have lost which would have been to have lost its soul. "'Teratology,' 'marvellousness,'" explains Von Dobschütz,[44] "is the fundamental element of these Christian romances also. This is made very clear," he goes on to say, "by the circumstance that it is regularly magic of which the Apostles are represented as being accused. Of course they do not admit that the accusation is just. Magical arts are demonic arts, and it was precisely every kind of demonic power against which they set themselves in the almighty name of Jesus Christ. It is most impressively shown that to this name every knee in heaven and on earth and under the earth is to bow. We cannot help seeing, however, that only another form of magic, a Christian magic, steps here into the place of the heathen. The name of Jesus serves as the all-powerful spell, the cross as the irresistible charm, by which bolts can be sprung, doors opened, idols overturned, poison rendered harmless, the sick healed, the dead raised. The demonic flight of the magician is confounded by the prayer of the Apostles; they are none the less themselves carried home on the clouds, through the air." Something new entered Christianity in these wonder-tales; something unknown to the Christianity of the Apostles, unknown to the Apostolic churches, and unknown to their sober successors; and it entered Christianity from without, not through the door, but climbing up some other way. It brought an abundance of miracle-working with it; and, unfortunately, it brought it to stay. But from a contemplation of the swelling flood of marvels thus introduced into Christianity, obviously, the theory of the gradual cessation of miracle-working in the church through three centuries, which we are now examining, can derive no support.[45]

It may be justly asked, how it can be accounted for that so large a body of students of history can have committed themselves to a view which so clearly runs in the face of the plainest facts of the very history they are setting themselves to explain. The answer is doubtless to be found in the curious power which preconceived theory has to blind men to facts. The theory which these scholars had been led to adopt as to the cessation of miraculous powers in the church required the course of events which they assume to have happened. They recognized the abundant development of miraculous gifts in the Apostolic Church, and they argued that this wide-spread endowment could scarcely fail suddenly, but must have died out gradually. In estimating the length of time through which the miracle-working might justly be supposed to subsist, and at the end of which it might naturally be expected to have died out, they were unfortunately determined by a theory of the function of these miracles in the Apostolic Church which was plausible indeed, and because plausible attractive, but which was not founded on an accurate ascertainment of the teaching of the New Testament on the subject, and therefore so missed the truth that, in its application to the history of the early church, it exactly reversed it. This theory is in brief, I may remind you, that the miraculous powers present in the early church had for their end supernatural assistance in founding the church; that they were therefore needed throughout the period of the church's weak infancy, being in brief, as Fuller calls them, "the swaddling-clothes of the infant churches"; and that naturally they were withdrawn when their end had been accomplished and Christianity had ascended the throne of the empire. When the protection of the strongest power on earth was secured, the idea seems to be, the power of God was no longer needed.[46]

But whence can we learn this to have been the end the miracles of the Apostolic age were intended to serve? Certainly not from the New Testament. In it not one word is ever dropped to this effect. Certain of the gifts (as, for example, the gift of tongues) are no doubt spoken of as "signs to those that are without." It is required of all of them that they be exercised for the edification of the church; and a distinction is drawn between them in value, in proportion as they were for edification. But the immediate end for which they were given is not left doubtful, and that proves to be not directly the extension of the church, but the authentication of the Apostles as messengers from God. This does not mean, of course, that only the Apostles appear in the New Testament as working miracles, or that they alone are represented as recipients of the charismata. But it does mean that the charismata belonged, in a true sense, to the Apostles, and constituted one of the signs of an Apostle. Only in the two great initial instances of the descent of the Spirit at Pentecost and the reception of Cornelius are charismata recorded as conferred without

the laying on of the hands of Apostles.[47]   There is no instance on record of their conference by the laying on of the
hands of any one else than an Apostle.[48]   The case of the
Samaritans, recorded in the eighth chapter of Acts, is not
only a very instructive one in itself, but may even be looked
upon as the cardinal instance.   The church had been propagated hitherto by the immediately evangelistic work of
the Apostles themselves, and it had been accordingly the
Apostles themselves who had received the converts into
the church.   Apparently they had all received the power
of working signs by the laying on of the Apostles' hands at
their baptism.   The Samaritans were the first converts to
be gathered into the church by men who were not Apostles;
and the signs of the Apostles were accordingly lacking to
them until Peter and John were sent down to them that
they might "receive the Holy Ghost" (Acts 8 : 14-17).
The effect on Simon Magus of the sight of these gifts springing up on the laying on of the Apostles' hands, we will all
remember.   The salient statements are very explicit.
"Then laid they their hands upon them, and they received
the Holy Ghost."   "Now when Simon saw that through
the laying on of the Apostles' hands the Holy Ghost was
given."   "Give me also this power, that, on whomsoever
I lay my hands, he may receive the Holy Ghost."   It could
not be more emphatically stated that the Holy Ghost was
conferred by the laying on of the hands, specifically of the
Apostles, and of the Apostles alone; what Simon is said to
have seen is precisely that it was through the laying on of
the hands of just the Apostles that the Holy Ghost was
given.   And there can be no question that it was specifically
the extraordinary gifts of the Spirit that were in discussion; no doubt is thrown upon the genuineness of the conversion of the Samaritans; on the contrary, this is taken as
a matter of course, and its assumption underlies the whole
narrative; it constitutes in fact the very point of the narrative.

This case of the Samaritans was of great importance in the primitive church, to enable men to distinguish between the gifts of grace and the gifts of power. Without it there would have been danger that only those would be accredited as Christians who possessed extraordinary gifts. It is of equal importance to us, to teach us the source of the gifts of power, in the Apostles, apart from whom they were not conferred: as also their function, to authenticate the Apostles as the authoritative founders of the church. It is in accordance with this reading of the significance of this incident, that Paul, who had all the signs of an Apostle, had also the power of conferring the charismata, and that in the entire New Testament we meet with no instance of the gifts showing themselves—after the initial instances of Pentecost and Cornelius—where an Apostle had not conveyed them. Hermann Cremer is accordingly quite right when he says[49] that "the Apostolic charismata bear the same relation to those of the ministry that the Apostolic office does to the pastoral office"; the extraordinary gifts belonged to the extraordinary office and showed themselves only in connection with its activities.[50]

The connection of the supernatural gifts with the Apostles is so obvious that one wonders that so many students have missed it, and have sought an account of them in some other quarter. The true account has always been recognized, however, by some of the more careful students of the subject. It has been clearly set forth, for example, by Bishop Kaye. "I may be allowed to state the conclusion," he writes,[51] "to which I have myself been led by a comparison of the statements in the Book of Acts with the writings of the Fathers of the second century. My conclusion then is, that the power of working miracles was not extended beyond the disciples upon whom the Apostles conferred it by the imposition of their hands. As the number of these disciples gradually diminished, the instances of the exercise of miraculous powers became continually less

frequent, and ceased entirely at the death of the last individual on whom the hands of the Apostles had been laid.
That event would, in the natural course of things, take place
before the middle of the second century—at a time when
Christianity, having obtained a footing in all the provinces
of the Roman Empire, the miraculous gifts conferred upon
the first teachers had performed their appropriate office—
that of proving to the world that a new revelation had been
given from heaven. What, then, would be the effect produced upon the minds of the great body of Christians by
their gradual cessation? Many would not observe, none
would be willing to observe, it. . . . They who remarked
the cessation of miracles would probably succeed in per-
suading themselves that it was only temporary and designed by an all-wise Providence to be the prelude to a
more abundant effusion of the supernatural powers upon
the church. Or if doubts and misgivings crossed their
minds, they would still be unwilling to state a fact which
might shake the steadfastness of their friends, and would
certainly be urged by the enemies of the gospel as an argument against its divine origin. They would pursue the
plan which has been pursued by Justin Martyr, Theophilus,
Irenæus, etc.; they would have recourse to general assertions of the existence of supernatural powers, without attempting to produce a specific instance of their exercise. . . ." The bishop then proceeds to recapitulate the
main points and grounds of this theory.[52]

Whatever we may think of the specific explanation which
Bishop Kaye presents of the language of the second-cen-
tury Fathers, we can scarcely fail to perceive that the confinement of the supernatural gifts by the Scriptures to those
who had them conferred upon them by the Apostles, affords
a ready explanation of all the historical facts. It explains
the unobserved dying out of these gifts. It even explains
—what might at first sight seem inconsistent with it—the
failure of allusion to them in the first half of the second

century. The great missionary Apostles, Paul and Peter, had passed away by A. D. 68, and apparently only John was left in extreme old age until the last decade of the first century. The number of those upon whom the hands of Apostles had been laid, living still in the second century, cannot have been very large. We know of course of John's pupil Polycarp; we may add perhaps an Ignatius, a Papias, a Clement, possibly a Hermas, or even a Leucius; but at the most there are few of whom we know with any definiteness. That Justin and Irenæus and their contemporaries allude to miracle-working as a thing which had to their knowledge existed in their day, and yet with which they seem to have little exact personal acquaintance, is also explained. Irenæus's youth was spent in the company of pupils of the Apostles; Justin may easily have known of, if not even witnessed, miracles wrought by Apostolically trained men. The fault of these writers need have been no more than a failure to observe, or to acknowledge, the cessation of these miracles during their own time; so that it is not so much the trustworthiness of their testimony as their understanding of the changing times which falls under criticism. If we once lay firm hold upon the biblical principle which governed the distribution of the miraculous gifts, in a word, we find that we have in our hands a key which unlocks all the historical puzzles connected with them.

There is, of course, a deeper principle recognizable here, of which the actual attachment of the charismata of the Apostolic Church to the mission of the Apostles is but an illustration. This deeper principle may be reached by us through the perception, more broadly, of the inseparable connection of miracles with revelation, as its mark and credential; or, more narrowly, of the summing up of all revelation, finally, in Jesus Christ. Miracles do not appear on the page of Scripture vagrantly, here, there, and elsewhere indifferently, without assignable reason. They belong to revelation periods, and appear only when God is speaking to His people through accredited messengers, declaring His gracious purposes. Their abundant display in the Apostolic Church is the mark of the richness of the Apostolic age in revelation; and when this revelation period closed, the period of miracle-working had passed by also, as a mere matter of course. It might, indeed, be *a priori* conceivable that God should deal with men atomistically, and reveal Himself and His will to each individual, throughout the whole course of history, in the penetralium of his own consciousness. This is the mystic's dream. It has not, however, been God's way. He has chosen rather to deal with the race in its entirety, and to give to this race His complete revelation of Himself in an organic whole. And when this historic process of organic revelation had reached its completeness, and when the whole knowledge of God designed for the saving health of the world had been incorporated into the living body of the world's thought—there remained, of course, no further revelation to be made, and there has been accordingly no further revelation made. God the Holy Spirit has made it His subsequent work, not to introduce new and unneeded revelations into the world, but to diffuse this one complete revelation through the world and to bring mankind into the saving knowledge of it.

As Abraham Kuyper figuratively expresses it,[53] it has not been God's way to communicate to each and every man a separate store of divine knowledge of his own, to meet his separate needs; but He rather has spread a common board for all, and invites all to come and partake of the richness of the great feast. He has given to the world one organically complete revelation, adapted to all, sufficient for all, provided for all, and from this one completed revelation He requires each to draw his whole spiritual sustenance. Therefore it is that the miraculous working which is but the sign of God's revealing power, cannot be expected to continue, and in point of fact does not continue, after the revelation of which it is the accompaniment has been completed. It is unreasonable to ask miracles, says John Calvin—or to find them—where there is no new gospel.[54] By as much as the one gospel suffices for all lands and all peoples and all times, by so much does the miraculous attestation of that one single gospel suffice for all lands and all times, and no further miracles are to be expected in connection with it. "According to the Scriptures," Herman Bavinck explains,[55] "special revelation has been delivered in the form of a historical process, which reaches its endpoint in the person and work of Christ. When Christ had appeared and returned again to heaven, special revelation did not, indeed, come at once to an end. There was yet to follow the outpouring of the Holy Ghost, and the extraordinary working of the powers and gifts through and under the guidance of the Apostolate. The Scriptures undoubtedly reckon all this to the sphere of special revelation, and the continuance of this revelation was necessary to give abiding existence in the world to the special revelation which reached its climax in Christ—abiding existence both in the word of Scripture and in the life of the church. Truth and life, prophecy and miracle, word and deed, inspiration and regeneration go hand in hand in the completion of special revelation. But when the revelation of God in Christ had taken place, and had become in Scripture and church a constituent part of the cosmos, then another era began. As before everything was a preparation for Christ, so afterward everything is to be a consequence of Christ. Then Christ was being framed into the Head of His people, now His people are being framed into the Body of Christ. Then the Scriptures were being produced, now they are being applied. New constituent elements of special revelation can no longer be added; for Christ has come, His work has been done, and His word is complete." Had any miracles perchance occurred beyond the Apostolic age they would be without significance; mere occurrences with no universal meaning. What is important is that "the Holy Scriptures teach clearly that the complete revelation of God is given in Christ, and that the Holy Spirit who is poured out on the people of God has come solely in order to glorify Christ and to take of the things of Christ." Because Christ is all in all, and all revelation and redemption alike are summed up in Him, it would be inconceivable that either revelation or its accompanying signs should continue after the completion of that great revelation with its accrediting works, by which Christ has been established in His rightful place as the culmination and climax and all-inclusive summary of the saving revelation of God, the sole and sufficient redeemer of His people.

At this point we might fairly rest. But I cannot deny myself the pleasure of giving you some account in this connection of a famous book on the subject we have been discussing—to which indeed incidental allusion has been made. I refer to Conyers Middleton's *A Free Inquiry into the Miraculous Powers which are supposed to have subsisted in the Christian church from the earliest ages through several successive centuries. By which it is shown that we have no sufficient reason to believe, upon the authority of the primitive fathers, that any such powers were continued to the church, after the days of the Apostles.* Middleton was a doughty controversialist, no less admired for his English style, which was reckoned by his contemporaries as second in purity to that of no writer of his day except Addison (though John Wesley more justly found it stiff and pedantic), than feared for the sharpness and persistency of his polemics. He was of a somewhat sceptical temper and perhaps cannot be acquitted of a certain amount of insincerity. We could wish at least that it were clearer that John Wesley's description of him were undeserved, as "aiming every blow, though he seems to look another way, at the fanatics who wrote the Bible." [56] In this, his chief theological work, however, Middleton had a subject where scepticism found a proper mark, and he performs his congenial task with distinct ability. His controversial spirit and a certain harshness of tone, while they may detract from the pleasure with which the book is read, do not destroy its value as a solid piece of investigation.

Conscious of the boldness of the views he was about to advocate and foreseeing their unpopularity, Middleton sent forth in 1747 as a sort of preparation for what was to come an *Introductory discourse to a larger work designed hereafter to be published, concerning the miraculous powers which are supposed to have subsisted in the Christian church from the earliest ages through several successive centuries; tending to show that we have no sufficient reason to believe upon the authority of the primitive fathers, that any such powers were continued to the church after the days of the Apostles. With a postscript* . . . (London, 1747). In this *Discourse* he points out the helplessness of the Anglican position in the face of Romish claims. There is no reason for allowing miracles for the first three centuries which is not as good or better for allowing them for the succeeding centuries: and yet the greater portion of the miracles of these later centuries were wrought in support of distinctively Romish teaching, which, it would seem, must be accepted, if their attesting miracles are allowed. Next year (1748) he published *Remarks on two Pamphlets* . . ., which had appeared in reply to his *Introductory Discourse;* and at length in December, 1748, he permitted the *Free Inquiry* itself to see the light, fitted with a preface in which an account is given of the origin of the book, and the position taken up in the *Introductory Discourse* is pressed more sharply still —that the genuineness of the ecclesiastical miracles being once allowed, no stopping-place can be found until the whole series of alleged miracles down to our own day be admitted. At the end of this preface Middleton's own view as to the cause of the cessation of the spiritual gifts is intimated, and this proves to be only a modification of the current Anglican opinion—that miracles subsisted until the church had been founded in all the chief cities of the empire, which, he held, had been accomplished in the Apostolic times. It is interesting to observe thus that Middleton reached his correct conclusion as to the time of the cessation of these gifts without the help of a right understanding of the true reason of their cessation with the Apostolic age; purely, that is to say, on empirical grounds.

The *Free Inquiry* itself is a scholarly piece of work for its time, and a competent argument. It is disposed in five parts. The first of these simply draws out from the sources and presents in full the testimony to miraculous working found in the Fathers of the first three centuries. The meagreness and indefiniteness of their witness are left to speak for themselves, with only the help of two closing remarks. The one of these presses the impossibility of believing that the gifts were first withdrawn during the first fifty years of the second century and then restored. The other contrasts the patristic miracles with those of the New Testament, with respect both to their nature and the mode of their working. The second section discusses the persons who worked the ecclesiastical miracles. It is pointed out that no known writer claims to have himself wrought miracles, or names any of his predecessors as having done so. The honor is left to unknown and obscure men, and afterward to the "rotten bones" of saints who while living did no such works. The third section subjects the character of the early Fathers as men of wisdom and trustworthiness to a severe and not always perfectly fair criticism, with a view to lessening the credit that should be given to their testimony in such a matter as the occurrence of miraculous workings in their day. The fourth section then takes up the several kinds of miracles which, it is pretended, were wrought, and seeks to determine from the nature of each, in each instance of its mention, whether its credibility may be reasonably suspected. Finally, in the fifth section, the principal objections which had been raised, or which seemed likely to be raised, to the tenor of the argument are cited and refuted.

The book was received with a storm of criticism, reprobation, even abuse. It was not refuted. Many published careful and searching examinations of its facts and arguments, among others Doctor William Dodwell [57] (the younger) and Doctor Thomas Church,[58] to whom Middleton replied in a *Vindication*, published posthumously (1751). After a century and a half the book remains unrefuted, and, indeed, despite the faults arising from the writer's spirit and the limitations inseparable from the state of scholarship in his day, its main contention seems to be put beyond dispute.[59]

PATRISTIC AND MEDIÆVAL MARVELS

PATRISTIC AND MEDIÆVAL MARVELS

As over against the effort made more especially by Anglican writers to confine genuine ecclesiastical miracles to the first, and in their view the purest and most authoritative, centuries of Christianity, the Romish theologians boldly declare that God has been pleased in every age to work a multitude of evident miracles in His church. Before this assertion, as we have seen, the Anglican theory is helpless, on the ground whether of fact or of principle. Of fact, because the evidence for the later miracles, which it denies, is very much greater in volume and cogency than that for the earlier miracles, which it accepts. Of principle, because the reason which it gives for the continuance of miracles during the first three centuries, if valid at all, is equally valid for their continuance to the twentieth century. What we shall look upon as the period of the planting of the church is determined by our point of view. If the usefulness of miracles in planting the church were sufficient reason for their occurrence in the Roman Empire in the third century, it is hard to deny that it may be sufficient reason for the repetition of them in, say, the Chinese Empire in the twentieth century. And why go to China? Is not the church still essentially in the position of a missionary church everywhere in this world of unbelief? When we take a really "long view" of things, is it not at least a debatable question whether the paltry two thousand years which have passed since Christianity came into the world are not a negligible quantity, and the age in which we live is not still the age of the primitive church? We must adjudge, therefore, that the Romish theory is the more consistent and reasonable of the two. If we are to admit that the miracles of the first three centuries happened, slightly and only generally witnessed as they are, we should in all reason go on and admit that the much more numerous and much better attested miracles of the fourth century happened too—and those of the fifth, and of the sixth, and of every subsequent century down to our day.

The force of this reasoning is interestingly illustrated by the conversion by it of Edward Gibbon, in his youth, to Roman Catholicism. Sir James Fitzjames Stephen gives a somewhat caustic account of the circumstances. "At Oxford," he says,[1] "'the blind activity of idleness' impelled him to read Middleton's *Free Inquiry*. Yet he could not bring himself to follow Middleton in his attack on the early Fathers, or to give up the notion that miracles were worked in the early church for at least four or five centuries. 'But I was unable to resist the weight of historical evidence that within the same period most of the leading doctrines of Popery were already introduced in theory and practice; nor was the conclusion absurd that miracles are the test of truth, and that the church must be orthodox and pure which was so often approved by the visible interposition of the Deity.'

"From the miracles affirmed by Basil, Chrysostom, Augustine, and Jerome, he inferred that celibacy was superior to marriage, that saints were to be invoked, prayers for the dead said, and the real presence believed in; and whilst in this frame of mind he fell in with Bossuet's *Exposition* and his *History of the Variations*. 'I read,' he says in his affected way, 'I applauded, I believed'; and he adds with truth in reference to Bossuet, 'I surely fell by a noble hand.' 'In my present feelings it seems incredible that I ever should have believed in transubstantiation; but my conqueror oppressed me with the sacramental words, and dashed against each other the figurative half-meanings of the Protestant sects. . . .'

"No one, we will venture to say, has been converted in

the nineteenth century by a belief that, as a fact, miracles were worked in the early church, and that, as a consequence, the doctrines professed at the time must be true. As a rule the doctrines have carried the miracles. . . . The fact that the process began at the other end with Gibbon is characteristic both of the man and of the age; but it is put in a still stronger light by the account which he gives of his reconversion. . . . The process from first to last was emphatically an intellectual one. . . . Gibbon himself observes: 'I still remember my solitary transport at the discovery of a philosophical argument against the doctrine of transubstantiation: that the text of Scripture which seems to inculcate the real presence is attested only by a single sense—our sight; while the real presence itself is disproved by three of our senses—the sight, the touch, and the taste.'"

Only a brief account will be necessary of the state of the case for the fourth and later centuries. When we pass from the literature of the first three into that of the fourth and succeeding centuries, we leave at once the region of indefinite and undetailed references to miraculous works said to have occurred somewhere or other—no doubt the references increase in number and definiteness as the years pass—and come into contact with a body of writings simply saturated with marvels. And whereas few writers were to be found in the earlier period who professed to be eye-witnesses of miracles, and none who wrought them were named to us, in the later period everybody appears to have witnessed any number of them, and the workers of them are not only named but prove to be the most famous missionaries and saints of the church. Nor must we imagine that these marvels are recounted only by obscure and otherwise unknown hero-worshippers, whose only claim to be remembered by posterity is that they were the overenthusiastic admirers of the great ascetics of their time. They are rather the outstanding scholars, theologians, preachers,

organizers of the age. It is Jerome, the leading biblical
scholar of his day, who wrote the distressing lives of Paul,
Hilarion, and Malchus; Gregory of Nyssa, one of "the
three great Cappadocians," who narrates the fantastic
doings of his thaumaturgic namesake;[2] the incomparable
Athanasius himself, who is responsible for the life of Antony. And not to be left behind, the greatest preacher
of the day, Chrysostom; the greatest ecclesiastic, Ambrose; the greatest thinker, Augustine,—all describe for us
miraculous occurrences of the most incredible kind as having taken place within their own knowledge. It will be
not only interesting but useful for our purpose, as well, if
a specimen instance be brought before us of how these
great men dealt with miracles.

Augustine no doubt will serve our purpose here as well
as another. In the twenty-second book[3] of the *City of
God*, he has circumstantially related to us a score or more
of miracles which had come under his own observation,
and which he represents as only a tithe of those he could
relate. A considerable number of these were wrought by
the relics of "the most glorious martyr, Stephen." The
bones of Stephen had come to light in Jerusalem in 415.
Certain portions of them were brought into Africa and
everywhere they were taken miracles were wrought.
Somewhere about 424 Hippo obtained its fragments and
enshrined them in a small chapel opening into the cathedral church, on the archway of which Augustine caused
four verses to be cut, exhorting worshippers to ascribe to
God all miracles wrought upon Stephen's intercession.
Almost seventy miracles wrought at this shrine had been
officially recorded in less than two years, while incomparably more, Augustine tells us, had been wrought at the
neighboring town of Calama, which had received its relics
earlier. "Think, beloved," he cries, in the sermon which
he preached on the reception of the relics, "what the Lord
must have in store for us in the land of the living, when

He bestows so much in the ashes of the dead." Even the
dead were raised at these shrines, with great promptness
and facility. Here are some of the instances recorded by
Augustine with complete confidence.[4]

"Eucharius, a Spanish priest residing at Calama, was
for a long time a sufferer from stone. By the relics of the
same martyr (Stephen) which the bishop Possidius brought
him, he was cured. Afterward the same priest sinking
under another disease, was lying dead, and already they
were binding his hands. By the succor of the same martyr
he was raised to life, the priest's cloak having been brought
from the oratory and laid upon the corpse. . . . Audurus
is the name of an estate where there is a church that contains a memorial shrine of the martyr Stephen. It happened that, as a little boy was playing in the court, the
oxen drawing a wagon went out of the track and crushed
him with the wheel, so that immediately he seemed at his
last gasp. His mother snatched him up and laid him at
the shrine, and not only did he revive but also appeared
uninjured. A religious female who lived at Caspalium, a
neighboring estate, when she was so ill as to be despaired
of, had her dress brought to this shrine, but before it was
brought back she was gone. However, her parents wrapped
her corpse in the dress, and, her breath returning, she became quite well. At Hippo, a Syrian called Bassus was
praying at the relics of the same martyr for his daughter,
who was dangerously ill. He too had brought her dress
with him to the shrine. But as he prayed, behold, his servants ran from the house to tell him she was dead. His
friends, however, intercepted them and forbade them to
tell him, lest he should bewail her in public. And when
he returned to his house which was already ringing with the
lamentations of his family, and had thrown on his daughter's body the dress he was carrying, she was restored to
life. There, too, the son of a man, Irenæus, one of the tax-
gatherers, took ill and died. And while his body was lying

lifeless, and the last rites were being prepared, amidst the weeping and mourning of all, one of the friends who were consoling the father suggested that the body should be anointed with the oil of the same martyr. It was done and he was revived. Likewise, Eleusinus, a man of tribunitian rank among us, laid his infant son, who had died, on the shrine of the martyr, which is in the suburb where he lived, and, after prayer, which he poured out there with many tears, he took up his child alive."[5]

Not all the miracles which Augustine includes in this anthology were wrought, however, by the bones of Stephen. Even before these bones had been discovered, miracles of the most astonishing character had occurred within his own personal knowledge. He tells us, for example, of the restoration of a blind man to sight at Milan—"when I was there," he says—by the remains of the martyrs Protasius and Gervasius, discovered to Ambrose in a dream. And he tells us with great circumstantiality of a miraculous cure of fistula wrought in Carthage—"in my presence and under my own eyes," he says—when he and Alypius had just returned from Italy. A special interest attaches to these early instances, because Augustine, although an eye-witness of them, and although he insists on his having been an eye-witness of them as their attestation, does not seem to have recognized their miraculous character until long afterward. For Augustine's hearty belief in contemporary miracles, illustrated by the teeming list now before us, was of slow growth. It was not until some years after his return to Africa that it became easy to him to acknowledge their occurrence. He arrived in Africa in 388, but still in his treatises, *On the True Religion*, which was written about 390, and *On the Usefullness of Believing*, written in 391 or 392, we find him speaking on the hypothesis that miracles no longer happened. "We perceive," he writes in the former of these treatises,[6] "that our ancestors, by that measure of faith by which the ascent is made from temporal things to eternal, obtained visible miracles (for thus only could they do it); and through them it has been brought about that these should no longer be necessary for their descendants. For when the Catholic Church had been diffused and established through the whole world, these miracles were no longer permitted to continue in our time, lest the mind should always seek visible things, and the human race should be chilled by the customariness of the very things whose novelty had inflamed them." Similarly, in the latter treatise, after enumerating the miracles of our Lord, he asks,[7] "Why do not these things take place now?" and answers, "Because they would not move unless they were wonderful, and if they were customary they would not be wonderful." "Even the marvels of nature, great and wonderful as they are," he continues, "have ceased to surprise and so to move; and God has dealt wisely with us, therefore, in sending his miracles once for all to convince the world, depending afterward on the authority of the multitudes thus convinced."

Subsequently at the close of his life, reviewing these passages in his *Retractations*, he supposes it enough to say that what he meant was not that no miracles were still wrought in his own day, but only that none were wrought which were as great as those our Lord wrought, and that not all the kinds our Lord wrought continued to be wrought.[8] "For," says he,[9] "those that are baptized do not now receive the Spirit on the imposition of hands, so as to speak in the tongues of all the peoples; neither are the sick healed by the shadow of the preachers of Christ falling on them as they pass; and other such things as were then done, are now manifestly ceased." What he said, he insists,[10] is not to be taken as meaning that no miracles at all were to be believed to be performed still in Christ's name. "For I myself, when I wrote that book"—the book *On the True Religion*—"already knew that a blind man had been given his sight at Milan, by the bodies of the martyrs in that city; and certain other things which were done at that time in numbers sufficient to prevent our knowing them all or our enumerating all we knew." This explanation seems scarcely adequate; but it suggests that the starting-point of Augustine's belief in contemporary miracles is to be sought in Milan—although it appears that some time was required after he had left Milan for the belief to ripen in his mind.

A sufficiently odd passage in one of his letters—written in 404—seems to illustrate at once the Milanese origin of his miracle-faith and the process of its growth to maturity.[11] There had been a scandal in the household; one member of it had accused another of a crime, and Augustine was in doubt which of the two was really at fault. "I fixed upon the following as a means of discovering the truth," he writes. "Both pledged themselves in a solemn compact to go to a holy place, where the awe-inspiring works of God might much more readily make manifest the evil of which either of them was conscious, and compel the guilty to confess, either by judgment or through fear of judgment." God is everywhere, it is true; and able to punish or reward in secret as He will. "But," continues Augustine, "in regard to the answers of prayer which are visible to men, who can search out the reasons for appointing some places rather than others to be the scenes of miraculous interpositions?" The grave of a certain Felix suggested itself to him as a suitable place to send his culprits. True, no supernatural events had ever occurred there. But, he writes, "I myself knew how, at Milan, at the tomb of the saints, where demons are brought in a most marvellous and awful manner to confess their deeds, a thief, who had come thither intending to deceive by perjuring himself, was compelled to own his thefts and restore what he had taken away." "And is not Africa also," he asks, "full of the bodies of holy martyrs?" "Yet we do not know of such things being done here," he confesses. "Even as the gift of healing and the gift of discerning of spirits," he explains, "are not given to all saints, as the Apostle declares; so it is not at all the tombs of the saints that it hath pleased Him who divideth to each severally as He will, to cause such miracles to be wrought." As late as 404, then, there were as yet no miracle-working shrines in Africa. Augustine, however, is busily at work producing them. And twenty years later we see them in full activity.

It was naturally a source of embarrassment to Augustine that the heretics had miracles to appeal to just like his own; and that the heathen had had something very like them from time immemorial. The miracles of the heretics he was inclined to reject out of hand. They never happened, he said. On the other hand, he did not dream of denying the actual occurrence of the heathen miracles. He only strained every nerve to put them in a different class from his own. They stood related to his, he said, as the marvels wrought by Pharaoh's magicians did to Moses' miracles. Meanwhile, there the three sets of miracles stood, side by side, apparently just alike, and to be distinguished only by the doctrines with which they were severally connected. A passage in the thirteenth tractate on John on Donatist miracles (he calls them "miracle-ettes"), is very instructive. This tractate seems to have been delivered subsequently to 416, and therefore represents Augustine's later views. "Let no one tell you fables, then," he cries,[12] "saying, 'Pontius wrought a miracle, and Donatus prayed and God answered him from heaven.' In the first place, either they are deceived or they deceive. In the last place, grant that he removes mountains: 'And have not charity,' says the Apostle, 'I am nothing.' Let us see whether he has charity. I would believe that he had, if he had not divided unity. For against those whom I may call marvel-workers, my God has put me on my guard, saying, 'In the last times there shall arise false prophets doing signs and wonders, to lead into error, if it were possible, even the

elect. Lo, I have foretold it to you.' Therefore the Bridegroom has cautioned us, that we ought not to be deceived
even by miracles." Similarly the heathen and Christian
miracles are pitted against one another, and decision between them sought on grounds lying outside the miracles
themselves. "Which, then, can more readily be believed
to work miracles? They who wish themselves to be reckoned gods by those on whom they work miracles, or those
whose sole object in working any miracles is to induce faith
in God, or in Christ also as God? . . . Let us therefore
believe those who both speak the truth and work miracles." [13]　It is not the empirical fact which counts—there
were all too many empirical facts to count—but the truth
lying behind the empirical fact.[14]

What now are we to think of these miracles which Augustine and his fellows narrate to us in such superabun-
dance?

We should perhaps note at the outset that the marvellous
stories do not seem to have met with universal credence
when first published. They seem indeed to have attracted
very little attention. Augustine bitterly complains that
so little was made of them.[15]　Each was known only in the
spot where it was wrought, and even then only to a few
persons. If some report of it happened to be carried to
other places no sufficient authority existed to give it prompt
and unwavering acceptance. He records how he himself
had sharply rebuked a woman who had been miraculously
cured of a cancer for not publishing abroad the blessing she
had received. Her physician had laughed at her, she said;
and moreover she had not really concealed it. Outraged,
however, on finding that not even her closest acquaintances
had ever heard of it, he dragged her from her seclusion and
gave the utmost publicity to her story. In odd parallelism
to the complaint of his somewhat older contemporary, the
heathen historian Ammianus Marcellinus, who in wistful
regret for the portents which were gone, declared stoutly

that they nevertheless still occurred, only "nobody heeds them now,"[16] Augustine asserted that innumerable Christian miracles were constantly taking place, only no notice was taken of them.[17]

It was not merely indifference, however, which they encountered, but definite disbelief. Many (*plurimi*) shook their heads at what Sulpitius Severus told in the second book of his *Dialogues* of the deeds of Martin of Tours—so many that he felt constrained carefully to give his authorities in the next book for each miracle that he recorded. "Let them accept," he says in announcing his purpose to do so,[18] "the evidence of people still living, and believe them, seeing that they doubt my good faith." In the first book of his *Dialogues*,[19] indeed, he represents his collocutor—his Gallic friend Postumianus—as saying to him frankly: "I shudder to tell what I have lately heard—that a miserable man (I do not know him) has said that you have told many lies in that book of yours"—that is, in his *Life of Martin*. The reason Postumianus gives for his shuddering, however, is what most interests us. It is that doubt of the actual occurrence of these miracles is a constructive assault upon the credibility of the Gospels. "For," Postumianus argues, "since the Lord Himself testified that such works as Martin's were to be done by all the faithful, he who does not believe that Martin did them simply does not believe that Christ uttered such words." In point of fact, of course, Christ did not utter these words; the appeal is to the spurious "last twelve verses of Mark." We see, however, that the belief that Christ uttered these words was a powerful co-operating cause inducing belief in the actual occurrence of the alleged marvels. It seemed an arraignment of Christ to say that His most distinguished followers did not do the works which Christ had promised that all His followers should do. The actual occurrence of the miracles was proved quite as much by the fancied promise of the Gospel as by ocular evidence.[20]

It is a very disturbing fact further that the very Fathers who record long lists of miracles contemporary with themselves, yet betray a consciousness that miracles had nevertheless, in some sense or other, ceased with the Apostolic age. When Ambrose, for example, comes to speak of the famous discovery of the bodies of the two martyrs, Protasius and Gervasius, at Milan, and the marvels which accompanied and followed their discovery, he cannot avoid expressing surprise and betraying the fact that this was to him a new thing. "The miracles of old time," he cries,[21] "are come again, when by the advent of the Lord Jesus a fuller grace was shed upon the earth." Augustine, in like manner, in introducing his account of contemporaneous miracles which we have already quoted, begins by adducing the question: "Why do not those miracles take place now, which, as you preach, took place once?" "I might answer," he replies, "that they were necessary before the world believed, that it might believe," and then he goes on to say, as we have seen, that "miracles were wrought in his time, but they were not so public and well attested as the miracles of the Gospel." Nor were the contemporary miracles, he testifies, so great as those of the Gospels, nor did they embrace all the kinds which occur there. So Chrysostom says:[22] "Argue not because miracles do not happen now, that they did not happen then. . . . In those times they were profitable, and now they are not." Again:[23] "Why are there not those now who raise the dead and perform cures? . . . When nature was weak, when faith had to be planted, then there were many such; but now He wills not that we should hang on these miracles but be ready for death." Again: "Where is the Holy Spirit now? a man may ask; for then it was appropriate to speak of Him when miracles took place, and the dead were raised and all lepers were cleansed, but now. . . ." Again: "The Apostles indeed enjoyed the grace of God in abundance; but if we were bidden to raise the dead, or open the eyes of the blind, or cleanse lepers, or straighten the lame, or cast out devils and heal the like disorders. . . ." Chrysostom fairly teems with expressions implying that miracle-working of every kind had ceased;[24] he declares in the crispest way, "Of miraculous powers, not even a vestige is left";[25] and yet he records instances from his day! Isodore of Pelusium similarly looks upon miracles as confined to the Apostolic times, adding:[26] "Perhaps miracles would take place now, too, if the lives of the teachers rivalled the bearing of the Apostles; though even if they did not, such a life would suffice for the enlightenment of those who beheld it." The same significant distinguishing of times follows us down the years. Thus Gregory the Great at the end of the sixth century, though the very type of a miracle-lover, nevertheless, writing on Mark 16 : 17, says:[27] "Is it so, my brethren, that because ye do not these signs, ye do not believe? On the contrary, they were necessary in the beginning of the church; for, that faith might grow, it required miracles to cherish it withal; just as when we plant shrubs, we water them until we see them to thrive in the ground, and as soon as they are well rooted we cease our irrigation." He proceeds to say that the wonders of grace are greater than miracles. Isodore of Seville at the opening of the next century writes in precisely the same spirit.[28] "The reason why the church does not now do the miracles it did under the Apostles," he explains, "is, because miracles were necessary then to convince the world of the truth of Christianity; but now it becomes it, being so convinced, to shine forth in good works. . . . Whoever seeks to perform miracles now as a believer, seeks after vainglory and human applause. For it is written: 'Tongues are for a sign, not to them that believe, but to them that believe not.' Observe, a sign is not necessary for believers, who have already received the faith, but for unbelievers that they may be converted. For Paul miraculously cured the father of Publius of a fever for the benefit of unbelievers;

but he restores believing Timothy when ill, not by prayer, but by medicine; so that you may clearly perceive that miracles were wrought for unbelievers and not for believers." Even in the thirteenth century, Bernard, commenting on Mark 16 : 17, asks:[29] "For who is there that seems to have these signs of the faith, without which no one, according to this Scripture, shall be saved?" and answers just as Gregory did, by saying that the greatest miracles are those of the renewed life. The common solution of this inconsistent attitude toward miracles, that the ecclesiastical miracles were only recognized as differing in kind from those of the Scripture, while going a certain way, will hardly suffice for the purpose. Ecclesiastical miracles of every conceivable kind were alleged. Every variety of miracle properly so-called Chrysostom declares to have ceased. It is the contrast between miracles as such and wonders of grace that Gregory draws. No doubt we must recognize that these Fathers realized that the ecclesiastical miracles were of a lower order than those of Scripture. It looks very much as if, when they were not inflamed by enthusiasm, they did not really think them to be miracles at all.[30]

It is observable further that, throughout the whole patristic and mediæval periods at least, it is difficult to discover any one who claims to have himself wrought miracles. "It may seem somewhat remarkable," says Gibbon,[31] "that Bernard of Clairvaux, who records so many miracles of his friend, St. Malachi, never takes any notice of his own, which in their turn, however, are carefully related by his companions and disciples. In the long series of ecclesiastical history, does there exist a single instance of a saint asserting that he himself possessed the gift of miracles?" There is certainly a notable phenomenon here which may be brought to its sharpest point by recalling along with it two facts. First, Christ and His Apostles present a strong contrast with it. Our Lord appeals to His own works, and Paul to his own, in proof of their mission. Secondly, Bernard, for example, not only does not claim to have worked miracles himself, but, as we have seen, seems to speak at times as if he looked upon miracles as having ceased with the Apostles.

It is very instructive to observe how J. H. Newman endeavors to turn the edge of Gibbon's inquiry. "I observe then, first," he says,[32] "that it is not often that the gift of miracles is even ascribed to a saint. In many cases miracles are only ascribed to their tombs or relics; or where miracles are ascribed to them when living, these are but singular or occasional, not parts of a series." "Moreover," he adds as his second answer, "they are commonly what Paley calls *tentative* miracles, or some out of many which have been attempted, and have been done accordingly without any previous confidence in their power to effect them. Moses and Elijah could predict the result; but the miracles in question were scarcely more than experiments and trials, even though success had been granted to them many times before. Under these circumstances, how could the individual men who wrought them appeal to them themselves? It was not till afterward, when their friends and disciples could calmly look back upon their life, and review the various actions and providences which occurred in the course of it, that they would be able to put together the scattered tokens of divine favor, none or few of which might in themselves be a certain evidence of a miraculous power. As well might we expect men in their lifetime to be called saints as workers of miracles." There still remains in reserve a third argument, which amounts to saying that the workers of ecclesiastical miracles were modest men, "as little inclined to proclaim them aloud as to make a boast of their graces."

The whole tenor of this representation of the relation of the miracle-workers of the patristic and mediæval church to their miracles is artificial. It is nothing less than ludicrous to speak of the miracles ascribed to a Martin of

Tours or a Gregory Thaumaturgus as "tentative," or as attempted with incomplete confidence. It is equally ludicrous to represent incomplete assurance on the part of a saint with respect to his miracles before they were wrought as prolonging itself throughout his life, after they were wrought. Meanwhile the fact remains that throughout the history of the church miracles have rather been thrust upon than laid claim to by their workers.[33] Nor did there ever lack those who openly repudiated the notion that any necessary connection existed between saintliness and miracle-working. Richard Rolle of Hampole, who also became posthumously a miracle-worker, was in his lifetime pronounced no saint because he wrought no miracles. His reply was to the effect that the inference was inconsequent. "Not all saints," he said,[34] "do or have done miracles, neither in life nor after death; nor do all reprobates either in life or after death lack miracles; frequently the mediocre good and less perfect do miracles, and many who are seated highest in the heavens before the face of God remain quiet within." [35] "Many bodies," he says, "have been translated on earth whose souls perchance have not yet attained heaven." "Saints are not carried to the supernatural seats for the reason that they have showed wonders, for some wicked men, too, have done this; but truth has desired that the more ardently one loves, the more highly shall he be elevated, the more honorably shall he be seated among the angels." [36] "It is not necessary now," he continues quite in the vein of Augustine, "that miracles should be shown, since throughout the whole world many abide in memory; but there is need that before the eyes of all should be shown the example of that work. . . ."

In remarks like these there is manifested a certain depreciation of the value of miracles, assuredly not strange in the circumstances. And we are bound to carry this a step further and to recognize that a great mass of these miracles are alleged to have been wrought in the interest of what we must pronounce grave errors. J. H. Newman, in a passage just quoted, remarks that many miracles are ascribed to the tombs or relics of the saints, rather than to the saints themselves; and this is only an example of the uses to which they have been put. So many were wrought in connection with superstitions which grew up about the Eucharist, for instance, that "wonders wrought by the Eucharist" is made one of the main divisions of the article, "Wonders," in Smith and Cheatham's *Dictionary of Christian Antiquities*.[37] Thus, for example, "Cyprian speaks of a person who had lapsed in persecution attempting to communicate; when on opening the arca or receptacle in which the consecrated bread was reserved, fire burst out from it and prevented her. Another, on attending church with the same purpose, found that he had received from the priest nothing but a cinder."[38] Ambrose relates that one of his friends called Satyrus was piously inclined but not yet admitted to the sacrament. "In this state he happened to suffer shipwreck in his passage from Africa." "Says Ambrose: 'Satyrus, not being afraid of death, but to die only before he had taken of these mysteries, begged of some of the company, who had been initiated, that they would lend him the divine sacrament'" (which they carried about with them—according to the superstitious habit of the day—as an amulet or charm), "'not to feed his curiosity by peeping inside the bag, but to obtain the benefit of his faith, for he wrapped up the mysteries in his handkerchief, and then tying it about his neck threw himself into the sea; never troubling himself to look out for a plank, which might help him to swim, since he wanted nothing more than the arms of his faith; nor did his hopes fail him, for he was the first of the company who got safe to the shore.'"[39] Optatus relates that certain members of the Donatist sect once cast the Eucharistic bread of the Catholics to the dogs —which promptly went mad and bit their masters.[40] Sozomen tells that a woman who had received some Eucharistic bread of the Macedonians, found it turned to a stone.[40] Gregory the Great narrates that a young monk who had gone to visit his parents without permission, died on the day of his return, but could not rest quiet in his grave until Benedict, his superior, had the host laid on it.[40] In the time of Justinian, we are told, when it was the custom to distribute the Eucharistic bread left over after the communion to the children, it happened once that a Jewish child received and ate a fragment of it. The enraged father cast the child into a furnace, but it was miraculously preserved from harm.[40] Gregory of Tours tells of a deacon of unholy life, who, carrying one day the Eucharist into a church, had the bread fly of itself out of his hand and place itself on the altar.[40] According to the same writer the host on one occasion shed blood when broken.[40] A bishop named Marsius is related to have let his portion of the Eucharistic bread, received from the hands of the administrator, fall into the folds of his robe because he did not wish to break his fast. It at once turned into a serpent, and wrapped itself about his waist whence it could be dislodged only by a night of prayer for him on the part of the administrator.[40] This is matched by the miracle of Bolsena, which Raphael has rendered famous. A priest saying the mass—it is dated 1264—let a drop of wine fall on his *corporal*, and doubled up the garment upon it. It was found to have left the impression of the wafer in blood on every fold which touched it.[41]

We have seen Augustine constrained to allow the principle that miracles alleged in the interests of false doctrines are self-condemned; that no miracle can be accepted against the truth, but is at once to be set aside if presented in the interests of error. The principle is a scriptural one[42] and has repeatedly been rationally validated. It is so validated, for example, in a solid argument by Lyman H. Atwater, speaking immediately of spiritualism.[43] "A corrupt doctrine," says he suggestively, "destroys a pretended miracle just as strong counter circumstantial evidence would invalidate the testimony of a single witness." A good deal of confusion seems to be abroad on this matter. An impression appears to exist that the proper evidence of truth—or at least of religious truth—is miracle, and that therefore there can be no decisive criterion of religious truth offered for our acceptance except miracles wrought in support of it. It is at least very commonly supposed that we are bound to examine carefully into the pretensions of any alleged miracle produced in support of any propositions whatever, however intrinsically absurd; and, if these alleged miracles cannot be at once decisively invalidated, we are bound to accept as true the propositions in support of which they are alleged. No proposition clearly perceived to be false, however, can possibly be validated to us by any miracle whatever; and the perception of the proposition as clearly false relieves us at once from the duty of examining into the miraculous character of its alleged support and invalidates any claim which that support can put in to miraculous character—prior to all investigation. A matter so clear could not be missed, of course, by Augustine, and we have his support, accordingly, in pointing out that the connection of alleged miracles with erroneous doctrines invalidates their claim to be genuine works of God.

We must not imagine, however, that ecclesiastical miracles are distinguished from the biblical miracles by nothing except the nature of the doctrines in connection with which they are alleged to be wrought. They differ from them also, fundamentally, in character. This difference is not denied. J. H. Newman, for example, describes it thus:[44] "Ecclesiastical miracles, that is, miracles posterior to the Apostolic age, are, on the whole, different in object, character, and evidence from those of Scripture on the whole." At a subsequent point, he enlarges on this.[45] "The Scripture miracles," says he, "are for the most part evidence of a Divine Revelation, and that for the sake of those who have been instructed in it, and in order to the instruction of multitudes; but the miracles which follow have sometimes no discoverable or direct object, or but a slight object; they happen for the sake of individuals and of those who are already Christians, or for purposes already effected, as far as we can judge, by the miracles of Scripture. . . . The miracles of Scripture are, on the whole, grave, simple, majestic; those of ecclesiastical history often partake of what may be called a romantic character, and of that wildness and inequality which enters into the notion of romance. The miracles of Scripture are undeniably beyond nature; those of ecclesiastical history are often scarcely more than extraordinary accidents or coincidences, or events which seem to betray exaggerations or errors in the statement." In a word,[46] "Scripture is to us a Garden of Eden, and its creations are beautiful as well as 'very good'; but when we pass from the Apostolical to the following ages, it is as if we left the choicest valleys of the earth, the quietest and most harmonious scenery, and the most cultivated soil, for the luxuriant wilderness of Africa or Asia, the natural home or kingdom of brute nature, uninfluenced by man." Newman labors to show that this is only a general contrast; that there are some miracles in Scripture which, taken by themselves, would find their place in the lower class; and some in ecclesiastical history which rise to the higher class; and in later life he would somewhat modify his statement of the contrast. But the admission that the contrast exists is unavoidable; some measure of recognition of it runs, as we have seen, through the literature of all the Christian ages, and it is big with significance.

I have frequently quoted in the course of this lecture Newman's essay on *The Miracles of Ecclesiastical History compared with those of Scripture, as regards their nature, credibility and evidence*. Indeed, I have purposely drawn a good deal of my material from it. Perhaps I owe you some account of this book, which is, perhaps, an even more famous book than Middleton's, formerly described to you. Newman had written in 1825-6 a paper on *The Miracles of Scripture, compared with those reported elsewhere, as regards their nature, credibility, and evidence.* That was in his Protestant days, and in this paper he takes sufficiently strong ground against the genuineness of ecclesiastical miracles. Then came the Oxford movement of which he was the leader; and afterward his drift Romeward. As this drift was reaching its issue in his passing into the Roman church —in 1842-3—he wrote the subtle plea for the genuineness of ecclesiastical miracles with which we are now concerned, primarily as a preface for a translation of a portion of Fleury's *Ecclesiastical History.*[47] How well pleased he, as a Catholic, was with his performance is evidenced by his republication of the two papers together, without substantial alteration, in repeated editions after his perversion.

The essay now claiming our attention is probably the most specious plea for the credibility and reality of the whole mass of ecclesiastical miracles ever penned. I say the whole mass, although Newman, with great apparent candor, admits that there is to be found among them every variety of miracle, of every degree of intrinsic credibility or incredibility, and supported by every degree of evidence or no-evidence. For, after he has, under the cover of this candor, concentrated attention upon what seem to him the particular miracles most deserving to be true, and supported by the most direct and weighty evidence, he subtly suggests that, on their basis, many more in themselves doubtful or distasteful may be allowed, that insufficiency of proof is not the same as disproof, and that very many things must be admitted by us to be very likely true for the truth of which we have no evidence at all—inasmuch as we must distinguish sharply between the fact and the proof of the fact, and must be prepared to admit that failure of the latter does not carry with it the rejection of the former.

The disposition of matter in this famous essay is as follows. First, the antecedent probability of the ecclesiastical miracles is estimated; then, their internal character is investigated; then, the argument in their behalf in general is presented; and finally the major portion of the essay is given to a detailed attempt to demonstrate that a few selected miracles of greater intrinsic likelihood and better attestation than the mass, actually happened—such as those of the thundering legion, the changing of water into oil by Narcissus, the alteration of the course of the Lycus by Gregory Thaumaturgus, the appearance of the cross to Constantine, the discovery of the cross by Helena, the death of Arius, the fiery eruption which stopped Julian's attempt to build the temple at Jerusalem, the cure of blindness by relics, and the speech of the African confessors without tongues. Everywhere the reader is charmed by the delightful style, and everywhere he is led on by the hand of a master-reasoner bending facts and reason alike to follow the path appointed for them.

The opening argument runs as follows. Although there may be a certain antecedent probability against this or that particular miracle, there can be no presumption whatever against miracles generally after the Apostles, because inspiration has borne the brunt of any such antecedent prejudice, and, in establishing the certainty of the supernatural histories of the Scriptures, has disproved their impossibility in the abstract. The skilfulness of this is beyond praise. By keeping his reader's attention fixed on the possibility of miracles in the abstract, Newman quite distracts it from the decisive question in the case—whether the scriptural histories of miracles do not themselves raise a presumption against the alleged miracles succeeding them. At a later point, to be sure, this question is raised. But only in a special form, namely, whether the difference between the biblical and ecclesiastical miracles is not so great that the latter become improbable if the former be admitted. A difference is allowed; but its implications are avoided by an appeal to the analogy of nature, in professed imitation of Joseph Butler. It is argued, namely, that the case is very much like that of a man familiar only with the noblest animals, which have been subjected to human dominion, who is suddenly introduced into a zoological garden and, perceiving the great variety of animal nature, the hideousness and uselessness of much of it, is led to deny that all could have come from God. Thus, says Newman, one accustomed to only the noble miracles of Scripture may be pardoned some doubt when introduced into the jungles of ecclesiastical history. But doubt here too should pass away with increasing knowledge and a broadening outlook on the divine power and works. This is the argument of the second section, on the "internal character of ecclesiastical miracles." But the real grounds of the presumption against ecclesiastical miracles are never adverted to—namely that Scripture represents miracles to be attached to the Apostles, the vehicles of revelation, as their signs, and thus raises an antecedent presumption against any miracles having occurred after their age; that on the testimony of history miracles accordingly ceased with the Apostolic age, and only after an interval are heard of again; that, when heard of again, they are the apparent progeny of the apocryphal miracles of the Gnostic and Ebionitic romances of the second and third centuries and not of the miracles of the New Testament; that they accordingly differ not only *toto cœlo* from the miracles of the Scripture in kind, but are often wrought in support of superstitions not only foreign to the religion of the Bible, but in contradiction to it. Of all this Newman says not a word, and he manages to carry the reader so along with him by an exhibition of candor when candor is harmless that there is danger of its being forgotten that of all this anything ought to be said.

The section on the state of the argument begins polemi-

cally, but soon returns to the main point, namely that the
case is to be settled on the ground of antecedent probability.
This is then at once resolved into the question of the doctrine of the church. Newman, it is true, expresses himself
as if what he was handling was the reality of Christianity.
He warns us that scepticism here may, nay, must, be at
bottom "disbelief in the grace committed to the church."
He suggests that those who realize that the bodies of the
saints in life are the Temples of the Highest ought not to
feel offense if miracles are wrought by these bodies after
death. Finally, he enunciates the proposition that "it
may be taken as a general truth that, where there is an
admission of Catholic doctrines, there no prejudice will
exist against ecclesiastical miracles; while those who disbelieve in the existence among us of the hidden Power will
eagerly avail themselves of every plea for explaining away
its open manifestation." [48]

This again is very skilfully put. But there is no reason
why the judgment expressed should not be concurred in
without debate. A Catholic, believing first in the divinity
of the church as the organ of the Holy Ghost, in which He
is made a deposit for the whole world, and from which
alone He can be obtained; and believing, next, in the truth
of all the distinctive teachings of this church, as to monasticism and asceticism, relics and saints, transubstantiation,
and the like, in honor of which the alleged miracles are
performed—will naturally be predisposed to believe these
miracles real. A Protestant, believing none of these things,
but looking upon them as corruptions of the Gospel, will
as naturally be predisposed to believe them spurious. In
this sense, every Protestant must deny the existence of
"the hidden Power among us" which Newman affirms,
and hence cannot either expect or allow "open manifestations" of it. We believe in a wonder-working God; but
not in a wonder-working church. Thus the effect of Newman's argument, when once it is probed, is to uncover the

root of the matter, and to make clear just what the presumption against ecclesiastical miracles is. It matters not that he proceeds to cite the last twelve verses of Mark and to build an argument upon the promise included in them. The spuriousness of the passage evacuates the argument. It is a meaningless excrescence, however, upon his argument in any case. That ultimately comes merely to the historical *causa finita est: ecclesia locuta est.*

The examination of the evidence for selected miracles which is presented at the end of the volume is an interesting piece of work, but is unconvincing for the main matter. That the conclusion in each case lacks cogency may be shown in one way or another; but it is not necessary to do this. Newman himself allows that the general conclusion reached rests on the antecedent presumption; and that that depends on our attitude to Roman doctrine. For its inherent interest, however, we may glance for a moment at the last, and perhaps the most striking, of the instances of miracles the evidence for which Newman treats fully. It is the miracle of the continued speech of the African confessors deprived of their tongues by the cruelty of Hunneric in 484. The evidence, which is especially profuse and good, is detailed with great skill. We really cannot doubt the underlying fact. The tongues of these martyrs were cut out, cut out by the roots; and one or more of them were known at Constantinople as having still the power to speak. The miracle is inferred. The inference, however, is not stringent. It curiously emerges as a physiological fact that a man with half a tongue cannot speak, but a man with no tongue at all can. Newman knew this fact. Middleton had adduced two French cases—one of a girl born without a tongue who yet talked distinctly and easily, the other of a boy who had lost his tongue without losing his faculty of speech. Newman judged that these instances left his miracle untouched. But other evidence was soon adduced. It happens that the excision of the tongue is a

form of punishment repeatedly inflicted in the East, and
a body of evidence has grown up there which puts it beyond cavil that excision of the tongue, if thoroughly done,
does not destroy the power of speech.   In his later editions,
while recording this evidence in an appendix, Newman is
still unable frankly to allow that this is what happened to
the African martyrs.[49]

Perhaps I ought to mention before leaving Newman's
book that it has been subjected to a very thorough examination, and has been given a very complete refutation by
Edwin A. Abbott, in a volume devoted wholly to it, published under the significant title of *Philomythus*.[50] And,
having mentioned this book, perhaps I ought to say further
that the same writer has also published a very extended
discussion of the miracles of Thomas à Becket,[51] under the
impression that some sort of a parallel might be drawn
between them and the miracles of the New Testament,
to the disadvantage of the acknowledgment of the truly
miraculous character of the latter.   Nothing further need
be said of this than what has been briefly said by A. G.
Headlam in the course of a discussion of miracles, which
he read at the Church Congress at Middlesbrough (1912).[52]
"Reference has been made to miracles of St. Thomas of
Canterbury," he says, "and it is maintained that those
miracles are supported by as good evidence as the Gospel
narratives, and that they represent just the same strong
ethical character that our Lord's work did.   I do not
think that any one who makes assertions of this sort can
have looked at the evidence for a moment.   We have very
full accounts of the life of Thomas à Becket, and we have
many letters written by him.   In none whatever of the
early narratives is there any reference to miracles performed in his lifetime.   Neither he himself nor his contemporaries claimed that he could work miracles.   The stories
of miraculous happenings are entirely confined to the miracles believed to have been worked by his dead body after

his death, and these narratives are exactly of the same character as those recorded at Lourdes, for example, at the present day. Many of them represent answers to prayers which were offered up in different parts of the world in the name of St. Thomas, many of them are trivial, and some repellent. Some doubtless represent real cures, which were worked among those who went on a pilgrimage, just as there can be no doubt that real cures are experienced by those who go to Lourdes. What their character may be we need not discuss at this moment, but the whole tone of the narrative represents something quite different from anything that we experience when reading the story of the Gospel."

We return now to the main question: What are we to think of these miracles? There is but one historical answer which can be given. They represent an infusion of heathen modes of thought into the church. If we wish to trace this heathen infusion along the line of literary development, we must take our start from those Apocryphal Acts of Encratite tendency which, in a former lecture, we had occasion to point to as naturalizing the heathen wonder-tales—then a fashionable literary form—in the church. Once naturalized in the church, these Christian wonder-tales developed along the line of the church's own development. As time went on, E. von Dobschütz explains, the church drew ever closer to the Encratite ideals which were glorified in the Apocryphal Acts, and it was this which gave their tendency to the new Christian romances which began to multiply in the later fourth century, and are represented to us especially by Athanasius' *Life of Antony*, and Jerome's *Lives of Paul, Hilarion*, and *Malchus*. "Whether there is any historical kernel in them or not," remarks Von Dobschütz,[53] "they are exactly like the older Christian romances, described already, in their fundamental traits— loose structure, miraculousness and asceticism." The state of the case is fairly brought before us by R. Reitzen-

stein, when, after expounding at length the relevant details,
he states his conclusion thus:[54] "I think I may now venture to say that the prophet and philosopher aretalogies
supplied the literary model for the Christian Acts of the
Apostles. . . . But in order properly to feel the extent
and influence of this literature, we must follow the Christian aretalogy a step further. . . . This new literature
arose, as is well known, when, after the victory of Christianity, the interest of the community shifted from the
portrait of the ideal missionary to the strange figures of
the hermits and monks. For us there come especially into
consideration Athanasius' *Life of Antony*, and the two great
collections of the *Historia Monachorum* and the *Historia
Lausiaca;* only in the second rank, the *Lives of Paul* and
Hilarion by Jerome."

It has been much disputed of late, whether the work
which stands at the head of this literature, Athanasius'
Life of Antony, is really Athanasius' or is a work of fiction.
Perhaps we do not need to treat the alternative as absolute.
The book can scarcely be denied to Athanasius, and if we
conceive it as a work of fiction, it ceases to be wholly un-
worthy of him. "In spite of its bad Greek—Athanasius
was anything but a master of form"—writes Reitzenstein,[55]
"the book belongs distinctly to the category of 'great literature,' and its appearance may be spoken of as an event
of world-historical importance." T. R. Glover, who con-
siders that it has been demonstrated that the book is a
"work of fiction," points out[56] that "it was fiction as
Uncle Tom's Cabin was fiction," and wrought even more
powerfully; "of all the books of the fourth century it had
the most immediate and wide-spread influence, which,
though outgrown by us, lasted on to the Renaissance."
How great the misfortune was that the ascetic ideal should
be commended to the world-weary people of God in this
age of dying heathenism through the medium of a romance
of such undeniable power, the event only too sadly showed.

The elevation of the work above its successive imitators—Jerome's *Paul* and *Hilarion* and *Malchus*, Sulpitius Severus's *Martin* and beyond—is immense. Reitzenstein suggests it to us[57] in the contrast he draws between it and Jerome's *Life of Hilarion*. It is Jerome's obvious purpose to outvie Athanasius, and he does it with vigor. "The difference between the two works," says Reitzenstein, "is certainly very great. Athanasius handled the miraculous narrative as a concession to his public, laid all the stress on the discipline of the monk, and precisely thus raised the work to a value which must be felt even by one who is filled with horror by this pedagogically presented union of the fervor of Christian faith and Egyptian superstition. Jerome has retrenched even the preaching and the exhortation which form the religious kernel of the heathen as well as the Christian aretalogy; the miracle narrative is its own end; it is 'great history' which he is giving, and he presents it by this means." [58]

Thus a new literature sprang up synchronously with monasticism—a monkish belletristic, as A. Harnack calls it.[59] "Feuilletonists in monks' clothing made romances and novels out of the real and invented experiences of the penitents, and the ancient world delighted itself with this preciosity of renunciation." The miraculous was in this literature a matter of course; and the ever-swelling accounts of miracles in that age of excited superstition transferred themselves with immense facility to life. "The martyr-legend," says H. Günter strikingly, at the opening of his *Legend-Studies*,[60] "is older than the Christian martyrs—of course with a grain of salt—in its presuppositions"; and the same is true of the monk-legends. Günter illustrates what the martyr-legend did with Bible passages by bidding us observe what is done in the *Acts of Peter and Andrew* with Christ's saying about the camel passing through the eye of a needle. This aretalogist is so zealous for the saving of rich men that he makes a camel actually pass repeatedly through the eye of the smallest needle that can be found, before our very eyes.[61] There is nothing too hard for the monkish legend. A veil of miracle settles down over everything, covering up all historical and individual traits.

An admirable summary of what took place in the church itself, parallel with this literary development, is drawn up by Robert Rainy in the course of his general description of the effects of the introduction of monasticism into the church. "The stimulus which was applied to the fancy and to nervous tendencies," says he,[62] "is revealed also by the extraordinary harvest of visions, demoniacal assaults, and miracles which followed in its wake. The occurrence of some marvels had been associated all along with Christian history, in times of persecution especially, and in other cases of great trial. But both in type and in number these had hitherto occupied a comparatively modest place, and the Christian feeling had been that miracles comparable to the Gospel miracles had for good reasons passed away. But from Antony onward the miraculous element increases, and by the end of the fourth century it had overflowed the world. Asceticism was one cause; another, which operated in the same way, was the mood of mind now prevailing in regard to the relics of the saints. Illustrations of the first may be found abundantly in Sulpitius Severus. For the effect of relics, note how Augustine, who in earlier days recognized the comparative absence of the miraculous from Christian experience, in later life qualified and virtually retracts the statement. For in the meantime not only had asceticism begun to bear fruits, but the relics of St. Stephen had come into Africa, and miracles everywhere followed in their train; and such miracles!"

When we say that this great harvest of miracles thus produced in Christian soil, from the late fourth century on, in connection with the rise of the monastic movement, was a transplantation from heathendom, we do not mean to imply that the particular miracles thus produced owed nothing to the Christian soil in which they grew. As they were the products of human hopes and fears, and humanity is fundamentally the same in all ages and under all skies, miracle-stories of this kind present a general family likeness·in all times and in all religious environments. But they are, of course, colored also by the special modes of thinking and feeling of the peoples among whom they severally rise, and Christian miracle-stories will, therefore, inevitably be Christian in their ground tone. C. F. Arnold describes very strikingly the difference in character and underlying postulates between the miraculous stories which grew up among the Christian population of southern Gaul and those of the heathen which they supplanted. He is speaking of the time of Cæsarius of Arles, in the first half of the sixth century. "Besides marvels of healing," he says,[63] "many other marvels are also related. It is easy to say that mediæval barbarism reveals itself in such records. But we must not forget that not only are the books of Apuleius filled with the wildest superstitions, but even such a highly educated heathen as the younger Pliny believed in the silliest ghost-stories. We not only perceive in this a reflection of folk-belief among the educated, but we are especially struck with the naturalism, the passive character of heathen religiousness. Christian superstition as it meets us in the environment of Cæsarius, always differs from the heathen by its double ideal background. First, we are met in it with a childlike form of vital faith in Providence, which, in these days of practical pessimism and materialism, we might almost envy that time. Secondly, there speaks to us in it, not fear in the presence of the blind forces of nature, as in heathen superstition, but a certain confidence in the victory of the spirit over nature. From a practical point of view this superstition wrought great evil, because it hindered fighting against physical ills with the weapon with which they should have been fought—that is, by God-trusting labor. Sickness was fought as if it had been sin, with prayer; while, on the other hand, sin was fought as if it had been sickness, with diligence in ascetic practices." Even a man so great and wise as Cæsarius was not able to escape this deeply rooted superstition. He shared, as Arnold phrases it, the fundamental error which, from a theological standpoint, underlay this whole miracle thirst: the error of failing to distinguish between the epoch of the creation of salvation and that of its appropriation. But Cæsarius was wise enough, while not denying that miracles still happened, to minimize their importance, and to point rather to spiritual wonders as the things to be sought.[64] "What is the example of Christ that we are to follow?" he asks. "Is it that we should raise the dead? Is it that we should walk on the surface of the sea? Not at all; but that we should be meek and humble of heart, and should love not only our friends but also our enemies."

As the miraculous stories of the populace thus took on a Christian complexion when the people who produced them became Christian, and became now the vehicles of Christian faith in Providence and of hope in the God who is the maker and ruler of the whole earth; so they reflect also the other currents of popular belief and feeling of the day. A long series might be gleaned from the mediæval records, for example, which reflect the ingrained belief in magic which tinged the thought of an age so little instructed in the true character of the forces of nature, and especially its deeply seated conception of the essentially magical nature of religion and its modes of working. Paul Sabatier, in his *Life of Francis of Assisi*, cites a number of instances of the kind,[65] from which we may cull the following. "In one case a parrot being carried away by a kite uttered the invocation dear to his master, '*sancte Thoma, adjuva me*,' and was immediately rescued. In another a merchant of Groningen, having purloined an arm of St.

John the Baptist, grew rich as if by enchantment, so long as he kept it concealed in his house, but was reduced to beggary so soon as, his secret being discovered, the relic was taken away from him and placed in a church." "A chronicler relates that the body of St. Martin of Tours had, in 887, been secretly transported to some remote hiding-place for fear of the Danish invasion. When the time came for bringing it home again, there were in Touraine two impostors, men who, thanks to their infirmity, gained large sums by begging. They were thrown into great terror by the tidings that the relics were being brought back; St. Martin would certainly heal them and take away their means of livelihood! Their fears were only too well founded. They had taken to flight; but being too lame to walk fast, they had not yet crossed the frontier of Touraine when the saint arrived and healed them." The mediæval chronicles are full of such stories in which the crass popular thought of the age expresses itself. Folk-tales are, after all, folk-tales, and must embody the people's ideas and sentiments.

One result is that the production of miraculous stories cannot be confined to authorized modes of thinking. If the dominant ecclesiastical powers avail themselves of the universal tendency to the manufacture of folk-stories in order to commend their system, they must expect to reckon with entirely similar stories supporting what they look upon as heresy. It accordingly happens that the heretics of all ages are at least as well provided with supporting miracles as the church itself. If Catholics took advantage of the tendency to superstition abroad in the world to conquer the unbeliever, it was but natural that "heretics often took advantage of this thirst for the marvellous to dupe the Catholics. The Cathari of Monceval made a portrait of the Virgin, representing her as one-eyed and toothless, saying that, in His humility, Christ had chosen a very ugly woman for mother. They had no difficulty in healing several cases of disease by its means; the image became famous, was venerated almost everywhere, and accomplished many miracles, until the day when the heretics divulged the deception, to the great scandal of the faithful." [66]

A more entertaining incident of the same kind occurred in France in the first half of the eighteenth century. The Jansenists had their miracles, you will understand, as well as the Jesuits. A young Jansenist cleric, François de Paris, was a particularly warm opponent of Clement XIV's bull *Unigenitus*. This did not prevent his acquiring a great reputation for sanctity. He died in 1727. Scarcely was this admirable man dead, says Mosheim,[67] than an immense crowd flocked around his body, kissing his feet, securing locks of his hair, books, and clothing he had used, and the like; and immediately the wonder-working power that was expected, appeared. Neither the excitement nor the miraculous phenomena showed any sign of ceasing after the burial of the good abbé. His tomb in the churchyard of St. Médard became the resort of the Jansenist *convulsionnaires*, and the constant scene of at once the most marvellous and the most fantastic miracles. In a few years his grave had grown into a famous shrine to which men came in crowds from all over France to be cured of their diseases, and at which prophecies, speaking with tongues, and ecstatic phenomena of all sorts daily took place. This could not be other than gravely displeasing to the Jesuits, and as the Jesuits were the power behind the throne, it could not be permitted to continue. To check it seemed, however, difficult if not impossible. At last the expedient was adopted of enclosing the tomb so that none might approach it. This, no doubt, brought miracles at the grave itself to an end, though it could not calm the general excitement. And some wag turned the tables on the Jesuits by chalking in great letters on the enclosure, after the manner of a royal proclamation, these words:[68]

> De par le Roy, défence à Dieu
> De faire miracle en ce lieu.

The whole incident of the miracles of St. Médard is full of instruction for us as to the origin and character of the miracle-working[69] which fills the annals of the patristic and mediæval church.[70]

ROMAN CATHOLIC MIRACLES

ROMAN CATHOLIC MIRACLES

It would be natural to suppose that the superstitions which flourished luxuriantly in the Middle Ages would be unable to sustain themselves in the clearer atmosphere of the twentieth century. "We shall have no repetition of mediæval miracles," says W. F. Cobb with some show of conviction,[1] "for the simple reason that faith in God has ousted credulity in nature." When we speak thus, however, we are reckoning without the church of Rome. For the church of Rome, while existing in the twentieth century, is not of it. As Yrjö Hirn crisply puts it:[2] "The Catholic Church is a Middle Age which has survived into the twentieth century." Precisely what happened to the church of Rome at that epoch in the history of Christianity which we call the Reformation, was that it bent its back sturdily to carry on with it all the lumber which had accumulated in the garrets and cellars of the church through a millennium and a half of difficult living. It is that part of the church which refused to be reformed; which refused, that is, to free itself from the accretions which had attached themselves to Christianity during its long struggle with invading superstition. Binding these closely to its heart, it has brought them down with it to the present hour.[3] The church of Rome, accordingly, can point to a body of miracles, wrought in our own day and generation, as large and as striking as those of any earlier period of the church's history. And when the annals of the marvels of the nineteenth and twentieth centuries come to be collected, there is no reason to suppose that they will compare unfavorably in point either of number or marvellousness with those of any of the "ages of faith" which have preceded

73

them. This continuous manifestation of supernatural powers in its bosom constitutes one of the proudest boasts of the church of Rome; by it, it conceives itself differentiated, say, from the Protestants; and in it it finds one of its chief credentials as the sole organ of God Almighty for the saving of the wicked world.[4]

We had occasion in a previous lecture to point out that this great stream of miracle-working which has run thus through the history of the church was not original to the church, but entered it from without.[5] The channel which we then indicated was not the only one through which it flowed into the church. It was not even the most direct one. The fundamental fact which should be borne in mind is that Christianity, in coming into the world, came into a heathen world. It found itself, as it made its way ever more deeply into the world, ever more deeply immersed in a heathen atmosphere which was heavy with miracle. This heathen atmosphere, of course, penetrated it at every pore, and affected its interpretation of existence in all the happenings of daily life. It was not merely, however, that Christians could not be immune from the infection of the heathen modes of thought prevalent about them. It was that the church was itself recruited from the heathen community. Christians were themselves but baptized heathen, and brought their heathen conceptions into the church with them, little changed in all that was not obviously at variance with their Christian confession. He that was unrighteous, by the grace of God did not do unrighteousness still; nor did he that was filthy remain filthy still. But he that was superstitious remained superstitious still; and he who lived in a world of marvels looked for and found marvels happening all about him still. In this sense the conquering church was conquered by the world which it conquered.

It is possible that we very commonly underestimate the marvellousness of the world with which the heathen imagination surrounded itself, crippled as it was by its ignorance of natural law, and inflamed by the most incredible superstition. Perhaps we equally underestimate the extent to which this heathen view of the world passed over into the church. Th. Trede bids us keep well in mind that Christianity did not bring belief in miracles into the world; it found it there. The whole religion of the heathen turned on it; what they kept their gods for was just miracles. As Theodore Mommsen puts it in a single sentence:[6] "The Roman gods were in the first instance instruments which were employed for attaining very concrete earthly ends"— and then he adds, very significantly, "a point of view which appears not less sharply in the saint-worship of present-day Italy." "The power," says Trede,[7] "which in the Roman Empire set the state religion going, as well as the numerous local, social, and family cults, was belief in miracles. The gods, conceived as protecting beings, as undoubted powers in the world, but as easily offended, were, by the honor brought to them in their worship, to be made and kept disposed to interpose in the course of nature for the benefit of their worshippers, in protecting, helping, succoring, rescuing them; that is to say, were to work miracles. Belief in miracles was involved in belief in the gods; only denial of the gods could produce denial of miracles." Enlarging on the matter with especial reference to the third century, Trede continues:[8] "In the third century religious belief was steeped in belief in miracles. In their thinking and in their believing men floated in a world of miracles like a fish in water. The more miraculous a story the more readily it found believing acceptance. There was no question of criticism, however timid; the credulity of even educated people reached an unheard-of measure, as well as the number of those who, as deceived or deceivers, no longer knew how to distinguish between truth and falsehood. Those of the old faith (the heathen) had no doubt of the miracles of those of the new faith (the

Christians), and *vice versa*. The whole population of the
Roman Empire was caught in a gigantic net of superstition,
the product of the combined work of East and West.
There never was a society so enlightened and so *blasé* that
lived so entirely in the world of the supernatural." And
he too draws the parallel with our own times. He adduces
the incredible things related by an Aristides and an Ælian,
and then adds:[9] "Things just like this are still related . . .
Ælian and Aristides are still living, as the miracle-stories
at the famous places of pilgrimage show. We mention
here the miracles at Lourdes and Pompeii *nuova*, which
afford a very close likeness of the doings of the third century. The miracles of the nineteenth century recall those
of the third."

Are we then to discredit out of hand the teeming multitudes of wonders which fill the annals of the church despite
their attestation in detail by men of probity and renown?
What credit can be accorded the testimony of men even
of probity and renown in matters in which they show themselves quite color-blind? Take Augustine, for example.
Adolf Harnack declares,[10] and declares truly, that he was
incomparably the greatest man whom the Christian church
possessed "between Paul the Apostle and Luther the Re-
former." And, perhaps more to our present purpose, there
was nothing in which he overtopped his contemporaries and
successors more markedly than in his high sense of the
sacredness of truth and his strict regard for veracity in
speech. In contrast with "the priests and theologians"
of his time, who, on occasion, "lied shamelessly," Harnack, for example, calls him[11] "Augustine the truthful,"
and that with full right. There is no one to whom we
could go with more confidence, whether on the score of his
ability or his trustworthiness, than to Augustine, to assure
us of what really happened in any ordinary matter. Yet,
whenever it is a case of marvellous happenings, he shows
himself quite unreliable. Here he is a child of his times and

cannot rise above them. What value can be attached to the testimony to wonders by a man, however wise in other matters and however true-hearted we know him to be, who can, for example, tell us gravely that peacock's flesh is incorruptible—he knows it because he has tried it? "When I first heard of it," he tells us,[12] "it seemed to me incredible; but it happened at Carthage that a bird of this kind was cooked and served up to me, and, taking a slice of flesh from its breast, I ordered it to be kept, and when it had been kept as many days as make any other flesh offensive, it was produced and set before me, and emitted no unpleasant odor. And after it had been laid by for thirty days more, it was still in the same state; and a year after, the same still, except that it was a little more shrivelled and drier."

Take another example which brings us closer to our present theme. Augustine tells us[13] that in the neighboring town of Tullium there dwelt a countryman named Curma, who lay unconscious for some days, sick unto death, and in this state saw into the other world, as in a dream. When he came to himself, the first thing he did was to say: "Let some one go to the house of Curma the smith, and see how it is with him." Curma the smith was found to have died at the very moment in which Curma the farmer "had returned to his senses and almost been resuscitated from death." He then told that he had heard in that place whence he had just returned that it was not Curma the farmer but Curma the smith who had been ordered to be brought to the place of the dead. Augustine, now, tells us that he knew this man, and at the next Easter baptized him. It was not until two years later, however, that he learned of his vision; but then he sent for him and had him bring witnesses with him. He had his story from his own lips and verified all the circumstantial facts carefully by the testimony of others who had first-hand knowledge of them—Curma's sickness, his recovery, his narrative of what had befallen him, and the timely death of the other Curma. He not only himself believes it all, but clearly expects his readers to believe it on the ground of his testimony.

This, however, is only the beginning. Gregory the Great tells the same story[14]—not, however, on the authority of Augustine as having happened to Curma of Tullium, but as having happened within his own knowledge to an acquaintance of his own—"the illustrious Stephen," he calls him, a man well known (and that means favorably known), he says, to Peter, the friend to whom he is writing. Stephen, he says, had related to him frequently his wonderful experience. He had gone to Constantinople on business, and, falling sick, had died there. The embalmers being a little difficult to get at, the body was fortunately left overnight unburied. Meanwhile the soul was conducted to the lower regions and brought before the judge. The judge, however, repelled it, saying: "It was not this one, but Stephen the smith that I ordered to be brought." The soul was immediately returned to the body, and Stephen the smith, who lived near by, died at that very hour. Thus it was proved that "the illustrious Stephen" had really heard the words of the judge; the death of Stephen the smith demonstrated it. Are we bound, on the credit of Augustine and Gregory, both of whom relate it as having happened within their own knowledge to acquaintances of their own, to believe that this thing really did happen, happened twice, and in both cases through one of the same name being mistaken for a smith?

We are not yet, however, at the end of the matter. The same story is related by the heathen satirist Lucian,[15] writing as far back as the third quarter of the second century—two hundred and fifty years before Augustine, and three hundred and fifty years before Gregory. Only, Lucian has this advantage over his Christian successors in his way of telling it, that he does not tell it as having really happened, but in a rollicking mood, laughing at the superstitions of his time. He brings before us a chance gathering of men, who, in their conversation, fall to vying with one another in "romancing" of their supernatural experiences. One of them, a Peripatetic, named Cleodemus, makes this contribution to the conversation. "I had become ill, and Antigonus here was attending me. The fever had been on me for seven days, and was now aggravated by the excessive heat. All my attendants were outside, having closed the door and left me to myself; those were your orders, you know, Antigonus; I was to get some sleep if I could. Well, I woke up to find a handsome young man standing by my side, in a white cloak. He raised me up from the bed, and conducted me through a sort of a chasm into Hades; I knew where I was at once, because I saw Tantalus and Tityus and Sisyphus. Not to go into details, I came to the judgment-hall, and there were Æacus and Charon, and the Fates and the Furies. One person of a majestic appearance—Pluto, I suppose it was—sat reading out the names of those who were due to die, their term of life having lapsed. The young man took me and set me before him, but Pluto flew into a rage: 'Away with him,' he said to my conductor; 'his thread is not yet out; go and fetch Demylus the smith; *he* has had his spindleful and more!' I ran off home, nothing loath. My fever had now disappeared, and I told everybody that Demylus was as good as dead. He lived close by, and was said to have some illness, and it was not long before we heard the voices of mourners in his house."

The late James Payne, the novelist, used whimsically to contend that fiction did not imitate life as was commonly supposed, but, on the contrary, life imitated fiction; a romancer could not invent a motive, he said, however *bizarre*, but a lot of people would soon be found staging copies of it in real life. Perhaps on some such theory we might defend the reality of the occurrences related by Augustine and Gregory as having happened within their own knowledge. Scarcely on any other. That the source of Augustine's and Gregory's stories lies in Lucian's is too obvious to require arguing; even the doomed smith is common to all three, and the strong heathen coloring of the story is not obscured, in Gregory's version at least, which clearly is independent of Augustine's. Heinrich Günter has an ingenious theory designed to save the credit of the saints. He supposes[16] that the story might have been so widely known that sick people would be likely to reproduce it in their fevered dreams. "To such an extent," he remarks, "had certain imaginary conceptions become the common property of the people that they repeated themselves as autosuggestions and dreams." [17] One would presume, even so, that when the dreamers woke up, they would recognize their dreams as old acquaintances; and how shall we account for Augustine and Gregory not recognizing such well-known stories circulating so universally among the masses, when they were told them as fresh experiences of the other world?

Hippolyte Delehaye frankly gives up the effort to save the credit of all parties. "It is impossible to be mistaken," he comments.[18] "That friend of St. Gregory's was an unscrupulous person, who bragged of having been the hero of a story which he had read in the books. To say nothing of St. Augustine, Plutarch could have taught it to him, and better still, Lucian." Nothing is said here to save Augustine's reputation for truthfulness; and if Gregory's honor is saved it is at the expense not only of his friend Stephen's, but also of his own intelligence. Could not Gregory, as well as Stephen, have read his Plutarch or his Lucian, to say nothing of his Augustine, whom of course he had read, though equally of course he had not remembered him? And how could he have listened to and repeated Stephen's tale without noting the heathen coloring of it, which alone should have stamped it to him as a bit of romancing? R. Reitzenstein is not so tender of the honor of the saints as Delehaye, and has theories of his own to consider. The close agreement of the details of the story as Augustine tells it with Lucian's version, as well as the use which Augustine makes of it, "leave no doubt," he thinks,[19] "that Augustine has simply transferred to his own time an early Christian miracle-tale, known to him in literary form, without taking offense at this ψευδός, which obviously belongs to the style; that early Christian story having been on its part taken almost verbally from a heathen motive." Gregory is supposed to have derived indirectly from Augustine—which, we may say in passing, is impossible, since Gregory's story is much closer to Lucian's than Augustine's is. And we may say, also in passing, that there is no proof of the circulation of the story in a written early Christian form, and no justification for representing Augustine as receiving it from any other source than that which he himself expressly indicates—namely the narrative of Curma. Augustine comes out of the affair with his feathers ruffled enough; we need not gratuitously ruffle them more.

With Reitzenstein we pass over from the theologians to the philologists, and the philologists' interest in the matter is absorbed in the formal question of the origin and transmission of the story. It occurs not only in Lucian, but also, in a form less closely related to that in which Augustine and Gregory repeat it, in Plutarch. Like Augustine and Gregory, Plutarch relates it in all seriousness as having happened within his own knowledge to a friend of his own.[20] Erwin Rohde[21] thinks that Lucian is directly parodying Plutarch's anecdote; L. Radermacher[22] pronounces this absurd; and Reitzenstein[23] agrees with him in this. All three, on grounds which appear very insufficient, declare the story to have been in popular circulation before even Plutarch, and all would doubtless contend that the Christians picked it up in the first instance from its oral circulation rather than took it over directly from Lucian—which again does not seem clear.

With such matters we have now little concern. Our interest is fixed for the moment on ascertaining the amount of credit which is due to Augustine and Gregory when they tell us marvellous stories. The outstanding fact is that they stake their credit in this instance on a marvellous story which very certainly did not happen. It is not necessary to go the lengths of Reitzenstein and charge Augustine with copying the story out of a book, and attributing it to quite another source than that from which he really derived it, elaborately inventing sponsors for his new story. That is a thing which, we may be sure, could not happen with Augustine; and the explanation of Radermacher that it belongs to the accepted methods of utilizing such materials that the sponsors for the story should, on each new telling, be altered into personages known to the teller, does not remove the difficulty of supposing that this happened with an Augustine. But the trustworthiness of the saints as relaters of marvels is not saved by supposing they were deceived by their informants, even though we could imagine those informants, with Günter, in some absurd fashion to have been self-deceived, and themselves honest in their narratives. Nothing can change the central fact that both Augustine and Gregory report as having happened within their own knowledge an absurd story which a Lucian had already made ridiculous for all the world some centuries before. Clearly their credit is broken, as witnesses of marvellous occurrences. The one fact which stands out in clear light, after all that can be said has been said, is that they were, in the matter of marvellous stories, in the slang phrase, "easy." [23a]

One of the reasons why we have chosen this particular incident for discussion lies in the illustration which it supplies of the taking over into Christianity of a heathen legend bodily. In this case it is only a little isolated story which is in question. But the process went on on the largest scale. Every religious possession the heathen had, indeed, the Christians, it may be said broadly, transferred to themselves and made their own. As one of the results, the whole body of heathen legends, in one way or another, reproduced themselves on Christian ground. The remarkable studies of the Christian legends which Heinrich Günter has given us,[24] enable us to assure ourselves of the fact of this transference, and to observe its process in the large. On sketching the legendary material found in the pagan writers, he exclaims:[25] "After this survey it will be seen that there is not much left for the Middle Ages to invent. They only present the same ideas in variations and Christianized forms, and perhaps also expanded on one side or another. There is no doubt as to the agreement of the conceptions." "With the sixth century," he says again,[26] "we find the whole ancient system of legends Christianized, not only as anonymous and unlocalized vagrants, but more and more condensed, in a unitary picture, into a logical group of conceptions, and connected with real relations of historical personalities, whose historical figures they overlie. . . . The transference of the legend became now the chief thing, the saint of history gave way to that of the popular desire." "Hellenism—Pythagoreanism—Neo-Platonism—Christian Middle Ages,"—thus he sums up[27]—"the parallelism of these has made it very clear that the legend in the grotesque forms of a Nicholas Peregrinus or Keivinos or of the Mary legend is not a specifically Christian thing." In one word, what we find, when we cast our eye over the whole body of Christian legends, growing up from the third century down through the Middle Ages, is merely a reproduction, in Christian form, of the motives, and even the very incidents, which already meet us in the legends of heathendom. We do not speak now of the bodily taking over of heathen gods and goddesses and the transformation of them into Christian saints; or

of the invention of saints to be the new bearers of locally
persisting legends; or of the mere transference to Christianity of entire heathen legends, such as that of Barlaam
and Joasaph, which nobody nowadays doubts is just the
story of Buddha.[28]   What we have in mind at the moment
is the complete reproduction in the conception-world of
the Christian legends of what is already found in the
heathen.   In this respect the two are precise duplicates.
We may still, no doubt, raise the question of the ultimate
origin of this conception-world.   That, remarks Günter,
"is not determined by the fact that it is the common possession of all.   In the last analysis," he declares,[29] "it has
come out of the belief of mankind in the other world.   It
is scarcely possible now to determine how old it is, or where
it originated.   The manner in which it flowered, and especially in which it discharged itself into Christianity,
however, gives an intimation also of the explanation of its
first origin."   It is this mass of legends, the Christianized
form of the universal product of the human soul, working
into concrete shape its sense of the other world, that the
church of Rome has taken upon its shoulders.   It is not
clear that it has added anything of importance to it.[30]

There is one type of miracle, it is true, which is new to
Christianity, though not to the church of Rome; for it
was invented by the mediæval church, and has been taken
from it with the rest.   We refer to stigmatization.   The
heathen world had no stigmatics; they are a specifically
Christian creation,[31] deriving their impulse from the contemplation of the wounds of Christ.   The first stigmatic
known to history is Francis of Assisi.[32]   After him, however,
there have come a great multitude, extending in unbroken
series down to our own day.   The earliest of these is
Catharine of Siena (1370), who, however, possessed the
stigmata only inwardly, not in outward manifestation;[33]
the latest the fame of whom has reached the general public
is a certain Gemma Galgani of Lucca, who received the

five wounds in 1899, those of the crown of thorns being added in 1900, and of the scourging in 1901—the external signs, in her case too, being subsequently removed in answer to her prayers.[34]   A. Imbert-Gourbeyre[35] has noted 321 instances in all, only 41 of which have been men, along with 280 women; the nineteenth century supplies 29 of his instances.   Only 62 of the 321 have received the official recognition of the church in the form of canonization or beatification; and, indeed, it is sometimes hinted that the church is not absolutely committed to the supernatural character of the stigmata in more than two or three instances— in that of Francis of Assisi, of course, and with him perhaps also only in those of Catharine of Siena and Lucie de Narnia.[36]   A disposition is manifested in some Romanist writers, in fact, to speak with great reserve of the supernaturalness of the stigmata.   A. Poulain, who writes the article on the subject in *The Catholic Encyclopedia*, for example, will not distinctly assert that they are supernatural in origin, but contents himself with declaring that they have not been shown to be natural.   Others remind us that[37] "the learned pope, Benedict XIV, in his *Treatise on the Canonization of the Saints*, does not attach capital importance to stigmatization, and does not seek in it a demonstration of sanctity; but himself notes that nature may have some part in it as well as grace"; or that Ignatius Loyola, when "consulted one day about a young stigmatic, responded that the marks described to him might just as well have been the work of the devil as of God." [38]

The writer of the article on this subject in Migne's *Dictionnaire des Prophéties et des Miracles*[39] seems to speak with Loyola's warning ever in mind, and to be above all things anxious that it should not be forgotten that these stigmatic marks are no safe *indicia* of supernatural action.   He appears almost to bewail the multitudinousness of the instances, lest by it we should be betrayed into confusing the good and the bad.   Francis and Catharine, he says, "are

in fact the two most ancient examples related by history
. . . but since then," he sighs, "how many stigmatics has
the world not seen!" "It is a great pity," he goes on to
object, "that the ignorance of the people, always benevolent and pious in their judgments, should take for divine
favors natural marks resulting from certain maladies which
it is scarcely decent even to name, or from the artifices of
fraud; and it is a very horrible thing that fraud should have
a place in a matter so respectable and so holy." "The
Charpy of Troyes," he exclaims, "was stigmatized; the
Bucaille of Valogne was stigmatized; Marie Desrollée of
Coutance was stigmatized; the Cadière was stigmatized;
and how many others besides! We have known of those
who have deserved nothing so little as the name of saint
which was attached to them by a mocking or a credulous
public; there were *convulsionnaires* of St. Médard who were
stigmatized. But let us allow the curtain to fall on these
ignoble actors of sacrilegious comedies; the list is neither
short nor edifying." If any one wishes to know anything
more about the ladies he has just mentioned, he says, let
him go where the biographies of such ladies are wont to
be found. Meanwhile, speaking of the stigmatics of our
own day: "We know personally some of them," he says,[40]
"and we leave them in the obscurity from which it has not
pleased God to draw them. This phenomenon, natural or
divine, is not as rare as might be supposed. But natural
as it may be in many persons, it sanctifies itself, and divini-
tizes itself, so to speak, by the use which they" (the feminine "they") "know how to make of it, and the increase
of faith, of love divine, of patience, and of Christian resignation which it produces in them" (feminine "them").
"And permit me here a reflection which arises from our
subject but is applicable to many others. On the Day of
God, who knows all, and who judges all, there will be a
great disillusionment for many people who have thought
that they recognized the divine *cachet* where it was not,

and for many others who have dared to attempt to efface it where it was." "We have not greatly advanced the question of the stigmata," he confesses in closing,[41] "but if any of our readers, affected by an inclination to attribute all these phenomena to natural causes, has come in the end to doubt this conclusion or to understand that the question is always an individual one, and cannot be resolved in one sense or the other except after examination, and independently of all analogy, we shall not have entirely lost our time." It seems not an unfair paraphrase of this to say that the stigmata are in themselves no signs of the divine action; anybody can have them; but when he who has them is a saint it should be understood that they have been sent him by God. This, however, is obviously to make the saint accredit the stigmata, and not the stigmata the saint. And it clearly removes them out of the category of miraculous manifestations.

Such a cautious method of dealing with the stigmata is certainly justified by the facts of the case. The single circumstance that only ecstatics receive them[42] is suggestion enough of their origin in morbid neuroses.[43] It is sufficient to read over an account of the phenomena, written by however sympathetic an observer—say, for example, that by Joseph von Görres in his great book on *Christian Mysticism*[44]—to feel sure that we are in the presence of pathological phenomena. It is a crime to drag these suffering women into the public eye; and it is a greater crime to implant in their unformed intelligences[45] that spiritual pride which leads them to fancy themselves singled out by the Lord for special favors, and even permitted by Him to share His sufferings—nay, to join with Him in bearing the sins of the world. For we do not fully apprehend the place given to stigmatization in the Roman system of thought until we realize that the passion of the stigmatics is not expended in what we call the "imitation of Christ" —the desire to be like Him, and to enter into His sufferings

with loving sympathy—but presses on into the daring am-
bition to take part in His atoning work, and, by receiving
the same bodily wounds which He received, to share with
Him the saving of the world. "The substance of this
grace," explains Aug. Poulain,[46] "consists in pity for Christ,
participation in His sufferings, sorrows, *and for the same end
—the expiation of the sins increasingly committed in the
world*." The matter is expounded fully by G. Dumas,
professor of religious psychology at the Sorbonne, in the
course of an admirable general discussion of "Stigmatization in the Christian Mystics," printed in the *Revue des
Deux Mondes* for the 1st of May, 1907.[47] We avail ourselves of his illuminating statement.

"First of all," says he, "it is scarcely necessary to point
out the symbolical and profound sense which all the
mystics attach to the very fact of stigmatization.

"To bear the marks of the cross, of the crown of thorns,
of the lance, or of the nails is to be thought worthy by
Jesus to participate in His sufferings; it is according to the
very words of a historian of mysticism, 'to ascend with
Him to the Calvary of the crucifixion before mounting with
Him the Tabor of the Transfiguration.'[48] All the mystics,
accordingly, suffer violent pains in their stigmata, and they
hold these pains to be the essential part of their stigmatization, without which their visible stigmata would be in their
eyes only an empty decoration. They experience under
the cross, under the crown, under the nails, under the lance
the same sufferings as Jesus; they really languish and die
with Him; they participate in His passion with all the
force of their nerves. We have seen Francis and Veronica
suffer in their ecstasies all the pains of the crucifixion; they
all do this. Catherine de Ruconisio experienced violent
pains under the crown of blood which she let John Francis
de la Mirandola see; Archangelica Tardera seemed at the
point of rendering up her soul during the scene of her flagel-
lation; and Catherine de' Ricci, on coming out of the

swoon in which she was marked, 'appeared to her associates so wasted and so livid that she looked to them like a living corpse.'

"In suffering thus the mystics persuade themselves not only that they draw near to Jesus, but that they are admitted by a kind of divine grace to perpetuate the sacrifice of their God, to expiate like Him sins of which they are personally innocent. These sharp pains of the thorns, these piercing sufferings of the nails and of the lance, are not, in their minds, pains lost for men; they redeem sins, they constitute pledges of salvation, they are for them the religious and metaphysical form of charity. 'These reparative souls which recommence the terrors of Calvary,' says a contemporary mystic,[49] 'these souls who nail themselves in the empty place of Jesus on the cross, are therefore in some sort express images of the Son; they reflect in a bloody mirror His poor face; they do more: they give to this Almighty God the only thing which He yet lacks, the possibility of still suffering for us; they satiate this desire which has survived His death, since it is infinite like the love which engenders it.' The stigmata are for these new crucified ones the external notification of their transformation into Jesus Christ; they proclaim that Archangelica Tardera, that Veronica Giuliani, that Catherine de' Ricci are so like to their God that they succeed Him in His sufferings; they are the visible seals of their sanctity."

The connection of stigmatization with such doctrine is the sufficient proof that it is not from God.[50]

It is often urged in defense of the miraculousness of the stigmata that they have not yet been exactly reproduced in the laboratories.[51] It is not clear why a phenomenon so obviously pathological, and in many instances confessedly pathological, should be pronounced miraculous in others of its instances merely because the imitation of it produced in the laboratories is not exact. If, however, the precise thing has not been produced in the laboratories, something so like it has been that it is made quite clear that external suggestion is capable of producing phenomena of the same general order. William James may be appealed to to tell us the general state of the case. "I may say," writes he,[52] "that there seems no reasonable ground for doubting that in certain chosen subjects the suggestion of a congestion, a burn, a blister, a raised papule, or a bleeding from the nose or skin may produce the effect." "Messrs. Delbœuf and Liégeois have annulled by suggestion, one the effects of a burn, the other of a blister." Delbœuf "applied the actual cautery (as well as vesicants) to symmetrical places on the skin, affirming that no pain should be felt on one of the sides. The result was a dry scorch on that side, with (as he assures me) no after-mark, but on the other side a regular blister, with suppuration and a subsequent scar. This explains the innocuity of certain assaults made on subjects during trance. . . . These irritations, when not felt by the subject, seem to have no after-consequences. One is reminded of the non-inflammatory character of the wounds made on themselves by dervishes in their pious orgies. On the other hand, the reddenings and bleedings of the skin along certain lines, suggested by tracing lines or pressing objects thereupon, put the accounts handed down to us of the stigmata of the cross appearing on the hands, feet, side, and forehead of certain Catholic mystics in a new light."

Certainly the effects produced by external suggestion in the laboratories are very remarkable, and cannot fail to lead the mind in the direction of a natural explanation of the stigmata. When we see Doctor Rybalkin of St. Petersburg, by a mere command, produce a bad burn, which blisters and breaks and scabs, and slowly heals like any other burn; or Doctor Biggs of Santa Barbara a red cross on the chest which appears every Friday and disappears for the other days of the week;[53] we acquire a new sense of the extent of the possible action of the mind upon the body, and may perhaps begin to understand what can be meant when it is said:[54] "That I should be able to hold my pen because I wish to do it, is ultimately just as great a mystery as that I should develop stigmata from meditating on the Crucifixion." To do them justice, there were not wanting Catholic writers before the days of this new experimentation who had more than a glimpse of the producing cause of the stigmata. Francesco Petrarch felt no doubt that Francis' stigmata were from God, but neither had he any doubt—he says so himself, when writing, be it observed, to a physician—that they were actually produced by the forces of his own mind working on his body. "Beyond all doubt, the stigmata of St. Francis," he writes,[55] "had the following origin: he attached himself to the death of Christ with such strong meditations that he reproduced it in his mind, saw himself crucified with his Master, and finished by actualizing in his body the pious representations of his soul." Even Francis de Sales, though of course absolutely sure that the ultimate account of Francis' stigmata is that they represented "that admirable communication which the sweet Jesus made him, of His loving and precious pains," yet works out the actual mechanism of their production in elaborate but healthful naturalism. "This soul, then," he says,[56] "so mollified, softened, and almost melted away in this loving pain, was thereby extremely disposed to receive the impressions and marks of the love and pain of its sovereign Lover; for the memory was quite steeped in the remembrance of this divine love, the imagination strongly applied to represent to itself the wounds and bruises which the eyes there beheld so perfectly expressed in the image before them, the understanding received the intensely vivid images which the imagination furnished it with; and finally, love employed all the forces of the will to enter into and conform itself to the passion of the Well-Beloved; whence no doubt the soul found itself transformed into a second crucifixion. Now the soul, as form and mistress of the body, making use of its power over it, imprinted the pains of the wounds by which it was wounded in the parts corresponding to those in which its God had endured them." [57]

With all its three hundred and more examples, however, it is, after all, a small place which stigmatization takes in the wonder-life of the church of Rome. The centre about which this life revolves lies, rather, in the veneration of relics, which was in a very definite sense a derivation from heathenism. Hippolyte Delehaye, it is true, puts in a protest here. "The cult of the saints," says he,[58] "did not issue from the cult of the heroes, but from the cult of the martyrs; and the honors paid to them from the beginning and by the first Christian generations which had known the baptism of blood, are a direct consequence of the eminent dignity of the witnesses of Christ which Christ himself proclaimed. From the respect with which their mortal remains were surrounded, and from the confidence of Christians in their intercession, there proceeded the cult of relics with all its manifestations, with its exaggerations, alas! only too natural, and, why should we not say it? with its excesses, which have sometimes compromised the memory which it was wished to honor." These remarks, however, do not quite reach the point. What is asserted is not that the Christians took the heathen heroes over into their worship, though there were heathen heroes whom the Christians did take over into their worship. Neither is it that they continued unbrokenly at the tombs of these heroes the heathen rites which they were accustomed to celebrate there, only substituting another name as the object venerated. It is that under the influence of these old habits of thought and action they created for themselves a new set of heroes, Christian heroes, called saints, and developed with respect to their relics a set of superstitious practices which reproduced in all their essential traits those to which they had been accustomed with respect to the relics of the heathen heroes. There is certainly a true sense in which the saints are the successors of the gods,[59] and the whole body of superstitious practices which cluster around the cult of relics is a development in Christian circles of usages which parallel very closely those of the old heathenism.[60] The very things which Delehaye enumerates as the sources of the later cult of the saints and the veneration of their relics—the cult of the martyrs, the honor rendered to their remains, the confidence of Christians in their intercession—are themselves already abuses due to the projection into the Christian church of heathen habitudes and the natural imitation of heathen example.

There are no doubt differences to be traced between the Christian and the heathen cult of relics. And these differences are not always to the advantage of the Christians. There is the matter of the partition of relics, for example, and the roaring trade which, partly in consequence of this, has from time to time been driven in them. The ancient world knew nothing of these horrors. In it the sentiment of reverence for the dead determined all its conduct toward relics. Christians seem to have been inspired rather with eagerness to reap the fullest possible benefit from their saints; and, reasoning that when a body is filled with supernatural power every part of the body partakes of this power, they broke the bodies up into fragments and distributed them far and wide.[61] The insatiable lust to secure such valuable possessions begot in those who trafficked in them a callous rapacity which traded on the ignorance and superstition of the purchasers. The world was filled with false relics,[62] of which, however, this is to be said—that they worked as well as the true.[63] So highly was the mere possession of relics esteemed that the manner of their acquisition was condoned in the satisfaction of having them. Theft was freely resorted to—it was called *furtum laudabile*;[64] and violent robbery was not unknown—and that with (so it was said) the manifest approval of God. St.

Maximinus, bishop of Trèves, died at Poitiers (of which town he was a native) on a journey to Rome, and very naturally was buried there. But the inhabitants of Trèves wished their bishop for themselves, and stole him out of the church at Poitiers. When the Aquitanians pursued the thieves, heaven intervened and drove them back home, not without disgrace, while the thieves were left scathless,[65] and furthered on their journey.

All sorts of irreverent absurdities naturally found their way into the collections of relics, through an inflamed craving for the merely marvellous. The height of the absurd seems already to be reached when we read in Pausanias that in the shrine of "the daughters of Leucippus," at Sparta, the egg which Leda laid was to be seen.[66] The absurdity is equally great, however, when we hear of the Christians preserving feathers dropped from the wings of Gabriel when he came to announce to Mary the birth of Jesus; and it is only covered from sight by the shock given by the irreverence of it, when we read of pilgrim monks boasting of having seen at Jerusalem the finger of the Holy Spirit.[67] Any ordinary sense of the ridiculous, however, should be sufficiently satisfied by the solemn exhibition in the church of Saints Cosmas and Damien at Rome of a "vial of the milk of the Blessed Virgin Mary." But Ossa is piled on Pelion when we learn that this is far from the only specimen of Mary's milk which is to be seen in the churches. Several churches in Rome have specimens, and many in France—at Evron, and Soulac, and Mans, and Reims, and Poitiers, and St. Denis, and Bouillac, and the Sainte Chapelle at Paris; the Cathedral of Soissons has two samples of it; and the Cathedral at Chartres three. Then there is some more at Toledo and at the convent of St. Peter d'Arlanza in Spain, and of course in other countries as well. We are fairly astonished at the amount of it.[68]

This astonishment is only partly relieved when we are

told that not all of this milk need be that with which the
Virgin nourished her divine Son. The Virgin, it seems,
has been accustomed all through the ages to give nourishment to her children in their times of deadly need, and
even her statues and paintings may, on occasion, supply
it.[69] We are here in contact with a wide-spread legend of
mystical nourishment which was current toward the end
of the Middle Ages. "Mary was looked upon," as Yrjö
Hirn explains,[70] "not as an individual human being, but
as an incarnation of an eternal principle which had exercised its power long before it became embodied in the figure
of a Jewish girl. The Madonna's motherly care had previously been directed to all the faithful, who had been fed
by her 'milk' in the same way as the Child of Bethlehem.
In Mechthild's revelations it is even expressly said that the
Madonna suckled the prophets before Christ descended
into the world. Later, she fed, during His childhood,
'the Son of God and all of us,' and when He was full-grown
she offered her milk to the Christian Church. All friends
of God could get strength at her bosom. 'Eja, darnach
sollen wir bekennen—Die Milch und auch die Brüste—Die
Jesus so oft küsste.'"[71] There is symbolism here, but not
mere symbolism. Therefore Hirn continues:[72] "There is
no question of symbolism when, in the miracle-histories,
it is related that the Madonna cured pious individuals with
her healing milk.[73] It is also told of some holy men that
they were quite literally refreshed by Mary's breast. The
pious Suso relates without reserve, and in a description of
great detail, how he tasted 'den himmlischen Trunk';[74] and
Bernard of Clairvaux, who merited the Virgin's gratitude
more than any other man, was rewarded for all his panegyrics and poems by Mary visiting him in his cell and letting
his lips be moistened by the food of the heavenly Child." [75]
"Thus," explains Heinrich Günter,[76] following out the
same theme, "in the age of the Mary-legend, the Virgin
also had to become a miraculous nourisher, and that—in

accordance with the exaggerated imagination of the times
—with her own milk. A monk gets sick; mouth and throat
are so swollen that he can take no nourishment; the brethren
expect the end. Then Mary appears—visible only to the
sick man—and gives him her breast and announces to him
his early recovery. Among the mystical women of the
convent of Töf the same thing happened to Sister Adelheit
of Frauenberg; she narrates it herself: Mary says to her
. . . '"I will fulfil your desire and will give you to drink
of the milk with which I suckled my holy Child," and she
put her pure, soft breast into my mouth; and when this
unspeakable sweetness was done to me I was on the point
of weeping.'"

As Mary, although the chief, is not the only sustainer of
God's people, so, in the incredible materialism of mediæval
thought, it is not she alone whose milk has been given to
succor them in their extremities. One and another of the
saints, without careful regard to sex, have been recorded
as performing the same service. Lacking another, Christina Mirabilis was fed from her own virgin breast.[77] Even
the veins of saints, in token of their functions as sustainers
of God's people, have flowed with milk as well as with
blood.[78] This was the case, for example, with Pantaleon,
and there was preserved in Constantinople a vessel containing the combined blood and milk which had issued
from his martyred body. "Every year," we read,[79] "they
changed places; when 'once in our time, under the Emperor
Michael (that is, Paleologus, 1259–82), the blood remained on top, it was a year filled with troubles.'" Pantaleon was a great saint, and his preserved blood even acted
as a palladium, giving oracles of weal or woe to the for-
tunate cities which possessed it. As soon as the famous
liquefying blood of Januarius appeared at Naples, Günter
tells us, "the blood of Pantaleon, too, all at once spread
over all Italy, everywhere exhibiting the same quality—
in Naples itself in three churches, in Ravello, Bari, Valli-

cella, Lucca, Venice—without San Gennaro, however, suffering in the least by the concurrence." The celebrated miracle of the liquefaction of the blood of Januarius is not then unexampled. In the single Church of the Holy Apostles at Rome you may see the perpetually liquid blood of St. James the Less, and the miraculous blood of St. Nicholas of Tolentino, which exudes from his arms whenever they are separated from his body. And at the near-by nunnery of St. Cyriacus, where Cyriacus's head is kept, that head has been said, since the time of Gregory IX (1241), to have become red with blood on the anniversary of the martyr's death, and the reliquary to have become moist.[80] Of all the miracles of this kind, however, the liquefaction of Januarius's blood is the most famous. It is exhibited annually at Naples, on the day of the saint's festival. Günter speaks of it with the prudence which becomes a historian who is also a Catholic. "A problem before which criticism is compelled to pause," says he.[81] "The fact is assured; the explanation is not yet discovered. The historian may content himself with registering that the blood-miracle first appears suddenly in the late Middle Ages, and that an older notice of a Neapolitan miraculous vial exists, which the popular belief brought into connection, however, with the magician Vergil." This vial enclosed in it an image of the city, and it was believed that so long as the vial remained intact, so would the city. It was esteemed, in other words, as the palladium of the city, as the vial of Januarius now is.

Relics, however, have not been venerated for naught, and it is not merely such spectacular miracles which have made them the object of the eager regard which is paid them. As Pfister puts it:[81a] "The basis of the Christian cult of relics, as in the case of the antique cult, lies in the belief that the men whose remains are honored after their death, were in their lifetime filled with special power by virtue of which they were in position to work extraordinary things: then, that this power still filled their remains, in the first instance, of course, their bodily remains, but, after that, all that had come into contact with the deceased." It was because much was hoped from these relics that they were cherished and honored; and since mankind suffers most from bodily ills the relics have naturally been honored above everything else as instruments through which bodily relief and bodily benefit may be obtained. Günter can write,[82] no doubt: "In the times of the inventions and translations of the relics there were naturally innumerable relic-miracles promulgated. It was not only that the 'blind saw, the lame walked, the lepers were cleansed, the deaf heard, and the dead were raised,' when they were brought to the graves of the saints; the sanctuaries and healing shrines had something greater still in the incorruptibility of the bodies of the saints,[83] or of their severed limbs, or in astonishing manifestations of power and life of other kinds. Gregory's *Gloria martyrum* and *Gloria confessorum*, and the activity of the miraculous goldsmith of Limoges, and of the later bishop of Noyon, Eligius, served almost exclusively to glorify the graves of the saints. Eligius was endowed from heaven especially for the discovery of relics. He himself, when his grave was opened a year after his death (December 1, 660) was wholly uncorrupted, just as if he were yet alive; beard and hair, which according to custom had been shaved, had grown again." But Günter requires to add: "It is in their power to help (*Hilfsmacht*) that, on the basis of old experiences, the significance of the graves of the saints for the people still lies, down to to-day." In point of fact the great majority of the miracles of healing which have been wrought throughout the history of the church, have been wrought through the agency of relics.[84] Not merely the actual graves of the saints, but equally any places where fragments of their bodies, however minute, have been preserved, have become healing shrines, to many of which pilgrims have flocked in immense numbers, often from great distances, and from which there have spread through the world innumerable stories of the most amazing cures, and even of the restoration of the dead to life. We are here at the very centre of the miracle-life of the church of Rome.[85]

We have pointed out the affiliation of this whole development of relic-veneration with heathenism. We are afraid that, as we survey its details, the even uglier word, fetichism, rises unbidden to our lips: and when we find J. A. MacCulloch, for example, writing of miracles at large, speaking incidentally of "the use of relics" as "*at bottom* a species of fetichism,"[86] we cannot gainsay the characterization.[87] Heinrich, naturally, repels such characterizations. There is no heathenism, fetichism, in the cult of relics, he insists,[88] because that cult is relative, and that with a double relativity. "Our cult terminates really on God, whom we venerate in the saints," he says, "and thus the cult becomes actually a religious one; it is a relative cult in a double relation: it does not stop with the relics but proceeds to the saints; it does not stop with the saints but proceeds to God Himself." We are afraid, however, that this reasoning will not go on all fours with Heinrich's fundamental argument for the propriety of venerating relics. "The veneration of the saint," he argues,[89] "terminates on the *person* as the total object, more particularly, of course, on the soul than on the body; for the formal object, that is, the ground of the veneration, is the spiritual excellences of the saint. . . . But during life the body also shares in the veneration of the person to which it belongs. It must, therefore, be esteemed holy also after death; the veneration always terminates on the person." We may miss the logical nexus here; it may not seem to us to follow that, because the body shared in the veneration offered to the saint while it was part of the living person, it ought therefore—Heinrich actually says "therefore"—to share in this veneration when it is no longer a part of the living person —any more than, say, the *exuviæ* during life, which, how-

ever, the relic-worshippers, it must be confessed, do make
share in it. But Heinrich not only professes to see this
logical nexus, but hangs the whole case for the propriety
of the veneration of relics upon it. In that case, however,
the veneration of the relic is not purely relative; there is
something in. the relic as such which calls for reverence.
It is not merely a symbol through which the saint, now
separated from it, is approached, but a part of the saint,
though an inferior part, in which the saint is immediately
reached. "The Christian," says Heinrich himself,[90] "recog-
nizes in the body of the martyr, of the saint, more than a
mere instrument of the soul; it is, as our faith teaches us,
the temple of the Holy Ghost; it was the sacred vessel of
grace in life; it is to be glorified in unity again with the
glorified soul." Such scholastic distinctions as that between direct and relative worship—like that between *doulia*,
hyperdoulia, and *latria*—are, in any event, matters purely
for the schools. They have no real meaning for the actual
transactions, and nothing can be more certain than that
throughout the Catholic world the relics, as the saints,
have been continuously looked upon by the actual worshippers, seeking benefits from them, as themselves the vehicles
of a supernatural power of which they may hopefully avail
themselves.[91]

We have said that relics stand at the centre of the miracle-
life of the church of Rome. Many are prepared to go
further. Yrjö Hirn, for example, wishes to say that they
stand at the centre of the whole religious life of the church
of Rome. He does not mean by this merely that all
Catholic religious life and thought centre in and revolve
around the miraculous. This is true. The world-view of
the Catholic is one all his own, and is very expressly a
miraculous one. He reckons with the miraculous in every
act; miracle suggests itself to him as a natural explanation
of every event; and nothing seems too strange to him to be
true.[92] It is a correct picture which a recent writer draws

when he says:[93] "The really pious Catholic has a peculiar passion for miracles. The extremely numerous accounts of miraculous healings, not alone at Lourdes; the multiplied promises, especially in the little Prayer and Pilgrim Books, of physical healing of the sick in reward for many offered prayers and petitions; the enormous credulity of the Catholic people, as it is revealed to us in the Leo Taxil swindle—all this manifests a disposition for miracle-seeking which is altogether unaffected by the modern scientific axiom of the conformity of the course of nature to law." To say that relics lie at the centre of the miracle-life of Catholicism is not far from saying that they lie at the centre of the Catholic religious life; for the religious life of Catholicism and its miracle-life are very much one. Hirn is thinking here,[94] however, particularly of the organization of Catholic worship; and what he sees, or thinks he sees, is that the entirety of Catholic worship is so organized as to gather really around the relic-chest. For the altar, as it has developed in the Roman ritual, has become, he says, in the process of the years, the coffin enclosing the bones of a saint; and that is the fundamental reason why the rule has long been in force that every altar shall contain a relic,[95] and that a Gregory of Tours, for example, when speaking of the altar can call it, not "ara" or "altare," but "arca," that is to say, box or ark. Catholic piety, thus expressing itself in worship, has found its centre in a sealed case; for the table for the mass is not a piece of furniture which has been placed in a building, but a nucleus around which the building has been formed, and the table for the mass has become nothing more or less than "a chest which guards the precious relics of a saint." Thus, "the ideas connected with the abode of the dead remain for all time bound up with the church's principal place of worship." "Saint-worship has little by little mingled with the mass-ritual, and the mass-table itself has been finally transformed into a saint's shrine."[96]

Enthroned though it thus be at the centre of the miracle-life, and with it of the religious life, of the church of Rome,[97] the cult of relics, nevertheless, does not absorb into itself the entirety of either the one or the other. It has one rival which shares with it even its central position, and in our own day threatens to relegate it, in some sections of the Catholic world at least, to the background. This is the cult of the Virgin Mary, whose legend has incorporated into itself all other legends,[98] and whose power eclipses and seems sometimes almost on the point of superseding all other powers. There is a sense in which it may almost be said that the saints have had their day and the future belongs to Mary. It is to her, full of grace, Queen, Mother of Mercy, our Life, our Sweetness, our Hope,[99] that men now call for relief in all their distresses, and it is to her shrines that the great pilgrim-bands of the afflicted now turn their steps.[100] These shrines are not ordinarily relic-shrines. Mary had her "assumption" as her divine Son had His "ascension"; she has left behind her no grave, no body, no bodily parts to be distributed severally through the earth. Her relics consist exclusively of external things: of her hair, her milk, the clothes she wore, the house she dwelt in. They have had their part to play —a very great part—in the history of the relic-cult and of pilgrimages; as have also miraculous images of her. But the chief source of the newer shrines of Mary which have been founded one after another in these latter days, and have become one after another the goal of extensive pilgrimages and the seat of innumerable miracles of healing, has been a series of apparitions of Mary, which have followed one another with bewildering rapidity until they have almost seemed to become epidemic in France at least—in France, because France is the land of Mary as Italy is the land of the saints.

Let us put side by side these four apparitions: La Salette (1846), where the Virgin appeared as a "beautiful lady" to two shepherd children, a girl and boy, aged respectively fifteen and eleven; Lourdes (1858), where she appeared as "a girl in white, no bigger than me," to a little country-bred girl of fourteen; Pellevoisin (1876), where she appeared as "the Mother All-Merciful" to an ill serving-maid; Le Pontinet (1889), where she appeared as the Queen of Heaven, first to a little country girl of eleven, and then to a considerable number of others infected by her example. The last of these was disallowed by the ecclesiastical authorities, and has had no wide-spread effects.[101] The other three are woven together in the popular fancy into a single rich chaplet for Mary's brow. "Each of the series of apparitions of the Blessed Virgin in this century," we read in a popular article published in the early nineties,[102] "bears a distinct character. At La Salette Mary appeared in sorrow, and displaying the instruments of the Passion on her heart; at Lourdes, with a gold and white rosary in her hands, and with golden roses on her feet, she smiled at the child Bernadette; at Pellevoisin she appeared in a halo of light, surrounded by a garland of roses, and wearing on her breast the scapular of the Sacred Heart." In each instance a new cult has been inaugurated, a new shrine set up, a new pilgrimage put on foot with the highest enthusiasm of devotion, and with immense results in miracles of healing—all of which accrue to the glory of Mary, the All-Merciful Mother of God.[103]

Among these apparitions, that at Lourdes easily takes the first place in point of historical importance. "Undoubtedly the greatest stimulus to Marian devotion in recent times," writes Herbert Thurston,[104] "has been afforded by the apparition of the Blessed Virgin in 1858 at Lourdes, and in the numberless supernatural favors granted to pilgrims both there and at other shrines that derive from it." No doubt the way was prepared for this effect by previous apparitions of similar character, at La Salette, for example, and perhaps above all by those to Zoe Labouré

(Sister Catherine in religion) in 1836, the external symbol of which was the famous "Miraculous Medal," which has wrought wonders in the hands of the Sisters of Charity.[105] And no doubt the impetus given by Lourdes has been reinforced by similar movements which have come after it, as, for example, by that growing out of the apparitions at Pellevoisin—whose panegyrists, however, praise it significantly only as "a second Lourdes." Meanwhile, it is Lourdes which occupies the proud position of the greatest shrine of miraculous healing in the world. We may predict the fading of its glory in the future, as the glory of other healing shrines in the past has faded. But there is nothing apparent to sustain this prediction beyond this bare analogy. We fear it is only the wish which has fathered the thought, when we find it put into somewhat exaggerated language by a French medical writer, thus:[106] "Let us see what has happened during a century only, in the most venerated sanctuaries of France. No more miracles at Chartres! Insignificant miracles at Notre Dame de Fourvières at Lyons. La Salette, incapable of the smallest cure, after having shone with an incomparable lustre. Paray-le-monial become useless in spite of the chemise of Marie Alacoque. To-day it is Lourdes which is the religious vogue; it is to Lourdes that the crowds demanding miracles go—waiting for Lourdes to disappear like the other shrines, when the faith of believers gradually fades like the flame of a candle coming to an end."

It must be admitted that the beginnings of Lourdes were not such as might have been expected of a great miraculous agency entering the world. It is possible to say, it is true, that they were better than has been the case in some similar instances. Bernadette Soubirous seems to have been a good child, and she seems to have grown into a good, if a somewhat colorless, not to say weak, and certainly very diseased, woman. The scandals of La Salette did not repeat themselves in her case.[107] And perhaps she cannot be spoken of with the same energy as "the little seer" of Le Pontinet, as the child of degenerated parents, weighted with the burden of bad heredity.[108] But it is a matter only of degree. Bernadette's parentage was not of the best omen; in her person she was, if not a degenerate, yet certainly a defective. It is of such that the Virgin apparently avails herself in her visions.[109] Nor does the vision itself reassure us. "The figure seen was one which, by the admission, we believe, of the Catholic clergy themselves, has been often reported as seen, mainly by young girls, under circumstances when no objective value whatever could be attributed to the apparition." [110] The communications made by the heavenly visitant, one would prefer to believe the dreams of the defective child. "As the times, so the saints," remarks Heinrich Günter,[111] with a very obvious meaning; and it may be added with an equally direct meaning: As the saints so the messages. Doctor Boissarie, it is true, seeks to forestall criticism by boldly affirming that the message given to Bernadette was lofty beyond the possibility of her invention:[112] "The name of the Virgin, the words which she uttered—all is out of proportion to the percipient's intelligence. Remembering the formal principle, admitted by all authorities, 'A hallucination is never more than a reminiscence of a sensation already perceived,' it is evident that the intelligence and the memory of Bernadette could never have received the image or heard the echo of what she received and heard at the grotto." To which the Messrs. Myers very properly respond:[113] "Doctor Boissarie does not tell us whether it is the divine command to kiss the earth for sinners, or the divine command to eat grass, which is beyond the intelligence of a simple child. He dwells only on the phrase, 'I am the Immaculate Conception'; and we may indeed admit that this particular mode of reproducing the probably often-heard statement that the Virgin was conceived without sin does indicate a mind which is either *supra* or *infra grammaticam.*" The plain fact is that the communications attributed to the Virgin are silly with the silliness of a backward child, repeating, without in the least comprehending their meaning, phrases with which the air was palpitant; it was in 1854 that the dogma of the Immaculate Conception of Mary was proclaimed in circumstances which shook the whole Catholic world with emotional tremors, some waves of which could not have failed to reach even Bernadette. The immense success of Lourdes as a place of pilgrimage has been achieved in spite of the meanness of its origin, and is to be attributed to the skill with which it has been exploited. Under this exploitation, it has distanced all its rivals, superseded all its predecessors, and has ended by becoming the greatest healing shrine in the world, counting the pilgrims who annually resort to it by the hundreds of thousands, and now even, so we are told, by the million.[114]

We cannot doubt that it is a true picture of Lourdes in its total manifestation, which is given by Émile Zola in his great novel.[115] He describes the colossal national pilgrimage which gathers there each August in an epic of human suffering. Looked at thus, it is a most moving spectacle. "It is difficult to remain strictly philosophical," writes an English physician after witnessing the scene;[116] "impossible to be coarsely sceptical in that strange assembly. Hard indeed would be the heart of any medical man which could remain unmoved by the sight which met my eyes that day. At no other spot in the wide world could the faculty behold at a glance so many of its failures. . . . Out of the thousands of pilgrims I could detect but few who were evidently of the poorest class; for the most part they were of the upper middle classes or, at least, well-to-do. . . . Surely so much misery has at no other spot been focussed in so small a space." It is, indeed, an "army of incurables" which gathers every year to Lourdes, driven to their last recourse. But of course not all the enormous masses of

pilgrims are seeking healing. Lourdes does not register her
failures; the proportion of her pilgrims who are seeking
healing, the proportion of those seeking healing who are
healed, can only be guessed. The late Monsignor R. H.
Benson, speaking of the great masses of the national pilgrimage, says, no doubt somewhat loosely:[117] "Hardly one
in a thousand of these come to be cured of any sickness."
During the twenty years from 1888 to 1907, inclusive, the
whole number of cures recorded was 2,665,[118] which yields
a yearly average of about 133.[119] It is generally understood that about 90 per cent of those seeking cure go away
unbenefited,[120] and this would lead us to suppose that between 1300 and 1400 seek healing at Lourdes annually.
Georges Bertrin tells us[121] that up to 1908—the fiftieth
anniversary of the vision—some 10,000,000 of pilgrims had
visited Lourdes, and that the whole number of cures,
"whether partial or complete," registered during that time
was 3,962. He thinks that nearly as many more may have
been wrought but not registered; let us say, then, that there
may have been some 8,000 cures in all during this half-
century—"whether partial or complete." Absolutely this
is a great number; but proportionately to the numbers of
pilgrims, not very large: about one cure being registered
to every 2,500 visitors, not more than one cure to every
1,250 visitors being even conjecturable. How many failures stand over against these 4,000 to 8,000 cures we have
no means of estimating; but if the proportion of 90 per
cent seeking cure be right, they would mount to the great
number of some 50,000. The heart sinks when it contem-
plates this enormous mass of disappointment and despair [122]

There are certain other circumstances connected with
the cures of Lourdes, which, on the supposition of their
miraculousness, evoke some surprise. The Bureau of
Constatation exhibits at times a certain shyness of expecting too much of a miracle—a shyness quite absent, it is
true, on other occasions, when, as it appears, anything

could be expected. We read,[123] for example, of a case of apparent hip-disease, and it was said that one leg had been seven centimetres shorter than the other; while now, after the cure, "the legs were of an exactly equal length." The cure was not admitted to registry, but was referred back for further investigation. "The doctors shook their heads considerably over the seven centimetres"; "seven centimetres was almost too large a measure to be believed." Why—if it was a miracle? And, after all, would the prolongation of a leg by seven centimetres be any more miraculous than the prolongation of it by six—or by one? Stress is sometimes laid on the instantaneousness[124] of the cures as proof of their miraculousness. But they are not all instantaneous. We read repeatedly in the records of slow and gradual cures: "At the second bath she began to improve"; "at the fourth bath the cure was complete."[125] Indeed the cures are not always ever completed. Gabriel Gargam, for example, one of Bertrin's crucial cases, he tells us,[126] "bears a slight trace of his old infirmity as the guarantee of its erstwhile existence. He feels a certain weakness in his back at the spot where Doctor Tessier supposed that a vertebra was pressing on the medulla." Similarly in the case of Madame Rouchel, a case of facial lupus, and another of Bertrin's crucial cases, "a slight ulceration of the inside of the upper lip," he says,[127] "remained after the cure." These cases are not exceptional: Bertrin informs us[128] that it is quite common for traces of the infirmity to remain. He even discovers the *rationale* of this. It keeps the cured person in grateful memory of the benefit received.[129] And it is even a valuable proof that the cure is truly miraculous. For, do you not see?[130] "had the disease been nervous and functional, and not organic, everything would have disappeared; all the functions being repaired, the disease would not have left any special trace." This reasoning is matched by that into which Bertrin is betrayed when made by the physicians of Metz—Madame

Rouchel's home—really to face the question whether she had been cured at all. They pointed out that the lip was imperfectly healed. Bertrin cries out[131] that the "question was not whether a slight inflammation of the lip remained, but whether the two perforations which had existed in the cheek and roof of the mouth before going to Lourdes had been suddenly closed on Saturday, September 6." The physicians point out inexorably that this is to reverse the value of the symptoms and to mistake the nature of their producing causes, and record the two findings: (1) that the lupus was not healed; (2) that the closing of the two fistulas in twelve days was not extraordinary. This celebrated case thus passes into the category of a scandal.[132]

It must remain astonishing, in any event, that miracles should be frequently incomplete. We should *a priori* expect miraculous cures to be regularly radical. No doubt we are not judges beforehand how God should work. But it is not wrong, when we are asked to infer from the very nature of an effect that it is the immediate work of God, that we should be disturbed by circumstances in its nature which do not obviously point to God as the actor. The reasons which Bertrin presents for the imperfections in the effects do not remove this difficulty. They bear the appearance of "covering reasons"—inventions to remove offenses. After all is said and done, it is mere paradox to represent the imperfections in the cures as evidences of the divine action. We may expect imperfections to show themselves in the products of second causes; we naturally expect perfection in the immediate operations of the First Cause. Bertrin strikes back somewhat waspishly when Zola makes one of the physicians at the Bureau of Constatation ask "with extreme politeness," why the Virgin contented herself with healing a sore on a child's foot, leaving an ugly scar, and had not given it a brand-new foot while she was about it—since "this would assuredly have given her no more trouble." Here, too, Bertrin says[133] that the

scar was left that it might be a standing proof of the reality
and greatness of the miracle of healing that had been
wrought, and adds, somewhat unexpectedly it must be
confessed at this point, that whatever God does, He does
well. Whatever God does, He certainly does well; and it
assuredly is our part only to endeavor to understand His
ways. But when the question is, Did God do it? we are
not unnaturally puzzled if it does not seem obvious that
what He is affirmed to have done, has been well done. The
physician's question was not foolish. It was the perhaps
not quite bland expression of a natural wonder—wonder at
the limitations which show themselves in these alleged
miracles. Why, after all, should miracles show limitations?[134]

We are far from wishing to suggest that the cures at
Lourdes are not in the main real cures. We should be glad
to believe that the whole of the four to eight thousand
which are alleged to have taken place there, have been
real cures, and that this great host of sufferers have been
freed from their miseries. Probably no one doubts that
cures are made at Lourdes; any more than men doubt that
similar cures have from the beginning of the world been
made in similar conditions elsewhere—as of old in the
temples of Asclepius, for example, and to-day at the hands
of the Christian Scientists. So little is it customary to
deny that cures are made at Lourdes that even free-thinking
French physicians are accustomed to send patients there.
Doctor Maurice de Fleury in his much-admired book, *La
Médecine de l'Esprit*,[135] writes: "The faith that heals is
only suggestion; that makes no difference, since it heals.
There is no one of us who has not sent some sick woman to
Lourdes, expecting her to return well." The same in effect
is said by Charcot,[136] Dubois,[137] even the polemic Rouby.
Rouby even goes to the length of pointing out a function
which Lourdes, according to him, may serve in the advance
of medical science. "Lourdes has not been without its

value to contemporary physicians," he writes;[138] "they have had in it a great field for the study of hysterosis, which a large number of them have misunderstood or only partially understood. Lourdes has put neurosis before them in a striking way. Those of our colleagues who have written into their certificates a diagnosis of incurability, have been profoundly disturbed when they saw their patients return cured; and those of them who have not believed in a miraculous cure have asked themselves the true account of these cures. They have come into actual touch at Lourdes with what they had read in their treatises on various diseases. They have learned what hysterosis really is, and what a great rôle it has played and will play still in the production of miracles; and they will sign no more certificates on which the Bureau of Constatation can depend for establishing the miraculous character of cures. This ignorance of hysterosis on the part of physicians, which has more than anything else made the fortune of the pilgrimage, will, it is to be hoped, no longer exist." [139]

Lourdes, naturally, repudiates this classification of her cures, and claims a place apart. She points to the unexampled multitude of cures wrought by her; she points to their intrinsic marvellousness. The great number of cures wrought at Lourdes is not due, however, to any peculiarity in the curative power which she possesses, but to the excellence of its exploitation. It will hardly be contended that her patients are miraculously brought to Lourdes. That the power by which her cures are wrought differs intrinsically from that at work elsewhere is not obvious. To all appearance, all these cures are the same in kind and are the products of the same forces set in action after essentially the same fashion. These forces are commonly summed up, in large part at least, under the somewhat vague term "suggestion." The term is, perhaps, not a very good one for the particular circumstances, and must be understood when used in this connection in a very wide sense. It means at bottom that the immediate curative agency is found in mental states induced in the patient, powerfully reacting, under the impulse of high exaltation, on his bodily functioning.[140] With his eye precisely on Lourdes, J. M. Charcot sketches with a few bold strokes the working of this suggestion in the mind of the patient. "In a general way," he says,[141] "the faith-cure does not develop the whole of its healing force spontaneously. If an invalid hears a report that miraculous cures take place in such and such a shrine, it is very rarely that he yields to the temptation to go there at once. A thousand material difficulties stand, at least temporarily, in the way of his moving; it is no light matter for a paralytic or a blind man, however well off he be, to start on a long journey. He questions his friends; he demands circumstantial accounts of the wonderful cures of which rumor has spoken. He receives nothing but encouragement, not only from his immediate surroundings, but often even from his doctor, who is unwilling to deprive his patient of his last hope, especially if he believes his malady to be amenable to the faith-cure —a remedy which he has not dared to prescribe himself. Besides, the only effect of contradiction would be to heighten the patient's belief in a miraculous cure. The faith-cure is now born, and it continues to develop. The forming of the plan, the preparation, the pilgrimage, become an *idée fixe*. The poor humiliate themselves to ask alms to enable them to reach the holy spot; the rich become generous toward the poor in the hope of propitiating the godhead; each and all pray with fervor, and entreat for their cure. Under these conditions the mind is not slow to obtain mastery over the body. When the latter has been shaken by a fatiguing journey the patients arrive at the shrine in a state of mind eminently receptive of suggestion. 'The mind of the invalid,' says Barwell, 'being dominated by the firm conviction that a cure will be effected, a cure is effected forthwith.' One last effort—an immersion at the pool, a last most fervent prayer, aided by the ecstasy produced by the solemn rites—and the faith-cure produces the desired results; the miraculous healing becomes an accomplished fact."

If any one wishes to feel the intensity with which the last stages of this process of suggestion are brought to bear on the sick at Lourdes, the perfect art with which the whole dramatic machinery is managed,[142] he need only read a few pages of the description of Monsignor Benson of what he saw at Lourdes. Like Bertrin,[143] Benson scoffs at the notion that "suggestion" can be thought of as the impulsive cause of the cures; but like Bertrin he defines suggestion in too narrow a sense and no one pictures more vividly than he does suggestion at work. Here is his description of the great procession and blessing of the sick.[144]

"The crowd was past describing. Here about us was a vast concourse of men; and as far as the eye could reach down the huge oval, and far away beyond the crowned statue, and on either side back to the Bureau on the left, and on the slopes to the right, stretched an inconceivable pavement of heads. Above us, too, on every terrace and step, back to the doors of the great basilica, we knew very well, was one seething, singing mob. A great space was kept open on the level ground beneath us—I should say one hundred by two hundred yards in area—and the inside fringe of this was composed of the sick, in litters, in chairs, standing, sitting, lying, and kneeling. It was at the farther end that the procession would enter.

"After perhaps half an hour's waiting, during which one incessant gust of singing rolled this way and that through the crowd, the leaders of the procession appeared far away —little white or black figures, small as dolls—and the singing became general. But as the endless files rolled out, the singing ceased, and a moment later a priest, standing solitary in the great space, began to pray aloud in a voice like a silver trumpet.

"I have never heard such passion in my life. I began to watch presently, almost mechanically, the little group beneath the *ombrellino*, in white and gold, and the movements of the monstrance blessing the sick; but again and again my eyes wandered back to the little figure in the midst, and I cried out with the crowd, sentence after sentence, following that passioned voice:

"'Lord, we adore Thee!'

"'Lord,' came the huge response, 'we adore Thee.'

"'Lord, we love Thee,' cried the priest.

"'Lord, we love Thee,' answered the people.

"'Save us, Jesus, we perish.'

"'Save us, Jesus, we perish.'

"'Jesus, Son of Mary, have pity on us.'

"'Jesus, Son of Mary, have pity on us.'

"Then, with a surge rose up the plain-song melody:

"'Spare, O Lord,' sang the people, 'spare Thy people! Be not angry with us forever.'

"Again:

"'Glory to the Father, and to the Son, and to the Holy Spirit.'

"'As it was in the beginning, is now and ever shall be, world without end, Amen.'

"Then again the single voice and the multitudinous answer:

"'Thou art the Resurrection and the Life!'

"And then an adjuration to her whom He gave to be our Mother:

"'Mother of the Saviour, pray for us.'

"'Salvation of the weak, pray for us.'

"Then once more the singing; then the cry, more touching than all:

"'Lord, heal our sick!'

"'Lord, heal our sick!'

"Then the kindling that brought the blood to ten thousand faces:

"'Hosanna! Hosanna to the Son of David!' (I shook to hear it.)

"'Hosanna!' cried the priest, rising from his knees, with arms flung wide.

"'Hosanna!' roared the people, swift as an echo.

"'Hosanna! Hosanna!' crashed out again and again, like great artillery.

"Yet there was no movement among those piteous prostrate lines. The bishop, the *ombrellino* over him, passed on slowly round the circle; and the people cried to Him whom he bore, as they cried two thousand years ago on the road to the city of David. Surely He will be pitiful upon this day—the Jubilee Year of His Mother's graciousness, the octave of her assumption to sit with Him on His throne!

"'Mother of the Saviour, pray for us.'

"'Jesus, Thou art my Lord and my God.'

"Yet there was no movement. . . .

"The end was now coming near. The monstrance had reached the image once again, and was advancing down the middle. The voice of the priest grew more persistent still, as he tossed his arms, and cried for mercy:

"'Jesus, have pity on us, have pity on us!'

"And the people, frantic with ardor and desire, answered him with a voice of thunder:

"'Have pity on us! Have pity on us!'

"And now up the steps came the grave group to where Jesus would at least bless His own, though He would not heal them; and the priest in the midst, with one last cry, gave glory to Him who must be served through whatever misery:

"'Hosanna! Hosanna to the Son of David!'

"Surely that must touch the Sacred Heart! Will not His Mother say one word?

"'Hosanna! Hosanna to the Son of David!'

"'Hosanna!' cried the priest.

"'Hosanna!' cried the people.

"'Hosanna! Hosanna! Hosanna! . . .'

"One articulate roar of disappointed praise, and then—*Tantum ergo Sacramentum!* rose in its solemnity."

There was no miracle, and Benson thinks that that is sufficient proof that the miracles are not wrought by "suggestion." "If ever 'suggestion' could work a miracle," he says, "it must work one now." But this was only the day of preparation, and the fever planted in the blood was working. And the next day the miracles came.[145] "The crowd was still, very still, answering as before the passionate voice in the midst; but watching, watching, as I watched. . . . The white spot moved on and on, and all else was motionless. I knew that beyond it lay the sick. 'Lord, if it be possible—if it be possible! Nevertheless, not my will but Thine be done.' It had reached now the end of the first line.

"'Lord, heal our sick,' cried the priest.

"'Lord, heal our sick,' answered the people.

"'Thou art my Lord and my God!'

"And then on a sudden it came.

"Overhead lay the quiet summer air, charged with the supernatural as a cloud with thunder—electric, vibrating with power. Here beneath, lay souls thirsting for its touch of fire—patient, desirous, infinitely pathetic; and in the midst that Power, incarnate for us men and our salvation. Then it descended swift and mightily.

"I saw a sudden swirl in the crowd of heads beneath the church steps, and then a great shaking ran through the crowd; but there for a few instants it boiled like a pot. A sudden cry had broken out, and it ran through the whole space; waxing in volume as it ran, till the heads beneath my window shook with it also; hands clapped, voices shouted, 'A miracle! A miracle!'"

The tension thus broken, of course other miracles followed. And Benson says he does not see what "suggestion" had to do with them!

We feel no impulse to insist on the word, "suggestion" as if it were a magic formula, which accounts with completeness for all the cures wrought at Lourdes. We should be perfectly willing to admit, on good reason being given for the admission, that, after all the cures which can be fairly brought under this formula have been brought under it, a *residuum* may remain for the account of which we should look further. We do not ourselves think that we are much advanced in the explanation of these *residuum* cases, if they exist, by postulating "a transferrence of vitalizing force either from the energetic faith of the sufferers, or from that of the bystanders"—as Benson intimates that Alexis Carrel was inclined to recommend.[146] At bottom, this is only a theory, and it does not seem to us a very complete theory, of how "suggestion" acts. Let us leave that to further investigation. For our part, we prefer just to leave these *residuum* cases themselves, if they exist, to this further investigation. We feel no necessity laid on us to explain them meanwhile. Bertrin makes himself merry[147] over the appeal, for their explanation, to the working of "unknown forces" as a mere shift to avoid acknowledging the presence of the supernatural. But surely we cannot pretend to a complete knowledge of all the forces which may work toward a cure in such conditions as are present at Lourdes. Unknown forces are assuredly existent, and it is not unnatural to think of them when effects occur, the causes of which are unknown. Meanwhile *residuum* cases suggesting reference to them, if they exist at all, are certainly very few. Doctor E. Mackey in a very sensible article published a few years ago in *The Dublin Review*,[148] seems inclined to rest the case for recognizing their existence on three instances. These are the cures of Pierre de Rudder, of a broken bone; of Joachine Dehant, of a dislocation; and of François Macary, of a varicose vein. "Such cases," he says,[149] . . . "cannot cure themselves, and no amount of faith and hope that the mind of man can imagine will unite a broken bone, reduce a dislocation, or obliterate a varicose vein. Such cases cannot be paralleled by any medical experience, or imitated by any therapeutic resource, and are as far removed from its future as its present possibilities. To the sceptic we may give without argument the whole range of nerve disorders, but what explanation is there of the sudden and permanent cure of an organic lesion? What, but the working of the uncovered finger of God?"

The cases selected by Doctor Mackey are famous cases. That of Pierre de Rudder may be said, in fact, to be Lourdes's star case, and is found duly set forth in detail at the head of well-nigh every argument for the miraculousness of the Lourdes cures. Perhaps Doctor Mackey might just as well have contented himself with appealing to it alone. Its salient features are that what was healed in it was a fracture of long standing of both bones of the lower leg, just below the knee, the two parts of the broken bone piercing the flesh and being separated by a suppurating wound an inch long. The healing was instantaneous. We have never seen a satisfactory natural explanation of how this cure was effected. If the facts, in all their details as published—say in Bertrin's extended account,—are authentic, it seems fairly impossible to imagine how it was effected. Doctor Rouby, it is true, offers a very plausible explanation of the healing, but, to make it plausible, he is compelled to assume that some of the minor details are not quite accurately reported.[150] We prefer simply to leave it, meanwhile, unexplained. Do you cry out that we are bound to supply a satisfactory natural explanation of it, or else acknowledge that a miracle has taken place in this case? We feel no difficulty in declining the dilemma. The healing of Pierre de Rudder's leg is not the only thing that has occurred in the world of the mode of the occurrence of which we are ignorant. After all, inexplicable and miraculous are not exact synonyms, and nobody really thinks

that they are. Is it wrong suddenly to turn the tables
and ask those who would compel us to explain Pierre de
Rudder's case, how they explain Charlotte Laborde's case,
which is certainly far more wonderful than Pierre de Rudder's?   Charlotte Laborde was a Jansenist cripple who
had no legs at all, as two surgeons duly testified; and yet
she literally had two good legs pulled out for her—as anybody may read in Montgeron's veracious narrative.[151]   No
doubt it will be at once said that the thing never happened.
Assuredly, it never did happen. But has everybody earned
the right to take up that attitude toward it? We recognize, of course, that not all testimony to marvels can be
trusted—at least not in all the details. It seems indeed
rather difficult to report marvels precisely as they happened, and few there be who attain to it.[152] We have seen
that even an Augustine cannot be implicitly trusted when
he reports marvels as occurring within his own knowledge.
Perhaps Doctor Rouby is right in suggesting that some
slight errors of detail have crept into the report of Pierre
de Rudder's case; and that this marvel too is one of the
things that never happened—precisely as it is reported.
Our personal interest in such adjustments, however, is at
best languid. In the nature of the case they are only con-
jectural. We are only beginning to learn the marvellous
behavior of which living tissue is capable, and it may well
be that, after a while, it may seem very natural that Pierre
de Rudder's case happened just as it is said to have happened. We are afraid to alter the facts as witnessed even
a little, in order to make them fit in better with the ignorance of to-day: and our guesses of to-day are sure to seem
very foolish to-morrow. We do not busy ourselves, therefore, with conjecturing how Pierre de Rudder's cure may
have happened. We are willing to believe that it happened
just as it is said to have happened. We are content to
know that, in no case, was it a miracle.

We must endeavor to make clear the grounds on which

this assertion is adventured. To do this we need to go back a little in the discussion. We take it up again at the point where we have said that bare inexplicableness cannot be accepted as the sufficient criterion of the miraculous. There are many things which we cannot explain, and yet which nobody supposes to be miraculous.[153] No doubt the appeal to "unknown laws," hidden forces of nature not yet discovered, may be made the mark of an easy ridicule. Yet we must not be stampeded into acknowledging as sheerly miraculous everything the laws of whose occurrence —the forces by which it is produced—are inscrutable to us. Even if absolute inscrutability be meant—inscrutability not to me (for my ignorance cannot be the measure of reality) but to any and every living man, or body of men, to any possible man—miracle cannot be inferred from this alone. Nature was made by God, not man, and there may be forces working in nature not only which have not yet been dreamed of in our philosophy, but which are beyond human comprehension altogether. Simple inexplicability, therefore, is not an adequate ground on which to infer miracle. There must be something else about an occurrence besides its inexplicableness to justify us in looking upon it as a direct act of God's.

Clearly, when we are bidden to accept an event as miraculous merely on the ground of its inexplicableness, it is forgotten that no event is merely an inexplicable event. It is always something else besides; and if we are to pass upon its origin we must consider not merely its abstract inexplicableness but the whole concrete fact—not merely that it has happened inexplicably, but what it is that has happened inexplicably—that is to say, not its bare occurrence, but its occurrence in all its circumstantials, the total thing which has occurred. The healing of Pierre de Rudder, for example, is not merely an inexplicable happening (if it be inexplicable) of which we need know no more than just that. It is the healing of a particular individual,

Pierre de Rudder, in a complex of particular circumstances, the whole complicated mass of which constitutes the thing that has occurred. The cause assigned to the occurrence must satisfy not only its inexplicableness, but also all these other circumstances entering into the event as an occurrence in time and space. No event, occurring in time and space—in a complex, that is, of other occurrences—no matter how marvellous it may seem to be, how sheerly inexplicable on natural grounds—can possibly be interpreted as a divine act, if there is anything about it at all in its concrete wholeness which cannot be made consistent with that reference.

If, for instance, to take an example so extreme that it could not occur, but one that may serve all the better as our illustration on that account, there were buried somewhere in the concrete wholeness of the occurrence the implication that twice two are five. It would be more inexplicable that God should not know His multiplication table than that any occurrence whatever, however inexplicable it may seem to us, should nevertheless be due to natural causation. God is not bare omnipotence; He is absolute omniscience as well. He cannot possibly be the immediate agent in an act in which a gross failure of "wisdom" is apparent, no matter how difficult it may be for us to explain that act without calling in omnipotence as its producing cause. Still less can He be supposed to be the immediate actor in occurrences in which immoralities are implicated; or, in which, in their wholeness, as concrete facts, there are embodied implications of, say, irreligion or of superstition. Whether we can see how such occurrences are wrought, or not, we know from the outset that God did not work them. It would be more inexplicable that God should be directly active in them than that they should be the product of natural causation, though to suppose this to be the fact would be to confound all our previous conceptions of natural causation. Charles Hodge speaks not a whit too strongly when he asserts[154] that "we are not only authorized but required to pronounce anathema an apostle or angel from heaven who should call upon us to receive as a revelation from God anything absurd or wicked."

God, indeed, has Himself forewarned us here. He has said:[155] "If there arise in the midst of thee a prophet or a dreamer of dreams, and he give thee a sign and a wonder, and the sign or the wonder come to pass, whereof he spake unto thee, saying, Let us go after other Gods, which thou hast not known, and let us serve them; thou shalt not hearken unto the words of that prophet or unto that dreamer of dreams." Conformity in their implications to what God has already revealed of Himself, He Himself makes the test of all alleged miracles. It would be more inexplicable that God by His action should confuse the revelation which He has made of His Being, of men's relation to Him, and of the duty of service which they owe to Him and to Him alone, than that inexplicable things should yet be produced by natural causation. It is a primary principle, therefore, that no event can be really miraculous which has implications inconsistent with fundamental religious truth. Even though we should stand dumb before the wonders of Lourdes, and should be utterly incapable of suggesting a natural causation for them, we know right well they are not of God. The whole complex of circumstances of which they are a part; their origin in occurrences, the best that can be said of which is that they are silly; their intimate connection with a cult derogatory to the rights of God who alone is to be called upon in our distresses,—stamp them, prior to all examination of the mode of their occurrence, as not from God. We are far more sure that they are not from God than we ever can be sure, after whatever scrutiny, of precisely how they are wrought. It is doubtless something like this that is expressed—it ought to be at least this that is meant

—by Émile Zola's crisp remark:[156] "That two and two make four may have become trite—but nevertheless they do make four. It is less foolish and less mad to say so than to believe, for example, in the miracles of Lourdes." That God is one, and that He alone is to be served with religious veneration, is no doubt an old revelation. It is nevertheless a true revelation. And he who takes it as such can never believe that miracles are wrought at Lourdes.

Of course, as R. H. Benson puts it,[157] "those who believe in God and His Son and the Mother of God on quite other grounds," may declare that "Lourdes is enough." But this is not to make the miracles carry the doctrine, but the doctrine the miracles, in accordance with J. H. Newman's proposition that it is all a matter of point of view, of presuppositions.[158] To those, on the other hand, who believe in God and His Son, as they have revealed themselves in the pages of Holy Scripture, but not in a Mother of God, standing between us and God and His Son, and usurping their place in our hearts and worship, Lourdes very distinctly is not enough. It would require something very different from what happens at Lourdes to make them see the express finger of God there. It is not He who rules there so much as that incoherent goddess who has announced herself to her worshippers with as fine a disregard of the ordinary laws of grammar and intelligible speech as of the fundamental principles of Christianity, in the remarkable words, "I am the Immaculate Conception," as if one should say, "I am the procession of the equinoxes," or "I am the middle of next week." "The whole place," says Benson,[159] "is alive with Mary." That is the very reason why we are sure that the marvels which occur there are not the direct acts of God, but are of the same order as the similar ones which have occurred at many similar shrines, of many names, in many lands, serving many gods. How close all these lie to one another is singularly illustrated by what we are told of a daughter shrine of

Lourdes's own, in that Near East which is the meeting-place of peoples and religions. At least, we read:[160] "The sanctuary of Feri Keuï at Constantinople, dedicated to Our Lady of Lourdes, is a place of pilgrimage and a source of miraculous cures for Christians, Jews, and Mussulmans. Its silver-wedding was celebrated recently with an assemblage of people of the religions which live in the Turkish Empire." What Lourdes has to offer is the common property of the whole world, and may be had by men of all religions, calling upon their several gods.[161]

IRVINGITE GIFTS

IRVINGITE GIFTS

PRETENSIONS by any class of men to the possession and use of miraculous powers as a permanent endowment are, within the limits of the Christian church, a specialty of Roman Catholicism. Denial of these pretensions is part of the protest by virtue of which we bear the name of Protestants. "In point of interpretation, the history of Protestantism," as an Edinburgh reviewer, writing in trying conditions in 1831, justly puts it,[1] "is a uniform disclaimer of any promise in the Scriptures that miraculous powers should be continued in the Church." In point of fact (we may slightly modify his next sentence to declare), the claim to the possession and exercise of powers of this description by individuals has always been received in Protestant circles with a suspicion which experience has only too completely justified.

Protestantism, to be sure, has happily been no stranger to enthusiasm; and enthusiasm with a lower-case "e" unfortunately easily runs into that Enthusiasm with a capital "E" which is the fertile seed-bed of fanaticism. Individuals have constantly arisen so filled with the sense of God in their own souls, and so overwhelmed by the wonders of grace which they have witnessed, that they see the immediate hand of God in every occurrence which strikes them as remarkable, and walk through the world clothed in a nimbus of miracle. To them it seems a small thing that the God who has so marvellously healed their sick souls should equally marvellously heal their sick bodies; that the God who speaks so unmistakably in their spirits should speak equally unmistakably through their lips. Especially in times of wide-spread oppression, when whole communities have, in their hopeless agony, been thrown back upon their God as their only refuge, and have found in Him solace and strength, it has over and over again happened that out of their distresses words and deeds have come to them which to their apprehension seemed manifestly divine.

We may find an illustration of the former phenomenon in John Wesley, who, though he would have repelled the accusation of superstition, yet, as one of his biographers finely expresses it,[2] "was always far more afraid of being ungodly than of being credulous." He would not admit that there was any scriptural ground for supposing that miracles had ceased. "I do not know," he declares,[3] "that God hath any way precluded Himself from thus exerting His sovereign power, from working miracles in any kind or degree, in any age, to the end of the world. I do not recollect any Scripture where we are taught that miracles are to be confined within the limits either of the Apostolic or the Cyprianic age; or to any period of time, longer or shorter, even to the restoration of all things. I have not observed, either in the Old Testament or the New, any intimation at all of this kind." Feeling thus no preconceived chariness with reference to miracles, he recognized their occurrence with great facility in the past and in the present.[4] He twits Middleton with his readiness to believe, on the testimony of scientific observers, that it is possible to speak without a tongue, rather than to credit the miracle testified to as having been wrought in favor of the African confessors who had had their tongues cut out. "After avowing this belief," he cries,[5] "do you gravely talk of other men's credulity? I wonder that such a volunteer in faith should stagger at anything. Doubtless, were it related as natural only, not miraculous, you could believe that a man could see without eyes." After himself recording a sheerly incredible instance of mirror-gazing, he solemnly affirms his belief in it, and stoutly declares that those who can believe it all fiction "may believe a man's getting into a bottle."[6] William Warburton, who devotes the second book of his *Doctrine of Grace* almost entirely to criticisms of a series of extracts from Wesley's *Journal*, sums up his findings in the remark[7] that "this extraordinary man hath, in fact, laid claim to almost every Apostolic gift and grace; and in as full and ample a measure as ·they were possessed of old"; that, in fact, "of all the Apostolic gifts and graces there is but one with which we find him not adorned—namely, the gift of tongues." To such apparent lengths is it possible to be carried by the mere enthusiasm of faith.

A very good example of the wide-spread prevalence of apparently supernatural experiences in conditions of deep religious excitement is afforded by the history of the Camisards during the long period of their brutal persecution; and, indeed, beyond—for the same class of manifestations continued among their English friends, apparently by a kind of spiritual infection, long after some of them had taken refuge from persecution in England. These manifestations included prophesying and predictions, miracle-working and speaking with tongues, and they were by no means done in a corner. A Mr. Dalton, "who did not know one Hebrew letter from another," nevertheless uttered "with great readiness and freedom complete discourses in Hebrew, for near a quarter of an hour together and sometimes much longer." Mr. Lacy spoke in Latin and Greek and French, although himself unable to construe his Latin and Greek, "of which," the historian slyly remarks, "the syntax is certainly inexplicable." Unfortunately for themselves, these "French Prophets" believed sufficiently in themselves to venture upon the luxury of specific predictions. They foretold that a certain Doctor Emes, who died December 22, 1707, would rise again on March 25, 1708. He did not do so; and the prophets were reduced to publishing a paper giving "*Squire Lacy's reasons why Doctor Emes was not raised.*" They predicted that certain dreadful judgments would fall on London in three weeks, explained explicitly to mean three literal weeks. When the fulfilment did not take place, they re-explained that, after all, it was three prophetic weeks that were intended—which corrected dating also was, of course, stultified in the process of time. Above all, of course, they predicted the speedy coming of the Lord, and the setting up of His personal reign on earth, of which, they explained, the present diffusion of the spiritual gifts among them was the preparation and the sign. "Christians," cries John Lacy, "now only look upon Christ as dead and ascended into heaven. But where—where's the expectation taught of His coming again? A doctrine that has annexed to it the powers, the mighty gifts of the Holy Ghost engaged by promises. Is the state of Christianity now so perfect that the powers and gifts of the Holy Ghost extraordinary are not worthy expecting or regarding? . . . Therefore the extraordinary dispensation to prepare so extraordinary a revolution . . . sure there needs something extraordinary to prepare for so tremendous, useful, so joyous and blissful a state of the Church on earth. Nay, the wisest do need an extraordinary call for it."[8]

This case of the "French Prophets" has not been adduced because it is better fitted in itself than a number of similar movements to illustrate the general subject. It has commended itself to our notice because of its long history and its pathetic significance during its connection with the persecutions in the Cévennes; and particularly because of certain peculiarities of its English development which recall the Irvingite movement to which we wish to devote this lecture. Among these may be numbered its close connection with chiliastic vagaries and the expectation of the speedy coming of the Lord, and also the circumstance that it left behind it a new sect in Christendom, to preserve in some sort its memory. Out of the activities of some of the followers of the "French Prophets" originated the people called Shakers, who, like the Catholic Apostolic Church, sprung from the Irvingite movement, have protracted some sort of existence to our day.

The religious atmosphere of the earlier decades of the nineteenth century was exceedingly unsettled and filled with a restless desire for change. In particular premillenarian extravagances were rife, and men were heatedly looking for the early coming of the Lord. It was out of this soil that Irvingism grew, predicting the immediate advent of Christ, and proclaiming the restoration of the extraordinary offices and gifts of the Apostolic age, along with an elaborate church organization, in preparation for His coming. Never have pretensions to gifts and powers of a supernatural order suffered more speedily and definitely the condemnation of facts. The predicted coming of the Lord did not take place: the "Apostles" appointed to receive Him at His coming were gradually called to their eternal home, and still He came not; the pretenders to supernatural gifts one after another awoke to the true state of the case and acknowledged themselves deluded. But the sect of Irvingites, broken in spirit, torn with dissension, altered in its pretensions, still lives on and adjusts itself to its blasted hopes as best it may.[9]

The views of Edward Irving, the founder of the sect, on the special matter now before us, the persistence or revival of the Apostolic charismata in the modern church, may be read at large in two papers, entitled respectively "The Church with her endowment of holiness and power" and "The Gifts of the Holy Ghost commonly called supernatural," which are printed at the end of his *Collected Writings*, edited by his nephew, Gavin Carlyle. One or two extracts will bring before us the essential elements of his teaching.

"I have shown," he writes, "the great purpose and end of this endowment of Spiritual gifts: that purpose and end is not temporary but perpetual, till Christ's coming again;

when that which is perfect shall come, and that which is in part shall be done away. If they ask for an explanation of the fact that these powers have ceased in the Church, I answer, that they have decayed just as faith and holiness have decayed; but that they have ceased is not a matter so clear. Till the time of the Reformation, this opinion was never mooted in the Church; and to this day, the Roman Catholics and every other portion of the Church but ourselves, maintain the very contrary. . . . And I would say, that this gift hath ceased to be visible in the Church because of her great ignorance concerning the work of Christ at His second coming, of which it is the continual sign; because of her most culpable ignorance of Christ's crowned glory, of which it is the continual demonstration; because of her indifference to the world without, for preaching to which the gift of the Holy Ghost is the continual furnishing and outfit of the Church. . . . But things are taking a turn. Let the Church know that things are taking on a mighty turn. There is a shining forth of truth in these subjects beyond former days. The power and glory of a risen Lord, as well as the holiness of a Lord in flesh, is beginning to be understood and discussed of; and the enemy would spread a curtain of their sophistry between the Church and the bright dawn; he might as well hide the morning by drawing before our eyes the spider's web or the frost-work of the night, which the rising sun quickly dissipates. . . . The Church . . . will have her full dignity restored to her of testifying . . . of a risen Lord in power and glory, crowned for His Church and in His Church putting forth unto the world a first-fruit of that power and government over all creation which in her He will ever exercise over all creation. These gifts have ceased, I would say, just as the verdure, and leaves, and flowers, and fruits of the spring and summer and autumn cease in winter, because, by the chill and wintry blasts which have blown over the Church, her power to put forth her glorious beauty hath

been prevented. But because the winter is without a
green leaf or beautiful flower, do men therefore argue that
there shall be flowers and fruits no more? . . . If the
Church be still in existence, and that no one denies; and
if it be the law and end of her being to embody a first-fruit
and earnest of the power which Christ is to put forth in
the redemption of all nature; then what though she hath
been brought so low, her life is still in her, and that life
will, under a more fervent day, put forth its native forces."
"Unless men, therefore, be left so far to themselves as to
say that God hath ceased to testify to the work which
Christ performed in the flesh—of casting Satan out; of redeeming all flesh from death, and disease its precursor; of
restoring the animal and vegetable world, and all creation,
to their original sinlessness, innocency, and subserviency
to mankind—unless men be disposed to say, that they know
God hath ceased to be at any pains or charges in giving
testimony to this work of His Son, they have no ground for
believing that the age of miracles is past. . . . As to the
fact which they allege, that there have not of a long time
been any such seals; granting their allegation to be a truth,
which I do not believe, the answer to it is, that there hath
been no testimony to the great work of Christ's redemption
such as to be worthy of being so sealed unto . . . in Christendom, since the first three centuries. . . . The subject
of the gifts, commonly called extraordinary, and rashly
conceived of as given for a local and temporary end, is one
of far greater importance than the advocates of either
opinion have dared to conceive, or, at least, have ventured to
express: being as I judge, connected in the closest manner
with the edification of the Church in love and holiness;
with her witness among the nations for their conversion
unto Christ; with the glory of God as the creator of the
human soul for His shrine, agent, and interpreter; with the
glory of Christ, as the head of the Church, subordinating
all the members unto Himself for the use of the Creator;

with the glory of the Holy Ghost, as the very life and mind and substance of Godhead, inhabiting, informing and manifesting forth the being of God, in such wise that the Church should be God's manifested fullness, the fullness of God, who filleth all in all."[10]

It is not my purpose to enter on a formal examination and criticism of Irving's views; they have already been judged by the course of history. But having thus presented them to you in his own highly ornate language, we may turn our attention to some account of the rise of the movement called (but not by its adherents) "Irvingism," as to a theme far more interesting and certainly as instructive for the general object which we have in view. We have spoken of Edward Irving as its founder, and so he was, without whose susceptibility, enthusiasm, force, and eloquence it could never have come into existence. But in another sense he may be thought of rather as its chief victim. It presents a curious subject for speculation, to consider how little often the chief movers in events like this are the real originators of them or the true forces which produce them. Just as J. H. Newman was in every high sense the leader of the Oxford movement while yet he himself was rather pushed on by the activity of others, so that it is literally true that it was Hurrell Froude who was at the bottom of his Anglo-Catholicism and W. G. Ward who nagged him, against his will, into Romanism; so Edward Irving was in every high sense the founder and leader of "Irvingism," which justly bears his name, while yet it is equally true that he was driven into it step by step by the influence and force of other minds. With all his sensitiveness of heart, enthusiastic earnestness of purpose, soaring views of religious truth, and grandeur of style in its presentation; in a word, with all those qualities which in their combination gave him a certain measure of greatness; his simplicity, perhaps we must also say, within due limits, his vanity, and certainly we must say his intellectual weakness and deficiency in judgment and common sense, made him the easy prey of other and more energetic orders of mind. Henry Drummond was his Hurrell Froude; Alexander J. Scott was his W. G. Ward.

Irving had none too brilliant a career as the young assistant of Chalmers in Glasgow, and the summons to London in July, 1822, to take charge of the dying Caledonian Chapel there, came no less as a surprise than as an opportunity.[11] From the first, however, he achieved in London a popularity which began by being astonishing, and ended by being immense. He became the talk of the town. Statesmen and men of letters hung on his words. Society took him under its patronage. The little church in Hatton Garden was soon outgrown. This sudden and unexampled popular applause perhaps did not completely turn his head, but it distinctly injured him. It left him an enthusiastic, simple-minded man; but it gave him overweening confidence in himself; and it infected him with the illusion that some high and world-wide mission had been committed to him.

At the very beginning of his London career, he adopted the crass premillennial views which later colored his whole thought. This was the work in him of James Hatley Frere,[12] a man of incisive mind and strong individuality, who seems to have deliberately selected Irving to be the popular mouthpiece of his Apocalyptic speculations. These he succeeded in impressing on him with amazing completeness of detail. Then came "the little prophetic conferences" at Albury, Henry Drummond's beautiful Surrey residence, where "the students of prophecy," as they called themselves, began in 1826 to meet for annual conferences on the meaning of the prophetic Scriptures.[13] These conferees were men of high social position and easy financial circumstances—Gerard Noel, Hugh McNeile, Lewis Way, Joseph Wolf, with Henry Drummond, the richest and most eccentric of them all, at their head—"a singular mixture of all things," Carlyle describes him; "of the saint, the wit, the philosopher, swimming, if I mistake not, in an element of dandyism." [14] Irving's imaginative disposition took fire, and he soon became the chief figure of the coterie, and began to proclaim everywhere that the Lord was shortly to come, and that the chief duty of believers was to press the signs of the times on the attention of men.

In this excited state of mind Irving was called upon to endure great personal trials. His opinions on the person of Christ were very properly called in question; and he was compelled to meet ecclesiastical process in consequence. In the midst of these distracting occurrences, he undertook a journey to Scotland that he might proclaim there, as in London, the approaching coming of his Master. [15] On this journey he met at Row (McLeod Campbell's parish) a man whose influence on his subsequent life cannot be overestimated—Alexander J. Scott, an impracticable probationer of the church of Scotland, whose strong and acute but indocile and wilful mind imposed upon every one whom he met an overestimate of his intellectual ability. This was in the summer of 1828. Irving was at once taken captive and engaged Scott to come up to London with him and share his work, on the only terms on which Scott could either then or at any subsequent time have been engaged— "entirely unfettered by any pledge as to doctrine." [16] This "powerful and singular spirit," so sceptical of whatever others believed—his driftage carried him ultimately beyond the limits of Christianity—so confident of whatever his mind fixed itself upon at the moment, had already reached the conclusion that the charismata of the early church might and should be enjoyed by the church of all ages. He succeeded in imposing this belief upon Irving, who himself dates his conviction that the spiritual gifts of the Apostolic age were not exceptional or temporary from 1828—the year in which he became associated with Scott. [17]

Irving was inclined to be content with holding his view

as a theory. This, however, did not content "the restless soul" by his side. As Irving himself relates: "And as we went out and in together, he used often to signify to me his conviction that the Spiritual Gifts ought to be exercised in the Church; that we are at liberty, and indeed bound, to pray for them as being baptized into the assurance of the 'gift of the Holy Ghost,' as well as of 'repentance and remission of sins. . . .' Though I could make no answer to this," he adds, "and it is altogether unanswerable, I continued still to be very little moved to seek myself or to stir up my people to seek these spiritual treasures. Yet I went forward to contend and to instruct whenever the subject came before me in my public ministrations of reading and preaching the Word, that the Holy Ghost ought to be manifested among us all, the same as ever He was in any one of the primitive Churches." [18]   Scott, his assistant, doubtless did likewise. Here we see, at least, Scott's preparation of Irving himself and of his church for what was to come.

"But," says Mrs. Oliphant,[19] "Mr. Scott's influence did not end there. About the same period at which he was engaged in quickening this germ of expectation in the breast of Irving, circumstances brought him in the way of sowing a still more effectual seed." There was a district in Scotland suffering at this time under great religious excitement —roused partly by the preaching of John McLeod Campbell, and partly by the influence of the kindly life of Isabella Campbell of Fernicarry, a young saint whose death had just profoundly moved the community. There, just at this juncture, Scott appeared, a "master of statement and argument," as Irving describes him, and in Mrs. Oliphant's words, "bent all his powers to laying this train of splendid mischief." [20]   "When Isabella Campbell died, a portion of her fame—her pilgrim visitors—her position as one of the most remarkable persons in the countryside, a pious and tender oracle—descended to her sister Mary," [21] who seems to have been a young woman "possessed of gifts of mind and temperament scarcely inferior to genius," "with all the personal fascination of beauty," and endowed with a "young, fervid and impressionable imagination." [22]   On her the subtlest arguments of one of the acutest men of the day were poured.   Irving himself describes the result thus: "Being called down to Scotland upon some occasion, and residing for a while at his father's house, which is in the heart of that district of Scotland upon which the light of Mr. Campbell's ministry had arisen, he (Scott) was led to open his mind to some of the godly people of those parts, and among others to a young woman who was at that time lying ill of a consumption, from which afterwards, when brought to the very door of death, she was raised up instantaneously by the mighty hand of God.   Being a woman of very fixed and constant spirit he was not able with all his power of statement and argument, which is unequalled by that of any man I have ever met with, to convince her of the distinction of regeneration and baptism with the Holy Ghost; and when he could not prevail, he left her with a solemn charge to read over the Acts of the Apostles with that distinction in mind, and to beware how she hastily rejected what was, as he believed, the truth of God.   By this young woman it was that God, not many months after, did restore the gift of speaking with tongues and prophesying to the Church." [23]

How it came about, Irving describes as follows: "The handmaiden of the Lord, of whom he made choice on that night" (a Sunday evening in the end of March—*i. e.*, March 28, 1830) "to manifest forth in her His glory, had been long afflicted with a disease which the medical men pronounced to be a decline, and that it would soon bring her to her grave, whither her sister had been hurried by the same malady a few months before.   Yet while all around her were anticipating her dissolution, she was in the strength of faith meditating missionary labours among the heathen;

and this night she was to receive the preparation of the Spirit; the preparation of the body she received not until some days after. It was on the Lord's day; and one of her sisters, along with a female friend who had come to the house for that end, had been spending the whole day in humiliation, and fasting, and prayer before God, with a special respect to the restoration of the gifts. They had come up in the evening to the sick-chamber of their sister, who was laid on a sofa, and, along with one or two others of the household, were engaged in prayer together. When in the midst of their devotion, the Holy Ghost came with mighty power upon the sick woman as she lay in her weakness, and constrained her to speak at great length and with superhuman strength in an unknown tongue, to the astonishment of all who heard, and to her own great edification and enjoyment in God; 'for he that speaketh in a tongue edifieth himself.' She has told me that this first seizure of the Spirit was the strongest she ever had, and that it was in some degree necessary it should have been so, otherwise she would not have dared to give way to it." [24]

Meanwhile the "power" passed across the Clyde to the opposite town of Port Glasgow into another pious household. When James Macdonald returned from his work to his midday dinner one day "he found his invalid sister in the agonies of this new inspiration. The awed family concluded . . . that she was dying." But she addressed her brothers at great length and solemnly prayed that James might at that time be endowed with the Holy Ghost. "Almost instantly James calmly said, 'I have got it.'" With a changed countenance in a few moments, "with a step and manner of the most indescribable majesty—he walked up to his sister's bedside and addressed her in these words of the 20th Psalm: 'Arise and stand upright.' He repeated the words, took her by the hand, and she arose." [25] After this wonderful cure James Macdonald wrote to Mary Campbell, "then apparently approaching

death, conveying to her the same command that had been
so effectual in the case of his sister." She rose up at once
and declared herself healed. And here we have the restored gifts prepared for the church.

The only remaining step was to convey the gifts to Irving's church. Of course, he was at once informed of the
extraordinary events which had taken place in Scotland.
He seems to have caught the contagion of excitement at
once. John Bate Cardale, a lawyer of Irving's circle, who
afterward became the first Irvingite "Apostle," went to
Scotland at the head of a delegation to investigate and
report. Meanwhile the church at London was kept in an
attitude of strained expectancy. But the "gifts" did not
come at once. An isolated case of healing occurred in
October, 1830—a Miss Fancourt—but this instance seems
to have stood somewhat apart from direct relation whether
to the Scotch manifestations or to the coming events in
Irving's church.[26] Irving's baby son took sick and died,
and though they sought it anxiously with tears there was
no interposition to save him. During the next spring daily
prayer-meetings were held in the early mornings to ask
directly for the "gifts of the Spirit," news of the unbroken
exercise of which was now coming continually from Scotland. "Irving," says Mrs. Oliphant, "had no eyes to see
the overpowering force of suggestion with which such
prayers" "might have operated upon sensitive and ex-
citable hearts."[27] At last we hear incidentally in July,
1831, that two of the flock in London had received the
gifts of tongues and prophecy.[28] They had been in exercise, however, for some months before that, first in the
form of speaking with tongues at private devotions, then in
the presence of others, and at length both in speaking with
tongues and in prophesying at small prayer-meetings.[29]
The formal date of the beginning of the "power" is
usually given as April 30, 1831, when Mrs. Cardale spoke
solemnly with the tongues and prophesied. David Brown,

however, seems to imply[30] that the first to exercise the power in the presence of others, was Emily Cardale at a date apparently very near this. He is speaking of the early-morning prayer-meetings in the church, which, he says, began to be held two weeks before the General Assembly of 1831.[31] It was the custom of a party from the prayer-meeting to go home with the Irvings to breakfast. "At one of these breakfasts," he writes, "a sweet, modest, young lady, Miss Emily Cardale, began to breathe heavily, and increasingly so, until at length she burst out into loud but abrupt short sentences of English which after a few minutes ceased. The voice was certainly beyond her native strength, and the subject matter of it was the expected power of the Spirit, not to be resisted by any one who would hear. Mr. Irving asked us to unite in thanksgiving for this answer to our prayers." "Other such instances," adds Brown, "followed, but as yet all in private, first by the same voice, but afterwards by a Miss Hall, and then by a man who rather repelled me (a teacher by the name of Taplin) who professed to speak in an unknown tongue." It was through this Miss Hall that the voices were introduced into the public services of the church, on Communion Sunday, October 16, 1831. We have several accounts of the scene by eye-witnesses.[32] What they chiefly dwell upon is the startling effect of the outcry, and the rush of the young woman, either unable to restrain herself, or alarmed at what she had done, into the vestry, whence proceeded a succession of doleful and unintelligible cries, while the audience of fifteen hundred or two thousand people, standing up and straining to hear and see what was toward, fell into utter confusion.

It is not necessary to give an account here of the natural excitement which was raised in London; of the increasing confusion which the exercise of the "gifts" brought into the public service of the church; of the suit instituted by the trustees against Irving for breach of trust deeds, and

his exclusion from the church; of the founding of the first
Irvingite Congregation in Newman Street in a deserted
studio which had been erected for the use of the painter
West. The new "prophets" as a matter of course soon
began to exercise the authority which they found in their
hands as inspired servants of God. They drove Irving
along from step to step, until at last a new spirit appeared
on the scene in the person of Robert Baxter (first in August,
1831, but not as a force until early in 1832).[33] Instead of
unintelligible "tongues" and weak repetitions of pious
platitudes, Baxter, when the "power" was on him, delivered himself authoritatively in specific commands to Irving,
arrangements for church order, and the like, and even
definite predictions of the future. Here was something
new and dangerous. Irving was startled and filled with
doubt. But the "power" in Baxter argued him down,
and all the "prophets" bore witness to the genuineness of
Baxter's inspiration, so that the whole movement was committed to this new development. The dangers inherent
in it were not slow in showing themselves. The first shock
came when the "power" in Baxter commanded him to go
to the Court of Chancery and deliver a message which
would be there given him, whereupon he should be cast
into prison. He went, and no message came to him, and
he was not cast into prison. Other predictions that had
been made failed of fulfilment. Contradictions began to
emerge between the several deliverances by the same organ,
or between the several organs. Spirit was arrayed against
spirit. The spirit that had spoken acceptably in one, was
pronounced by another, speaking in the Spirit, nothing
other than an evil spirit. Some who had been very forward in speaking, and had received the indorsement of
others speaking in the Spirit, were convicted of having
framed their own messages. Baxter's eyes were opened,
and the very doctrinal basis of Irving's teaching having
become—as well it might—suspect to him, he found him-

self at last no longer able to believe that the manifestations in which he had himself taken so prominent a part were of God.[34]

The climax of this particular development is very dramatic. Having reached his conclusion, Baxter (who lived at Doncaster) naturally travelled at once up to London to communicate it to Irving. He arrived at the moment of a crisis in Irving's own affairs. It was the very morning when Irving was to appear in the suit brought against him by the trustees of the church for permitting in it practices contrary to the trust deed. Irving was at breakfast with a party of friends. "Calling him and Mr. J. C[ardale] apart," says Baxter,[35] "I told them my conviction that we had all been speaking by a lying spirit and not by the Spirit of the Lord." But we will let David Brown describe the scene from within. He had himself reached the conclusion that there was nothing supernatural in the "manifestations"—this was not exactly Baxter's conclusion—and had determined to separate himself from Irving. He had broken this to Mrs. Irving but had postponed announcing it to Irving himself until after the trial, which was to take place that day. "The select few of us," he writes,[36] "came home with him"—from the early-morning prayer-meeting —"to breakfast, in the midst of which Miss Cardale uttered, in the usual unnatural voice, some words of cheer in prospect of the day's proceedings. But scarcely had she ceased when a ring came to the door, and Mr. Irving was requested to speak with the stranger. After five minutes' absence, he returned, saying, 'Let us pray,' and kneeling down, all followed while he spoke in this strain: 'Have mercy, Lord, on Thy dear servant, who has come up to tell us that he has been deceived, that his word has never been from above but from beneath, and that it is all a lie. Have mercy on him, Lord, the enemy hath prevailed against him, and hither hath he come in this time of trouble and rebuke and blasphemy, to break the power of the testimony we have to bear this day to this work of Thine. But let Thy work and power appear unto Thy poor servant. . . .'"

So strong was the delusion to which Irving was now delivered—that Irving who had been hitherto plastic wax in the hands of everybody. He was soon established in his new church in Newman Street. In that church an elaborate order was set up, and an ornate ritual instituted according to the pattern of which Baxter himself had drawn the outlines, and which was ever more fully developed by deliverances from Baxter's followers.[37] "Before the opening of this church, the prophet himself had published the wonderful narrative in which he repeated the predictions which came from his own lips, and, appealing to the whole world whether they had been fulfilled, proclaimed them a delusion." [38] Nothing, however, could now stay the development of the "Catholic Apostolic Church," not even Irving himself, had he wished to do so. More and more overruled and set aside by the powers he had evoked and could not control, he sank into an ever more subordinate position in the edifice he had raised.[39]

Meanwhile it was not going much better with the "gifts" in Scotland, where they had originated, than in London, whither they had been transplanted. The report of their outbreak on the Clyde had found a ready response in the heart of Thomas Erskine of Linlathen. His whole religious life was intensely individualistic, and he too had become imbued with the same chiliastic hopes which in London were fostered by the prophetic studies of Albury. Predisposed to recognize the phenomena as endowments of the Holy Ghost, he repaired at once to Port Glasgow and became an inmate of the Macdonalds' house, living with them for six weeks and attending the daily prayer-meetings, where he witnessed the manifestations. His immediate conclusions he published to the world in a tract, *On the Gifts of the Spirit*, issued at the close of 1830, and in a more con-

siderable volume which appeared the same year under the
title *The Brazen Serpent or Life Coming through Death.*
"The world," said he,[40] "does not like the recurrence of
miracles. And yet it is true that miracles have recurred.
I cannot but tell what I have seen and heard. I have heard
persons, both men and women, speak with tongues and
prophesy, that is, speak in the Spirit to edification, exhortation, and comfort." A closer acquaintance with the
phenomena, however, first shook and then shattered this
favorable judgment. The developments in London were
a great trial to his faith, as indeed they were also to that
of the originators of the "gifts" at Port Glasgow, who did
not hesitate to denounce them as delusions. "James
Macdonald writes," [41] Erskine tells one of his correspond-
ents, "that the spirit among them declared the London
people to be 'deceitful workers transforming themselves
into the Apostles of Christ.' Strange things—spirit against
spirit." He discovered that some at least of the deliverances of the Macdonalds rested on no profounder inspiration than paragraphs in the current newspapers.[42] Before
the end of 1833 he required to write:[43] "My mind has undergone a considerable change. . . . I have seen reason
to disbelieve that it is the Spirit of God which is in M——,
and I do not feel that I have stronger reason to believe
that it is in others." His conviction grew ever stronger
that all the manifestations he had himself witnessed at
Port Glasgow were delusive,[44] and that the whole development had originated and been maintained through a dreadful mistake.[45]

Why he should have ever given himself to such a delusion
is the real puzzle. There is an article in the *Edinburgh
Review* for June, 1831, reviewing the new charismatic
literature, considering which the reviewer impatiently but
not unjustly exclaims that "theologians look for truth, as
children on excursions seek for pleasure, by leaving the
plain path and the light of day to penetrate into caverns

and scramble in the dark." [46] In this article occurs a pungent paragraph which ought itself to have awakened Erskine to the true nature of his procedure. The subject in hand is the criterion employed to discriminate between true and false manifestations of the Spirit. True to his spiritual individualism, his "enthusiasm," to give it an old name, Erskine had contended that the only possible criterion in such cases is our own spiritual discernment. "The only security," he wrote, "lies in having ourselves the seal of God—that gift of the Holy Ghost by which we may detect the lying wonders of Satan." "According to his account, therefore," the reviewer comes down with his sledge-hammer blow,[47] "the very fact of their being prepared to pass judgment between God and Satan in the affairs of Port Glasgow amounts to a direct pretence to inspiration." "The gift pretended," he continues, "is that 'discerning of spirits,' so celebrated by the Apostles, as the divine endowment by means of which Simon the magician was detected by Peter and Elymas the sorcerer confounded by Paul. It is not the first time, doubtless, that men have indemnified themselves for the absence of visible gifts by setting up a title to invisible ones. Their argument, if it entitles them to either, entitles them to both. Their claim is unfortunately confined to the case which admits no other proof than their mere personal assertion that they are inspired."

Certainly the claims made to "gifts" which admitted of external tests, failed to justify themselves in the application of these tests. Even poor Mary Campbell was, in the end, led to confess that she had not behaved quite honestly in the matter of her "gifts." "I had, before receiving your letter," she writes to Robert Story, "come to the resolution to write to you and to confess my sin and error for calling my own impressions the voice of God. Oh," she exclaims, "it is no light thing to use the holy name irreverently, as I have been made to feel." [48] "'She was not at all careful in her statements,' wrote an impartial spectator of the doings at Fernicarry, who knew the attractive prophetess well," R. H. Story tells us,[49] and then goes on to remark on what he calls her Celtic temperament, "impressive rather on the spiritual than on the moral side." It is rather a sordid story, all in all, and we leave it with only two remarks, both of which appear to us very relevant. The one concerns the pathetic circumstance that Robert Story sent Mary Campbell's confession to Irving, accompanied with a note exposing her "want of simplicity"— and remarking on how "disappointing a career hers had turned out, especially as she was considered the most remarkable and conclusive evidence of the Holy Ghost being again with power in the midst of the church"—just in time to be delivered after Irving's death.[50] The other concerns the completeness with which the criterion desiderated by the Edinburgh reviewer of the reality of the gift of spiritual discernment alleged to be laid claim to by Erskine, is supplied by the issue in these Scotch instances of claims to spiritual gifts, so confidently accepted by Erskine. This issue for a time profoundly and salutarily shook Erskine's confidence in his judgment in such cases. "The shake which I have received in the matter is, I find, very deep," he writes.[51] But he can only add: "I hope I shall not be led to shut my ear against the true voice because I have been deceived by a false one."[52] He does not seem able to find the right way.[53]

You will doubtless be glad to have some account of the nature of the "prophetic" deliverances, and other manifestations of this movement. You will find such an account with specimens of the Scotch "tongues" in the eighth appendix to Hanna's edition of Erskine's *Letters*, written during this period. Mrs. Oliphant, in the course of her biography of Irving, records quite a number of the utterances. In particular she gives the interjected "manifestations" of the first service at the Newman Street

Church.[54]   We cannot quote them at large; here are some examples.   In the course of his exposition of the first chapter of I Samuel, Irving mentions the church as barren . . . on which the ecstatic voice interposes: "Oh but she shall be fruitful: oh! oh! oh! she shall replenish the earth and subdue it—and subdue it!"   A little further on, another breaks in with less appositeness to the subject: "Oh, you do grieve the Spirit—you do grieve the Spirit! Oh! the body of Jesus is to be sorrowful in spirit!   You are to cry to your Father—to cry, to cry, in the bitterness of your souls!   Oh it is a mourning, a mourning, before the Lord—a sighing, and crying unto the Lord because of the desolations of Zion—because of the desolations of Zion— because of the desolations of Zion!"   There were seven of these voices heard during the course of the service.   They were all pious, but repetitious, and, one would think (with Mrs. Oliphant), quite unnecessary, interruptions of the service.

It is more difficult to convey a notion of what the "speaking with tongues" was like.   The "tongues" were thought at first to be real languages.   Observers of the Scotch instances are very clear that, although unintelligible to their hearers, they were languages with recognizable structure as such.[55]   Cardale easily separated in J. Macdonald's utterances two distinguishable tongues.[56]   Mary Campbell declared that the tongue which she spoke was ordinarily that of the Pelew Islanders.[57]   The opinion soon became settled, however, that the "tongues" were an ecstatic heavenly and no earthly speech.   The piercing loudness and strength of the utterance was its most marked characteristic.   One witness speaks of it as "bursting forth" from the lips of a woman, "with an astonishing and terrible crash." [58]   Baxter says that it fell on him at his private devotions so loudly that he stuffed his handkerchief into his mouth to keep from alarming the house.[59]   Irving's own description of it is as follows: "The whole utterance from the beginning to

the ending of it, is with a power, and strength, and fullness
and sometimes rapidity of voice, altogether different from
that of the person's ordinary utterance in any mood; and I
would say, both in its form and in its effects upon a simple
mind, quite supernatural. There is a power in the voice
to thrill the heart and overawe the spirit after a manner
which I have never felt." [60]   Carlyle once heard it, and he
gives· a characteristic description of it.[61] "It was in a
neighboring room. . . .   There burst forth a shrieky hysterical 'Lah lall lall!' (little or nothing else but *l*'s and *a*'s)
continued for several minutes. . . . 'Why was there not
a bucket of water to fling on that lah-lalling hysterical
madwoman?' thought we or said to one another."   Doubtless both accounts are somewhat colored by the personal
equation.

We may imagine what a public service would be like
liable to interruptions by such manifestations. Henry
Vizetelly, in his *Glances Back Through the Years* (1893),
gives us a vignette picture of Irving in his new chapel in
Newman Street. "What chiefly attracted me to the chapel
in Newman-street was the expectation, generally realised,
of the spirit moving some hysterical shrieking sister or
frantic Boanerges brother (posted in the raised recess behind Irving's pulpit), to burst forth suddenly with one of
those wild rapid utterances which, spite of their unintelligibility, sent a strange thrill through all who heard them
for the first time. . . . He had grown gray and haggard-
looking, and this, with his long, straggling hair and restless look, emphasized by the cast in his eye, gave him a
singularly wild and picturesque appearance. His voice,
too, was piercingly loud, and his gestures were as vehement
as those of any street ranter of the day."

I think you will not be sorry, however, to place by the
side of this a full-length portrait of one of those early-
morning prayer-meetings held in the Regent Street Church,
which were the scene of the first public displays of the

"power." You will bear in mind that the hour is six in the morning, which in the winter was before dawn. "The church appeared to me," writes our observer,[62] "to be pitch dark; only the lights from the gas lamps shining into the windows enabled us to grope our way forward. It seemed to be entirely full, but my friend accosted a verger, who led us to an excellent seat, nearly opposite the reading desk. After the people were seated the most solemn stillness prevailed. The sleet beating upon the windows was the only sound that could be heard. The clouded sky and the driving snow increased the obscurity, and it was not for some time that we could perceive our nearest neighbors, and assure ourselves that the place was full from one end to the other. I quite believe in the exquisite simplicity and entire sincerity of Mr. Irving's whole character. I believe him to have been incapable of deliberately planning the scene which followed. Had he, however, been the most consummate actor that ever lived, had he studied the art of scenic portraiture and display from his youth up, he could not have produced a finer effect than on this occasion. Just as the clocks outside struck six, the vestry door opened and he entered the church with a small but very bright reading lamp in his hand. He walked with solemn step to the reading desk, and placing the lamp upon it, immediately before him, he stood up facing the audience. Remember, this was the only light in the place. It shone upon his face and figure as if to illuminate him alone. He had on a voluminous dark blue cloak, with a large cape, with a gilt clasp at the throat, which he loosened at once, so that the cloak formed a kind of a background to his figure. Tall, erect, and graceful, he stood for a few moments in silence, his pale face in the white light, his long dark locks falling down upon his collar, his eyes solemn and earnest, peering into the darkness of the building. . . . After a few musical, earnest words of prayer he opened the Bible before him, and began to read the twenty-second chapter of Revelation. If I were to live a hundred years I should never forget the reading of that chapter. I believe it exceeded in effect the finest speech and most eloquent sermon ever uttered. The exquisite musical intonation and modulation of voice, the deep and intense pathos of delivery, as if the speaker felt every word entering into his own soul, and that he was pouring it out to create a sympathy with his own feelings in others—all this was very wonderful, and totally absorbing every thought of the audience. But when he came to that verse, 'I am the root and the offspring of David, and the bright and Morning Star,' the effect of the last five words was electrical. The people could not cheer nor applaud, nor in any way relieve their feelings. There was a kind of hard breathing, a sound of suppressed emotion, more striking than the loudest plaudits could have been. The reader himself stopped for a moment as if to allow his unwonted emotion to subside. Before he could resume there came from a woman who was two or three seats behind me, a sound so loud that I am sure it might have been heard on the opposite side of the square. I have been trying to find a word by which to describe it, and the only word I can think of is the word 'yell.' It was not a scream nor a shriek; it was a yell so loud and so prolonged that it filled the church entirely, and as I have said, must have been heard far beyond it. It was at first one single sound, but it seemed in a short time to resolve itself into many separate sounds—not into articulate words by any means. They were far more like the sounds uttered by a deaf and dumb child modulating its tones, but wholly innocent of speech. This was the beginning and the ending of the so-called 'unknown tongues' in Regent Square, by which I mean they never varied from nor improved upon this type. How any one could be so deluded as to fancy in them any words or syllables, to say nothing of any language, I could never understand. There was no articulation, and no attempt at it. Had there been now and then something like a word, it was mixed up in such a jargon of sound, it was uttered with such rapidity, and in such a long continued and prolonged yell that, led up to it as I had been by the adjuncts of the scene, by the weirdness and obscurity of the building, I was never deceived by it for one moment. After a few minutes' utterance of these 'unknown tongues,' the excited woman began to speak in articulate English words. It was still in the same loud yell, slightly subdued by the necessity of speech. The utterances were chiefly texts of Scripture of an exhortative kind—the first word being uttered three times over, each one louder than the last, the last calling forth the woman's powers to the utmost, her breast heaving and straining with the exertion. On this occasion the English began oddly enough, with the word, 'Kiss! Kiss!! Kiss!!! the Son, lest he be angry, and ye perish from the way.' This morning there was only one manifestation. Generally there were two; on several occasions I heard three, and once four. They proceeded, however, from the same women, for while the second was speaking the first recovered her strength, and as her companion's voice died away in subdued murmurs, she burst out anew, as if a dozen spirits were contending in her. When I look back on that first morning, I feel moved with the deepest pity and regret for poor Edward Irving. He was greatly excited and overcome. In his honest heart, he believed that God had honored him and favored him above all the ministers in London. I can see him now before me, as I saw him then, meekly and humbly saying, 'I will now finish reading the chapter in which I was interrupted by the Holy Spirit, speaking by this young woman.' Yes I heard him say this with my own ears. Already the charm of the service was gone. He seemed glad to conclude it, as if he were afraid his own gentle words could detract from and injure the holy impression that had been produced. . . ."

Edward Irving himself "never received the power, nor
attained to any supernatural utterance, though no one
more earnestly sought after it." [63]   As Erskine in Scotland,
so Irving in London, had to be content with the rôle of observer of others' endowments. Nor was the actual number of those who enjoyed the gifts at any time very large.
"Of the many hundred individuals who for the first twelve
months attended in London upon these utterances, and
who were, one and all, praying for the same gifts, not so
many as twelve attained to the utterances." "The leading persons who, for many months gave forth the utterances, and wrought the strong conviction of the work being
of God were two ladies" [64]—and one of them (Miss Hall)
was not only declared by her sister prophetess (Miss Cardale) to be a false prophetess,[65] but was constrained to
confess that on some occasions at least she was herself the
author of her utterances.[66]

Of course we are in the presence here of hysteria.[67]
There are those who take occasion from this fact to exon-
erate Irving, in whole or at least in large part, for his va-
garious course. "Oh," cries an appreciative biographer,
"that the whole sad tribe of prophetic pedants and hysterical pietists had gone their own way, leaving him to go
his!" [68] Did they not go their own way? And was it
their fault that Irving never had a way of his own? Why
burden "the Albury sages" or the crowd of hysterical
women which surrounded him, and to whom he gave all too
willing an ear, with "the shipwreck of Irving's genius and
usefulness"? Is not their own shipwreck burden enough
for them to bear? Were it not juster to say simply that
this was the particular kind of fire Irving chose to play
with, and that, therefore, this is the particular way in which
he burned his fingers? It is altogether probable, being
the man he was, that if it had not been in these, he would
have burned them in some other flames.[69]

FAITH–HEALING

FAITH-HEALING

I HAVE called your attention to the discrediting which befell the Irvingite gifts. This discrediting was wrought not only by the course of history which confounded all the expectations based on them, but also by the confession which was made by one and another of the "gifted" persons that they had suffered from delusion. Let me remind you of this, and at the same time point out that all the gifts are involved in this discrediting. The characteristic Irvingite gift was the "tongues," and the accompanying "prophecy." Robert Baxter introduced a new manifestation of authoritative and predictive deliverances, which was assumed to belong to the "Apostolic" gift. But all the "prophets" committed themselves, when speaking in "the power," to the genuineness of his inspiration. Their credit falls thus with his. But again, their gifts are inextricably bound up with the gift of "healing." You will remember that Mary Campbell "spoke with tongues" before she was healed; and that the descent of the "power" on Margaret Macdonald was preliminary to its descent on James Macdonald, who by it was made the first faith-healer of the movement. By him both Margaret Macdonald's and Mary Campbell's healing was performed—the initial steps of the restoration of the "gifts."

It is impossible to separate these cases of healing from the other gifts with which they are historically connected. And in general the several "gifts" appear on the pages of the New Testament together, and form so clearly connected a body that it would be difficult to separate them from one another. Nevertheless many attempt their separation, and, discarding or at any rate neglecting the other gifts

revived in the Irvingite movement, contend vigorously
that the gift of healing the sick is a permanent endowment
of the church, and has been illustrated by numerous cases
essentially like those of Margaret Macdonald and Mary
Campbell down to to-day. This assertion is very clearly
made by a clergyman of the church of England, Joseph
William Reynolds, in a book dealing with what he calls
The Natural History of Immortality. "Many facts, attested
by honest, capable, painstaking witnesses," he says,[1]
"show the reality in our own days of healings which exceed
the limits of all known natural and human means, so that
no reasonable doubt ought to exist as to their being given
of God in confirmation of our Christian faith. Clergy and
laity of the English church, various non-conforming ministers, medical men, lawyers, and professors of physical science, with a large number of healed persons, present indis-
putable evidence that the Gift of Healing is now, as in the
Apostolic Age, one of the signs which follow those who
believe." The claim is precise, and the belief which it
expresses is somewhat wide-spread. Already thirty years
ago (1887)[2] there were more than thirty "Faith-Homes"
established in America, for the treatment of disease by
prayer alone; and in England and on the European Conti-
nent there were many more. International conferences
had already been held by its advocates, and conventions of
narrower constituency beyond number. It counts adherents in every church, and, if for no other reason than its
great diffusion, it demands careful attention.

I am a little embarrassed to know how to take up the
subject so as to do it justice and to bring the full truth out
clearly. On the whole, I fancy it will be fairest to select a
representative book advocating this teaching, and to begin
with an analysis of its argument. The way being thus
opened, we shall probably be able to orient ourselves with
reference to the problem itself in a comparatively brief
space. The book I have selected for this purpose as, on

the whole, at once the most readable and the most rational presentation of the views of the Faith-Healers, is Doctor A. J. Gordon's *The Ministry of Healing, or Miracles of Cure in All Ages.* The copy of this book at my disposal belongs to the second, revised edition, issued in 1883. Gordon writes in a straightforward, businesslike style, in excellent spirit, with great skill in arranging his matter and developing his subject, and with a very persuasive and even ingenious disposition of his argument, so as to present his case in the most attractive way. He expresses his purpose as "to let the history of the church of all ages answer to the teaching of the Scriptures on this question, without presuming to dogmatize on it himself." [3] Already we get the impression that he knows how to present his matter so as not only to please readers, but also to remove such prejudices against his cause as may be lurking in their minds, and to predispose them to follow his guidance. We do not lose this impression as we read on. After an introductory chapter on "The Question and Its Bearings," we are at once given a series of chapters on "The Testimony of Scripture," "The Testimony of Reason," "The Testimony of the Church," "The Testimony of Theologians," "The Testimony of Missions," "The Testimony of the Adversary," "The Testimony of Experience," "The Testimony of the Healed." You will observe the power of such a disposition of the matter; it almost convinces us to read over the mere titles of the chapters. At the end there come two chapters on the "Verdict"—called respectively the "Verdict of Candor" and the "Verdict of Caution"—and finally the "Conclusion." We must now look a little more closely into the contents of this full and admirably marshalled argument.

Our logical sense meets with a shock at the first opening of the volume. On the very first page the author represents asking the question, What is a miracle? as "evading the issue"; and toward the close of the first chapter he formally declines to define a miracle. This, as the outcome of a chapter on "The Question and its Bearings," beginning a volume undertaking to give proof of the existence of "miracles of cure in all ages," is far from reassuring. We open our eyes wider, however, when we observe that this method of dealing with the subject is not peculiar to this author, but is somewhat characteristic of the advocates of Faith-Healing. Robert L. Stanton, for example, in an able essay printed in *The Presbyterian Review*, takes up the same position.[4] "It is well in the outset," he says, "to have a definite conception of the topic to be handled." He then proceeds by way of rendering the subject more definite to express a preference for "the category of the supernatural, instead of that of the miraculous." Such methods can bear only one of two meanings. They either yield the question in debate altogether—for no one who is a Christian in any clear sense doubts that God hears and answers prayer for the healing of the sick in a generally supernatural manner—or else they confuse the issue. The former is certainly not their intention; these writers do not mean to yield the point of the strict miraculousness of Faith-Healing. Stanton's selected instances, on which he rests his defense of Faith-Healing, are all such as are meant to demonstrate specifically miraculous working. Everywhere the use of means naturally adapted to bring the cure about, such as the surgeon's knife or the articles of the *materia medica*, are, if not forbidden, yet certainly discouraged by the practitioners of Faith-Healing, and represented as a mark of lack of trust in God; and dependence on God alone, apart from all use of natural means, is represented as the very essence of the matter.[5] After refusing at the outset to define a miracle, we observe Gordon, accordingly, showing no hesitancy later on in defining it sharply enough, and asserting that it is just this which is wrought in Faith-Healing. When the testimony is all in, and he comes to deliver the verdict, he declares decisively,[6] "a miracle is the immediate action of God, as distinguished from His mediate action through natural laws"—than which no definition could be clearer or better. This, he now says, this and nothing else, is what we pray for in Faith-Healing. It is plain, therefore, that these writers do not mean to yield the question when they decline to define a miracle at the beginning of their arguments. Precisely what they contend for is that express miracles of healing—healings by the "immediate action of God, as distinguished from His mediate action through natural laws"—still take place in numerous instances. The only effect of their refusal of definition at the outset, therefore, is to confuse the issue.

Now, this confusion of the issue is a very serious matter. It has first of all the effect of permitting long lists of unsifted cases to be pleaded as proofs of the proposition defended, although a large number of these cases would be at once excluded from consideration on a closer definition of exactly what is to be proved. Thus the verdict of the simple reader is forced, as it were: he is led to look upon every instance of answer to prayer as a case in point, and is gradually led on through the argument in the delusion that these are all miracles. It has next the effect of unjustly prejudicing the reader against those who feel constrained to doubt the reality of specifically miraculous Faith-Healing as if they denied the supernatural, or any real, answer to prayer, instead of merely the continuance through all time of the specific mode of answer to prayer which comes by miracle. The confusions thus engendered in the reader's mind are apt, moreover, to eat pretty deeply into his own modes of thinking, and to end by betraying him into serious errors. He is likely, for example, to be led to suppose that in the cases adduced for his consideration he has examples of what real miracles are; and thus to reduce the idea of miracles to the level of these Faith-Healings, assimilating the miracles of our Lord, for example, to them and denying that miracles in the strict sense have ever been wrought, even by our Lord. Or, on the other hand, under a more or less vague consciousness that the instances of Faith-Healing adduced do not prove what they are really adduced to prove, he may gain the impression that they do not prove what they are ostensibly adduced to prove, that is to say, the supernatural answer to prayer; and thus he may be betrayed into doubting the reality of any answer to prayer whatever. Readers of the literature of Faith-Healing will not need to be told that no merely hypothetical effects of this confusing way of arguing the question are here suggested. Each of these effects has actually been produced in the case of numerous readers.

So far is confusion between things that differ pressed, in the attempt to obtain some petty argumentative advantage, that, not content with refusing to discriminate miracles (the continued recurrence of which some deny) from special providences (which all heartily recognize as continually occurring), some writers make a vigorous effort also to confound the miraculous healing of the body with the supernatural regeneration of the soul, as not merely analogous transactions, but transactions so much the same in essence that the one cannot be denied and the other affirmed. Gordon permits himself, for example, to write: "Is it right for us to pray to God to perform a miracle of healing in our behalf? 'The truth is,' answers an eminent writer,[7] 'that to ask God to act at all, and to ask Him to perform a miracle are one and the same thing. . . .' We see no reason, therefore, why we should hesitate to pray for the healing of our bodies any more than the renewal of our souls. Both are miracles. . . ."[8] The effect of writing like this is obviously to identify miraculous Faith-Healing with the cause of supernaturalism in general; and thus the unwary reader is led, because he believes in the regeneration of the soul by the immediate operation of the

Holy Spirit and in a prayer-hearing. God, to fancy that he must therefore believe in miraculous Faith-Healing. A very unfair advantage is thus gained in the argument.

The deeper danger to the reasoner himself which comes from thus obscuring the lines which divide miracles, specifically so called, from the general supernatural, although already incidentally suggested, seems to require at this point more explicit notice.   When once the distinguishing mark of miracles is obliterated, it is easy to eliminate the specifically miraculous altogether by the simple expedient of sinking it in the general supernatural; and that not merely in contemporary Christianity, but in the origins of Christianity also.   Numerous recent advocates of Faith-Healing have definitely entered upon this path.   Thus Prebendary Reynolds, to whose book allusion has already been made, is perfectly sure that the miracles of Faith-Healing are as truly miracles as those that Christ wrought while on earth. But, the fence between miracles properly so-called and the general supernatural having been conveniently let down for him by his instructors, he is not so sure that miracles, in the sense of effects wrought immediately by God without the intervention of natural forces, ever occurred.   He seeks analogies in mesmerism, hypnotism, and the like, and permits himself to write a passage like this: "Dr. Rudolf Heidenhaim gently stroked once or twice along Dr. Kröner's bent right arm; at once it became quite stiff.   Other muscles, other members can be acted on in like manner.   The effects are similar to effects produced by catalepsy.   This shows how easy it was for our Lord, with His divine knowledge and power, to work every kind of healing." [9]   Even Prebendary W. Yorke Fausset insists that the healing works of our Lord were wrought by Him not in virtue of His Deity but on the plane of His humanity, and differ not in kind but in degree "from the wonderful works of human healing, or, at all events, of healers who have wrought 'in the name of Jesus Christ'"

—in which, it is needless to say, he finds nothing that is strictly miraculous, though everything that is "spiritual," that is to say, supernatural.[10]   Some may look upon this movement of thought, to be sure, with indifference.   The late Charles A. Briggs, for example, taught that "if it were possible to resolve all the miracles of the Old Testament into extraordinary acts of Divine Providence, using the forces and forms of nature in accordance with the laws of nature; and if we could explain all the miracles of Jesus, His unique authority over man and over nature, from His use of mind-cure, or hypnotism, or any other occult power," "nothing essential would be lost from the miracles of the Bible." [11]   Few of us will be able, however, to follow Doctor Briggs in this judgment, a judgment which would confound Moses with the magicians at Pharaoh's court, and reduce our Lord, in these of His activities at least, from the manifestation of God in the flesh to the exhibition of the occult powers of man.   It is not easy to view, therefore, with other than grave apprehension the breaking down of the distinction between miracles and the general supernatural; because it tends to obliterate the category of the miraculous altogether, and in the long run to assimilate the mighty works of our Lord to—we put it at its best—the wonders of science, and Him, as their worker, to—we still put it at its best—the human sage.[12]

There is yet another effect, coming, however, from the opposite angle, which follows on breaking down the distinction between miracle and the general supernatural, that we should not pass by without notice.   What is the natural attitude of a man expecting a miracle?   Simple expectancy, of course; just quiet waiting.   But what is the natural attitude of a man praying for help from God, which is expected to come to him through the ordinary channels of law?   Equally, of course, eager activity directed to the production of the desired result.   Hence the proverb, God helps those who help themselves; and the exhortation, on a higher plane, Work and pray. No man prays God for a good harvest and then neglects to plan and plant and cultivate. If he did he knows perfectly well he would neither deserve nor receive the harvest. Similarly God requires effort on the part of those who receive His supernatural salvation—even though there are elements in it which do not come by " law." "Work out your own salvation with fear and trembling," Paul commands, " for it is God who worketh in you both to will and to work, for his good pleasure." One would think that Gordon, who insists that the healing of our bodies and the renewal of our souls stand on the same plane with respect to the nature of the Divine activities involved, would infer from such a passage that since the gift of salvation from God does not supersede our duty to work out our own salvation, so the gift of bodily healing from God cannot supersede the duty of working out our own healing—each by the use of the appropriate means. But no; he requires us to discard means, and all seeking through means. Whence there follows, on the one hand, an additional proof that, despite his refusal to define "miracle" for his readers at the outset, he carries in his own mind a perfectly definite conception of what a miracle is; and, on the other hand, an indication of the fanatical character of his teaching as to Faith-Healing—if it does not turn out to be not merely supernatural but distinctively miraculous in its mode of occurrence. He who prays for a harvest, and does not plough, and sow, and reap, is a fanatic. He who prays for salvation and does not work out his own salvation is certainly a Quietist, and may become an Antinomian. He who prays for healing and does not employ all the means of healing within his reach—hygiene, nursing, medicine, surgery,—unless God has promised to heal him in the specific mode of precise miracle, is certainly a fanatic and may become also a suicide. Whence, at this stage of the inquiry, we may learn not merely the controversial unfairness and the logical error of refusing to define at the outset of a discussion like this what a miracle is, but also the grave practical danger which arises from such a procedure of leading men into destructive fanaticism. It is the essence of fanaticism to neglect the means which God has ordained for the production of effects.

We perceive that Gordon is bound to produce evidence not merely of supernatural healing but distinctively of miraculous healing in order to justify his contention. And with his manner of opening the discussion before us, we feel bound, not only for our own instruction but for our protection as well, to scrutinize the evidence he offers with care, in order to assure ourselves that it unambiguously justifies the conclusion that God has continued the gift of specifically miraculous healing permanently in the church. The heads of the chapters in which the proof is adduced have already been mentioned. The first of them appropriately invites us to consider the testimony of Scripture. Three scriptural passages are cited and commented upon at large. These are: Matt. 8 : 17: "And he cast out the spirits with his word, and healed all that were sick: that it might be fulfilled which was spoken by Esaias the prophet, saying, Himself took our infirmities, and bare our sicknesses"; Mark 16 : 17, 18: "These signs shall follow them that believe: in my name shall they cast out devils; they shall speak with new tongues; they shall take up serpents; and if they drink any deadly thing, it shall not hurt them; they shall lay their hands on the sick and they shall recover"; and James 5 : 14, 15: "Is any sick among you? let him call for the elders of the church; and let them pray over him, anointing him with oil in the name of the Lord: and the prayer of faith shall save the sick, and the Lord shall raise him up; and if he have committed sins, they shall be forgiven him." Elsewhere, and in treatises of other writers, we find hints of other passages supposed to bear on the subject, such

as John 14 : 12, 13: "Verily, verily, I say unto you, He
that believeth on me, the works that I do shall he do
also; and greater works than these shall he do; because I
go unto my Father"; [13] the enumeration of miraculous
gifts by Paul in the twelfth chapter of I Corinthians, without hint of their approaching cessation, and [14] "among
other powers which are conceded to belong to the Church
to the end or 'till He come'"; and especially numerous
instances of actual Faith-Healing in the Old and New
Testaments alike, particularly in the Acts of the Apostles,
which we are told, "is full of it." It is observable, however,
that the three passages on which Gordon rests his argument really constitute the case of the other writers as well.
We must take a look at them, though, naturally, as brief
a look as can be made serviceable.

We begin with the second of them, Mark 16 : 17, 18,
because we may rule it out of court at once as spurious.
Of course its spuriousness may be disputed, and some very
learned men have disputed it. The late Dean Burgon
published a lengthy treatise in its defense, and the Abbé
Martin wrote an even more lengthy one. Nevertheless
it is just as certain that it is spurious as anything of this
kind can be certain. The certainty that it was not originally a part of Mark's Gospel, for example, is the same
kind of certainty as that the beautiful verse

> "For Thy sorrows we adore Thee,
>   For the griefs that wrought our peace;
>   Gracious Saviour, we implore Thee,
>   In our hearts Thy love increase,"

which we now sing as the last verse of the hymn, "Sweet
the moments, rich in blessing," was not originally a part
of that hymn. Or if you prefer to put it so, the certainty
that the last twelve verses of Mark are spurious is the
same in kind as the certainty that the rest of Mark's
Gospel is genuine. And it may be added that it is just as

well for you and me that they are spurious. For the gifts
that are promised to "them that believe" seem not to be
promised to eminent saints merely, one here and there
who believes mightily, but to all believers; and what is
promised to believers is not one or two of these gifts but
all of them. "These signs," it is said, "shall accompany
them that believe." I should not like to have the genuineness of my faith made dependent upon my ability to speak
with new tongues, to drink poison innocuously, and to
heal the sick with a touch.[15] And, let us note in passing,
it certainly was not understood in the Apostolic Church
that these gifts were inseparable from genuine faith. The
incident of the conversion of the Samaritans recorded in
the eighth chapter of Acts stands there, as we have seen
in a previous lecture,[16] for the express purpose of teaching
us the contrary—that, to wit, these signs accompanied
not them that believed but them on whom the Apostles
laid their hands in order to confer these signs upon them.

The employment of this spurious passage by Gordon in
this connection brings him into inevitable embarrassment.
For although, when commenting on it here,[17] he insists,
as he must, that "this rich cluster of miraculous promises
all hangs by a single stem, faith"—"the same believing to
which is attached the promise of salvation"; and that
"whatever practical difficulties we may have in regard to
the fulfillment of this word, these ought not to lead us to
limit it where the Lord has not limited it "; yet, when he
comes, at a later point, to meet the objection that "if you
insist that miracles of healing are possible in this age, then
you must logically admit that such miracles as raising the
dead, turning water into wine, and speaking in unknown
tongues are still possible" [18]—he does "throw one half of
the illustrious promise into eclipse," denying that that part
of it, at least, which says that this sign shall follow believers,
"They shall speak with other tongues," does still follow
them. Nor will it be easy to show that "taking up ser-

pents," whatever that may mean, or drinking deadly things without harm, are not "miracles on external nature, like the turning of the water into wine." The truth is that these items bear an apocryphal appearance, and constitute one of the internal indications, answering to the sufficient external proof, that the passage is uncanonical and of uninspired origin.[19]

The third passage, that from James 5 : 14, 15, we are ourselves inclined to set aside with equal summariness as irrelevant. We allow, of course, that the presumption is "that the passage refers to an established and perpetual usage in the Church"; we should not find it difficult to believe that "the oil is applied as a symbol of the communication of the Spirit, by whose power healing is effected"; we agree that "the promise of recovery is explicit, and unconditional" to the prayer of faith.[20] But we see no indication in the passage that "a peculiar miraculous faith" is intended; no promise of a healing in a specifically miraculous manner; and no command to exclude medicinal means, or proof of their exclusion. If we read the passage with simple minds, free from preconceptions, I think we shall find in it nothing but a very earnest exhortation to sick people to turn to the Lord in their extremity, and a very precious promise to those who thus call upon Him, that the Lord will surely hearken to their cry.

The passage does not stand off by itself in isolation: it has a context. And the context throws light upon the simplicity of the meaning. "Is any among you suffering?" asks James, and advises, "let him pray. Is any cheerful? let him sing praises. Is any among you sick? let him call for the elders of the church; and let them pray over him, anointing him with oil in the name of the Lord; and the prayer of faith shall save him that is sick, and the Lord shall raise him up; and if he have committed sins, it shall be forgiven him." Is there anything here that is not repeated before our eyes every day, whenever any Christian is sick—except that we have allowed the formal churchly act of intercession for him to fall into desuetude? Here is really the gravamen of the passage to us. The explicit promise is to the official intercession of the church, the Apostolic enforcement, I take it, consonant to the entrance into history of the organized church, of our Lord's gracious promise, that "when two or three are gathered together in His name, there He is in the midst of them." Even nature itself should have taught us the value of this organic supplication; does not Émile Boutroux, for example, declare[21] that "a collective will has nothing to do with the mathematical sum of the individual wills"? And can we wonder that our Lord should honor the same principle? Apart from this failure, we have nothing in the passage that transcends universal Christian experience. Where is there any command in it to exclude the ordinary medicinal means? Where is there any promise of a specifically miraculous answer? When James says, "If any of you lacketh wisdom, let him ask of God who giveth to all men liberally and upbraideth not, and it shall be given him," are we to understand him to forbid that wisdom should be sought in the natural way of thoughtful consideration, and to promise that God will bestow it after a specifically miraculous fashion? When our Lord says, with complete absence of any hint of limitation as to the field in which the request moves, "Ask and ye shall receive," are we to understand Him to forbid all effort in any sphere of life, and to promise specifically miraculous provision for all our needs? Are we to expect to be fed with manna from heaven, or are we not rather to learn to work with our own hands, that we may have wherewith to give to the necessities of others as well as to supply our own wants? There seems to be no more reason in our present passage to exclude medicinal means from the healing of the sick, or to expect a miraculous answer to our prayers in their behalf, than there is in our Lord's promise to exclude the use of all means of seeking to supply our daily necessities and to depend wholly on miraculous gifts from heaven.

It is probable that the common impression received from this passage of the promise of a miraculous healing in large part arises from what seems the extreme formality of the transaction recommended. The sick man is to send for the elders of the church to pray for him, and they are to anoint him with oil. We are apt here to get the emphasis misplaced. There is no emphasis on the anointing with oil. That is a mere circumstantial detail, thrown in by the way. The emphasis falls wholly on the sick man's getting himself prayed for officially by the elders of the church, and the promise is suspended wholly on their prayer, on the supposition that it is offered in faith. The circumstantial clause, thrown in almost incidentally, "anointing with oil in the name of the Lord," is susceptible of two interpretations.[22] The reference may be to the use of oil as a symbol of the power of the Spirit to be exercised in the healing; or it may be to the use of oil as a medicinal agent. In neither view is the employment of medicinal agents excluded; but in the latter view their employment is distinctly alluded to. The circumstance that oil was well-nigh the universal remedy in the medical practice of the day favors the latter view, as does the employment of, as Archbishop Trench puts it, "the mundane and profane" instead of the "sacred and religious word" for the act of anointing.[23] The lightness of the allusion to the anointing points in the same direction. It scarcely seems that so solemn an act and so distinct an act as ceremonial anointing could be alluded to so cursorily.[24] If, on the other hand, the allusion is to the use of oil as a medicinal agent, everything falls into its place. The meaning then is in effect, "giving him his medicine in the name of the Lord." The emphasis falls not on the anointing, but on its being done "in the name of the Lord," and the whole becomes an exhortation to Christians, when they

are sick, to seek unto the Lord as well as to their physician
—nay, to seek unto the Lord rather than to their physician
—with a promise that the Lord will attend to their cry.
If any is sick among you, we read, let him call for the elders
of the church and let them pray for him, rubbing him with
his oil in the name of the Lord, and the prayer of faith
shall save him that is sick. Where is there promise of
miracle in that?[25]

What James requires of us is merely that we shall be
Christians in our sickness as in our health, and that our
dependence then, too, shall be on the Lord. It is just the
truly Christian attitude that he exhorts us to, precisely
as Prebendary Reynolds describes it. "We avail ourselves," says he,[26] "of all that science knows, and thank
God for it. The resources of civilization are ours, and we
use them to the utmost. We labour in wise and kindly
nursing, and thankfully call in the medical skill which the
devout and learned and experienced physician and surgeon
have at command. It is God, however, the real physician,
who gives the chief medicine; who makes drugs, operations, kindness, nursing to have true healing power; who
takes away sin, sickness, death, giving righteousness, healing, eternal life." Do you say this is a purely clerical
view? It is the physician's view also, if the physician
happens to be a Christian. "I dressed the wound and
God healed it," wrote Ambroise Paré, the great Huguenot
physician—the father of modern surgery—on the walls
of the École de Médecine at Paris.[27] Let me read you,
however, more at large how a more modern Christian
physician puts it. "In the healing of every disease of
whatever kind," writes Doctor Henry E. Goddard,[28] "we
cannot be too deeply impressed with the Lord's part of the
work. He is the operator. We are the co-operators. More
and more am I impressed that every patient of mine who
has ever risen up from his sick bed onto his feet again has
done so by the divine power. Not I, but the Lord, has

cured him. And it is this fact that the Lord does so much, that gives to different systems of healing their apparent cures. He has healed many a one in spite of medicine, in spite of mental healers, in spite of ignorance, in spite of negligence and poor and scanty food. [Nineteen out of twenty cases of grippe will get well without doing anything for it, if we are willing to bear it until that time. Pneumonia, even, is what the physician calls a self-limiting disease, and many cases will recover alone if we are willing to run our chances with it. The arm may drop into boiling water and become scalded. Nine times out of ten it will take care of itself and heal. But if that arm is mine it is going to have an outward application which will make it feel better the moment it touches it. And more important by far, it is going to be dressed aseptically to prevent blood poisoning. It might get well itself, probably would; but it is going to have my little co-operation, the most intelligent that I can render, that the Lord may have the open door through which He can come in and bless it." It is the very spirit of James, I take it, that speaks in this Christian physician. If you are sick, you will use means, all the means that exist; but you will use the means in the name of the Lord, and to Him you will look for the issue.

The scattered passages of Scripture which are appealed to here and there by Faith-Healers to buttress the chief proof texts need not delay us more than a moment. The examples of miraculous cures adduced from the Bible, are, of course, irrelevant. No one of the parties to this discussion doubts that they were truly miraculous. The question at issue is, whether such miraculous works may still be performed, now that the period of revelation has gone by. The appeal to the enumeration of gifts in the twelfth chapter of I Corinthians is equally irrelevant, since the question at issue is precisely whether they are ordinary gifts continued in the church, or extraordinary gifts connected (according to the eighth chapter of Acts) directly

with the Apostles.   John 14 : 12 is worthy of more attention.   The Faith-Healers do not even profess, however,
to do the great works which Christ did—His miracles on
nature, His raising of the dead—and much less can they
point to their healings as greater works than these.[29]   No
miracles, in the strict sense of the word, greater than those
which Christ did, have been done by any of His followers.
But in and through His followers He has, in fulfilment of
this promise, manifested the power of the Holy Spirit,
foreshadowed and begun at Pentecost, beyond anything
witnessed in His lifetime; and He is thus conquering the
world to Himself through the "greater works" of His disciples.   That He refers here to these spiritual works is
generally agreed.[30]

I have reserved to the last the passage which Gordon
appeals to first, because its application to the present
matter raises a question of doctrine which it seemed more
convenient to discuss at the end, rather than at the beginning of a scrutiny of proof texts.   When speaking of our
Lord's abounding miracles of healing, Matthew says that
He did them "that it might be fulfilled which was spoken
by Isaiah the prophet, saying, Himself took our infirmities
and bare our diseases" (Matt. 8 : 17).   The passage has,
of course, no direct bearing on the assertion that miraculous
cures continue to be performed in the church.   It speaks
only of Christ's own miraculous cures, and does not in the
remotest way suggest that His followers were to work similar ones.   It can be made useful to the Faith-Healing
hypothesis, not directly, but only indirectly, through the
doctrine which it is supposed to teach.   That doctrine is
declared to be this: "That we have Christ set before us
as the sickness-bearer as well as the sin-bearer of His people"; "that Christ endured vicariously our diseases as
well as our iniquities"; and, it being true "that our Redeemer and Substitute bore our sicknesses, it would be
natural to reason at once that He bore them that we

might not bear them." As, then, "we urge the transgressor to accept the Lord Jesus as his sin-bearer, that he may no longer have to bear the pains and penalties of his disobedience," so we should urge the sick " to accept Him as his pain-bearer." [31] Otto Stockmayer is quoted as teaching[32] "that if our Redeemer bore our sicknesses it is not his will that his children should remain under the power of disease, any more than that, having borne our sins, it is his will that they should remain under condemnation and disobedience." In enunciating the same doctrine, Stanton makes use of the remarkable expressions,[33] "that the Atonement was not only made for sin but for disease, the fruit of sin," and "that in atoning for our diseases of body, just as for our sins of soul, Christ took them upon Himself that He might *bear them away*, and thus relieve His people from the need of bearing them."

It would be difficult to find more confused expressions than these. What exact meaning can be attached, for example, to the phrase, "atonement for disease"? Is it intended to suggest that disease is fault for which we are responsible? Atonement can be made only for fault. And why should the phrase, "bear disease away" be employed in connection with this text? Does not the word employed here for "bearing sickness" express not bearing away, removing, but bearing, enduring? And by what right can Stockmayer—the "theologian of Faith-Healing," as he is called—parallel the "power of disease" with "condemnation and disobedience" as alike taken away by Christ's redemption, unless he means to convey the idea that, as there is now no condemnation to them in Christ Jesus, so there can now be no disease to them that are in Christ Jesus; and as all disobedience is wilful and sinful, so also is all sickness? If so, we can only infer that none of us are in Christ Jesus: our universal physical decay and death are but the external manifestations of our inward corruption and our eternal doom.[34]

It will doubtless be more profitable, however, to seek to lay our finger on the source of error in the statement of the doctrine, and to correct it, than to track out all its confusions. This error does not lie in the supposition that redemption is for the body as well as the soul, and that the saved man shall be renewed in the one as well as in the other. This is true. Nor does it lie in the supposition that provision is made in the atonement for the relief of men from disease and suffering, which are fruits of sin. This too is true.[35] It lies in confusing redemption itself, which is objective and takes place outside of us, with its subjective effects, which take place in us; and in failing to recognize that these subjective effects of redemption are wrought in us gradually and in a definite order. Ideally all of Christ's children were saved before the foundation of the world, when they were set upon by God's love, and given by the Father to the Son to be saved by Him. Objectively they were saved when Christ died for them on the tree, purchasing them to Himself by His own precious blood. This salvation was made their personal possession in principle when they were regenerated by the Holy Spirit, purchased for them by the death of Christ in their behalf. It was made over to them judicially on their believing in Christ, in the power of the Holy Ghost thus given to them. But it is completed in them in its full effects only when at the Judgment Day they stand, sanctified souls, clothed in glorified bodies, before the throne of God, meet for the inheritance of the saints in light. Here, you perceive, is a process. Even after we have believed in Christ, and have a title as justified men to the benefits bought for us by His blood and righteousness, entrance into the actual enjoyment of these several benefits remains a process, and a long process, to be completed in a definite order. This is true of the spiritual blessings which come to us through the atonement of Christ. We are no longer under the curse of sin. But we remain sinners. The struggle against indwelling sin, and therefore indwelling sin to struggle against, continues through life. We have not yet obtained, and we are not yet made perfect. It is little that we continue also physically weak, liable to disease, and certain to die. For the removal of these physical evils, too, provision is made in the atonement. But the benefit here too is not received all at once. For us, as in the broader sphere of the world's salvation, death is the last enemy to be conquered. Though the redeemed of the Lord and no longer under the dominion of sin, the results of sin remain with us: inwardly we are corrupt, outwardly we are the prey of weakness and disease and death. We shall not escape from either in this life. Who is there that sins not? And who is there that does not suffer and die? But ultimately we are relieved from both. Of indwelling corruption when our sanctification is completed and, having been made holy, we depart, which is far better, to be with the Lord, the Holy One. Of outward weaknesses, at that redemption of the body which, while here below, we only, groaning and travailing in pain, wait for in its due season—that is, at the resurrection, when death shall be swallowed up in victory. This is the teaching of the Bible; and this is what Christ illustrated when He healed the sick in His ministry on earth that men might see, as in an object-lesson, that provision was made in His substitutionary work for the relief of every human ill. There is included in this, however, no promise that this relief is to be realized in its completeness all at once, or in this earthly life. Our Lord never permitted it for a moment to be imagined that the salvation He brought was fundamentally for this life. His was emphatically an other-world religion. He constantly pointed to the beyond, and bade men find their true home, to set their hopes, and to place their aspirations, there.

But, we are asked, are there not to be prelibations here? Is there no "intermediate work of healing and recovery for the body" here as there is "a vast intermediate work of cleansing and renewal effected for the soul?" [36] Assuredly. The good man will not fail to be the better for his goodness even in his bodily life. Of course we may make an absurd application of even so obvious a maxim. That devout physician whom we had occasion to quote a while ago, warns us against such an absurd application. He is unwise, he declares,[37] who teaches "Obey the commandments, the laws of spiritual life, and you will thereby attain physical health." "That does not follow," he declares. "As well say, 'Obey the commandments and you will become large possessors of this world's goods,' or, 'Obey the commandments and you will therefore be exempt from the law of gravitation.'" What he means to say is that the Lord, in placing His people in this complex of forces whose regular working constitutes what we call the laws of nature, subjects them, of course, to these laws. We cannot expect to be emancipated from the laws which govern the action of the forces in the midst of which our life is cast. That would be to take us out of the world. No matter how holy we are we must expect, if we cast ourselves from a tenth-story window, to fall with the same certainty and with the same rate of accelerating velocity as other men. The law of gravity is not suspended in its action on us by our moral character. We cannot grow rich by simply rubbing some Aladdin's lamp and commanding supernatural assistance; economic law will govern the acquisition of wealth in our case as in that of others. When typhoid germs find lodgment in a body, even though it be the body of a saint, they will under favorable conditions, grow and produce all their dreadful effects, with the same certainty with which the seeds of corn which you cast into the ground grow and bring forth their harvest. The same laws on which you depend for the harvest of corn, you may equally depend on for the harvests of disease which you reap year after year. We live then in a complex of forces out of which we cannot escape, so long as we are in this world, and these forces make for disease and death. We are all left here, like Trophimus at Miletum, sick. And if we insist upon being relieved of this sickness we can expect only the answer which was given to Paul: "My grace is sufficient for you."

All this is true, and yet it too is not incapable of exaggeration in its application. And that for two very obvious reasons. In the first place it also is a law of nature that the pure in heart and clean in conduct escape many evils, among which must be ranged multifarious sicknesses. We need not labor so obvious a point.[38] We find even Matthew Arnold remarking on this law in his allusive manner. "Medical science," says he,[39] "has never gauged—never perhaps set itself to gauge—the intimate connection between moral fault and disease. To what extent, or in how many cases, what is called *illness* is due to moral springs having been used amiss, whether by being overused or by not being used sufficiently—we hardly at all know, and we too little inquire." But we do not found here solely on a law of nature. Even the laws of nature are under the control of God in their operation, and we point to the good providence of our God. The Lord is rich in mercy to them that trust in Him, and it would be strange indeed if there were no visible and tangible fruits of this His mercy perceptible in our bodily life. There is a promise for this life as well as for that which is to come, and it is definitely said that to those who seek first the kingdom of God and His righteousness, all these things shall be added. Are not the providence and grace of God enough for us in this "our little journey in the world"? Or, dissatisfied with these, are we to demand that the laws of nature be suspended in our case; that, though in the world, we shall, in this sense too, be not of it? What scriptural ground is there for expecting miraculous healings of the body through these ages of our earthly pilgrimage, in addition to that benefit which the body obtains from its animation by a renewed and sanc-

tifying soul, from our Lord's watchfulness over it as His
purchased possession, from the indwelling in it of the
Holy Spirit as His Temple, from the Father's listening to
the prayers of His saints for its keeping and healing, and
from all God's goodness to it in fulfilment of His word that
godliness has the promise of the life that now is as well as
that which is to come? None has been pointed to, and
we are constrained to believe none exists. For soul and
body we are in the Lord's loving keeping. We trust in
Him and He keeps us. There is no specific promise that
He will keep us otherwise than by His providence and grace.
Do not these suffice for all our needs?

We have examined all the scriptural passages formally
appealed to by Gordon. The considerations which he
places under the heading of "the testimony of reason,"
however, are closely related to the scriptural argument,
and no doubt require a passing word. They are these:
(1) that, "if miracles should cease, they would form quite
a distinct exception to everything else which the Lord introduced by His ministry"; and (2) that "the use of miracles of healing as signs seems to argue strongly for their
permanency; if the substance remains unchanged, why
should the sign which was originally chosen to exhibit it
be superseded?" The force of the argument here lies in
its assumptions. If we begin by assuming that miracle-
working was instituted by our Lord as an ordinance of the
Christian religion; was established, like Baptism and the
Lord's Supper, as a visible, permanent sign of the invisible
reality; why, of course, their cessation becomes a striking
exception to the rule and calls for explanation. But
clearly there is nothing to justify these assumptions. And
if there were, too much would be proved to suit the case.
For Gordon proceeds at once to argue that only miracles
of healing abide. But surely it cannot be contended that
only miracles of healing were introduced by our Lord by
His ministry, and only His miracles of healing were "signs."
If Gordon's argument is worth anything it proves that all

forms of miracle-working practised by Christ were continued as the permanent possession of His church. It is not even claimed that that is the fact.

It might not be absolutely fatal to the assertions of the Faith-Healers that the scriptural grounds on which they base them prove too precarious to bear their weight. It is conceivable that the fact of the continuance of miraculous healing could be made so clear that we should be compelled to confess its continuance though no Scripture had promised it. Stanton prefers to take this attitude toward the matter. He deprecates beginning with scriptural "theory" and thence proceeding to investigate "fact," as essentially an *a priori* method. He insists that "the question is pre-eminently one of fact"; which can only be fairly tested by a "process of rigid induction." "Facts are never heresies," he says, "either in science or religion." Accordingly he proposes to begin with facts and argue back from them to their true cause. He opens his discussion, therefore, with a collection of selected cases which he represents as undeniable in point of fact and details, and as of such inherent character, being immediate healings by prayer of organic diseases, that they necessitate the conclusion that they are veritable miracles. From the fact of miracle-working, thus established, he turns back to the Scripture, to see whether it is possible that it contains no warrant for such great transactions. There is a certain apparent strength in this mode of procedure. It involves, however, a confession of the weakness of the scriptural evidence. If the evidence of Scripture were felt to be in itself conclusive, its consideration would scarcely be postponed until facts were accumulated to guide in its interpretation. Gordon's method of appealing to Scripture first, certainly does more honor to Scripture and gives the impression that in dealing with it he feels himself on solid ground. The scriptural evidence having failed, however, his case too falls back on the bald facts of experience.

The titles of the chapters in which Gordon adduces the

testimony of the alleged miraculous facts, have already
been enumerated. He calls in turn upon the witness of the
church, of theologians, of missions, of the adversary, of
experience, and of the healed. There is an almost too
great completeness in this accumulation of sources of testimony. There is nevertheless observable a certain eclecti-
cism in dealing with it. The testimony of the church, for
instance, does not mean the testimony of the church speaking as an organized body—whether as a whole or in some
one or other of its organized sections. It means the testimony of Christians of the past, the record of which is
found in what is called "church history." It is a very
eclectic "church history," however, which is appealed to.
The testimony of the first three centuries is adduced, and
partly that of the fourth. Then comes a sharp break, at
the age of Constantine, at which time, as we have shown,
really explicit evidence only begins. Later, it is true, under the caption of "The Testimony of Theologians," Augustine's opinion is cited—with what consistency we may
judge when we observe that all the miracles of "the Apostate Church," which is said to have begun with the age
of Constantine,[40] are declared to be "the testimony of the
Adversary," working counterfeit miracles, and· only so
bearing witness to the currency of the true. In this chapter on "The Testimony of the Church" we are carried over
at once to the testimony of the Waldenses, Moravians,
Huguenots, Covenanters, Friends, early Baptists and
Methodists. With reference to these the remark is made
that, in every revival of primitive faith, "we find a profession of chaste and evangelical miracles." How far this
description applies to the marvels it has professedly in
view we must let the reader of the annals of those troubled
movements himself decide. We think ourselves that a
remark made by Gordon at an earlier point is far more
applicable to them: when he spoke of the likelihood of
every true upstirring of genuine emotion being accom-

panied by more or less fanaticism which ought not to be permitted to cloud our judgment as to the genuineness of the emotion itself. The testimony of theologians is, naturally, a matter of opinion, while that of missions, experience, and of the healed themselves is only a further record of facts, artificially divided into these heads, which constitute in their totality the whole evidence before us. It is to the facts thus gathered that we are to give our attention.

What now are these facts? What is their nature? And what are we to think of them? The first thing which strikes the observer, as he casts his eye over them, is that they stand sadly in need of careful sifting. What we are looking for is such facts as necessitate or at least suggest the assumption, in order to account for them, of the "immediate action of God, as distinguished from His mediate action through natural laws." That is Gordon's own definition of miracle,[41] and what is affirmed is that these facts argue miraculous action. The great body of the facts offered to us, however, argue nothing of the kind.

In many of them means are openly used, means which rank among the specifically best means known to medical science. This is the case, for example, with all the instances of cures made in the Faith-Houses. Who doubts that multitudes of the sick would find cure under the skilled and tireless nursing of a Dorothea Trüdel, who was known to pass the whole day without food, utterly forgetting the claims of her body in devotion to her work?[42] Who doubts that great physical benefit could be found by many in "the silence and retirement of the simple cure of Pastor Rein"? Doctor Weir Mitchell won fame as a physician through his "rest-cure." What medical man will not agree that good nursing and a quiet and restful state of body and mind are among the best of curative agents? The very existence of Faith-Houses, indeed, is the sufficient refutation of the doctrine of Faith-Healing which seeks support from them. By hypothesis a miraculous cure should be immediate, as in cause so in time—without delay as without means—on the exercise of simple faith.   The existence of Faith-Hospitals is a standing proof that it is not immediate, either in cause or in time: that a place of retirement is helpful, and that good nursing has its reward. Faith-Houses may raise a protest against the methods of current medical practice, but they do so by setting up a particular method of practice of their own—not by introducing miraculous healing as over against natural.

It is observable, further, that the cases which are successfully treated in the Faith-Houses have their natural limits.   Not every one is cured.   The brother of Samuel Zeller, who succeeded Dorothea Trüdel in her House in Switzerland, sought cure there for years in vain.   Dorothea Trüdel's own health remained throughout her life "very feeble"; she suffered from curvature of the spine from an early age and died at forty-eight of typhus fever.   Zeller himself "strongly repudiated the whole system of doctrine" of the typical Faith-Healers, especially "the idea that sickness in God's people is the result of unbelief"; and sharply reprobated the practice of holding public meetings and expecting cures at them, attributing failure to lack of faith. He did not require that medical treatment should be renounced; he merely put his own dependence on rest, quiet, and prayer to God.[43]   The failures of cure on this system cannot be accounted for merely by an appeal to the sovereignty of God in answering prayer.   They find their account also in the nature of the diseases treated.   We quote the following from the pen of one of the most eminent aurists of the last generation.   "The avoidance of tangible affections by faith-curers," says Doctor St. John Roosa,[44] "is a circumstance that tells unanswerably against their doctrines.   I was once sent for to see a lady who was living in what was called a faith-cure establishment in this city, in order that I might, if possible, relieve her from impairment of hearing.   This I found to be chiefly caused by a collection of wax in the outer canal of the ear, which was easily removed. The removal caused great improvement in the hearing. I had never seen a faith-cure establishment before, and I confess I was somewhat surprised that I was sent for. I asked, 'How is it possible, that, if without the use of any means except prayer to God, internal diseases are cured, affections of the organs that we cannot see, those that we can see, and that are susceptible of relief by the ordinary physician, believing or unbelieving, cannot be cured by prayer? . . .' It is a terrible shock to the believer in this system to think that God can cure a case of disease of the liver or of the nerves, and will cure it by the use of the prayer of faith alone, but (and I mean to speak reverently) He will have nothing to do with a case of deafness."

We think it fair to urge also that the sifting of cases must exclude all those cures which can be paralleled by cures that have, in similar circumstances, been effected obviously without miracle. If we are seeking instances which demonstrate that a miracle has been wrought, surely we must have cases essentially different from those which are known to be curable without miracle. Obviously, for example, we cannot confidently infer miracle to account for a cure which "the Apostate Church" can perform as well as we; which mind-cure can equally readily work on a pantheistic, the Buddhist on an atheistic, and the mesmerist on a purely materialistic basis. These cures may seem to us startling, but they cannot be thought by us to be miraculous. It is, however, no exaggeration to say that the great mass of the cures wrought by Faith-Healers are closely paralleled by some or all of these sister practitioners. Your time need not be taken up by descriptions here of the wonders worked by Doctor Perkins's metallic tractors, by mesmerism, mind-cure, the waters of Lourdes.[45] Let me give you but a single partial illustration of how completely they repeat one another's triumphs.

Stanton rests his case for Faith-Healing on a half-dozen wisely chosen instances. The first one which he gives is that of a young woman with "a withered hand which was bent in upon her wrist as no well hand by any act of the will can be, and presented nothing but a mass of skin and bones, with not a vein visible upon it." This withered hand was cured by prayer. Well, here is first a Roman Catholic parallel among the cures of Prince Hohenlohe: "Captain Ruthlein, an old gentleman of Thundorf, seventy years of age, who had long been pronounced incurable of paralysis which kept his hand clinched, and who had not left his room for many years, was perfectly cured." [46] And here is a parallel from mesmerism: "Edward Wine, aged seventy-five, who had been paralyzed ten years in an arm and leg. The left arm was spasmodically fixed to the chest, the fingers drawn toward the palm of the hand and wasted, quite incapable of holding anything." Perfectly cured by mesmerism.[47] And here is a parallel from imagination: Sir Humphrey Davy placed a thermometer under the tongue of a paralyzed patient simply to ascertain the temperature; the patient at once claimed to experience relief, so the same treatment was continued for two weeks, and by that time the patient was well.[48] And, finally, here is a somewhat similar case from pure deception. "The wife and mother of the house was suffering from inflammatory rheumatism in its worst form. She could not move, was terribly swollen, and could not bear to be touched. . . . One of the hands of the patient was fearfully swollen, so that the fingers were as large very nearly as the wrist of an ordinary child three years of age. . . . Nearly all the space between the fingers was occupied and the fist was clinched. It was plain that to open them voluntarily was impossible, and to move them intensely painful. . . . The hand had not been opened for several weeks." "I held," says Doctor Buckley, the operator,[49] "two knitting-needles about two inches from the ends of the woman's fingers, just above the clinched hand, and said, 'Now, Madam, do not think of your fingers, and above all do not try to move them, but fix your eyes on the ends of these needles.' She did so . . . and the fingers straightened out and became flexible without the least pain. I then moved the needles about, and she declared that all pain left her hand except in one spot about half an inch in length." The fact is that imagination and concentrated attention are powers which need to be reckoned with in all cures, and only such cures as exclude a possible appeal to them, or to shock, or the like, are available for evidence of the miraculous. The simulation of disease by hysteria is also very remarkable. There was a woman in St. Luke's Hospital, New York City, who had a tumor to all, even the most skilled, diagnosis. But the tumor simply disappeared on the administration of ether and the consequent withdrawal of nervous action.[50] When all these cases are excluded, the list left as available evidence for miraculous action will be short indeed.

Sifting is not even yet, however, at an end. We must exclude also all cures which seem to us, indeed, to have come in answer to prayer, but of which there is no evidence that they have come miraculously, that is, by the immediate action of God, without all means. The famous cure of Canon Basil Wilberforce is a typical instance of what we mean. He declares that he has no shadow of doubt that he "was healed by the Lord's blessing upon His own word, recorded in St. James 5 : 15, 16." "But," he adds, "as in so many other cases, there was sufficient margin of time, and possibility of change of tissue, between the anointing and the recovery to justify the sceptic in disconnecting the two." [51] All Christians believe in healing in answer to prayer. Those who assert that this healing is wrought in a specifically miraculous manner, need better evidence for their peculiar view than such as fits in equally well with the general Christian faith.

Finally it must be added with great firmness that sifting
is needed by the cases reported by the Faith-Healers to
isolate the instances the details of which can be trusted.
Of certain obvious facts any honestly disposed person is a
competent witness; of certain others few persons are competent witnesses.   Among these latter facts may safely be
classed the accurate diagnosis of disease.   Few physicians,
of even lifelong practice, are really good diagnosticians;
perhaps there is none of whatever eminence who has not
been more than once wholly deceived in the nature of the
disease he has been called upon to treat—as the autopsy
has proved.[52]   Every one who has sought to trace up alleged cases of Faith-Healing will have felt the grave doubt
which frequently rests upon the identification of the disease which is asserted to have been cured.   Yet we are
asked to believe in multifarious miracles on the faith of
the diagnosis of this, that, or the other unknown person.
Nothing is more remarkable than the scorn which the average Faith-Healer pours on physicians as healers, and the un-
bounded confidence which he reposes in them as diagnosticians.   It is with him the end of all strife if he can say that
the case was hopeless on the testimony of Doctor This or
Doctor That.

It is to be feared that it must even be said that Faith-
Healers, in their enthusiasm over the wonderful things
they are testifying to, are not always as careful as they
might be in ascertaining the actual facts of the cases of
cure which they report.   It may seem to them sometimes
almost a sacrilege to make so close an inquisition into the
facts, the cold facts, when so much has obviously been
done.   Gordon records,[53] with apparent approval, the reply of one of a visiting body of German preachers and professors, when inspecting Zeller's Faith-Home in Switzerland.
When asked to give his opinion of the work, he responded:
"When the Holy Spirit speaks with so much power, we
can do no otherwise than listen to His teaching; critical

analysis is out of the question." But the Holy Spirit Himself says, "Try the Spirits, whether they be of God," and it is no more good religion than good sense, in a matter of such moment, to abnegate the functions of a critic. It is necessary for even pious men to guard against misleading their fellows.

The matter may be illustrated by the case of one of the most celebrated instances of Faith-Healing ever wrought in America. It was deservedly celebrated, because it took place in a sphere of operation into which Faith-Healing rarely penetrates. It was nothing less than the instantaneous knitting of a broken bone in answer to prayer. Doctor Charles Cullis is said to have reported it to Doctor W. E. Boardman, who printed it in his book called *The Great Physician*. Gordon quotes it from Boardman, and Stanton makes it one of his test cases. The narrative comes ultimately from the father of the boy in question, "Doctor Reed a physician of Philadelphia." The story as reported in his words by Boardman is this: "The children were jumping off from a bench, and my little son fell and broke *both bones of his arm below the elbow*. My brother, who is a professor of surgery in the college at Chicago, was here on a visit. I asked him to set and dress the arm. He did so; put it in splints, bandages, and in a sling. The dear child was very patient, and went about without a murmur all that day. The next morning he came to me and said: 'Dear papa, please take off these things.' 'Oh no, my son, you will have to wear these five or six weeks before it will be well.' 'Why, papa, it is well.' 'Oh no, my dear child, that is impossible!' 'Why, papa, you believe in prayer, don't you?' 'You know I do, my son.' 'Well, last night when I went to bed, it hurt me very bad, and I asked Jesus to make it well.' I did not like to say a word to chill his faith. A happy thought came. I said, 'My dear child, your uncle put the things on, and if they are taken off he must do it.' Away he went to his uncle, who told him he would have to go as he was six or seven weeks, and must be very patient; and when the little fellow told him that Jesus had made him well, he said, 'Pooh! pooh! nonsense!' and sent him away. The next morning the poor boy came to me and pleaded with so much sincerity and confidence, that I more than half believed, and went to my brother and said: 'Had you not better undo his arm and let him see for himself?' . . . My brother yielded, took off the bandages and the splints, and exclaimed, 'It is well, absolutely well!' and hastened to the door to keep from fainting." Could anything be more conclusive? Here is expert medical testimony to the fracture and to the cure also. Here is the testimony of the father himself, a chief actor in the scene, to all its details. We have the additional guarantee of the repetition of it as authentic by a series of the chief advocates of Faith-Healing. And it is a case of a broken bone, and must be a miracle. But here comes the trouble. "The case was thoroughly investigated by Doctor J. H. Lloyd of the University of Pennsylvania, and in *The Medical Record* for March 27, 1886, Doctor Lloyd published a letter from this *very child*, who is grown up and become a physician. Dear Sir:" it reads, "The case you cite, when robbed of all its sensational surroundings, is as follows: The child was a spoiled youngster who would have his own way; and when he had a *green stick* fracture of the forearm, and, after having had it bandaged for several days, concluded he would much prefer to go without a splint, to please the spoiled child the splint was removed, and the arm carefully adjusted in a sling. As a matter of course, the bone soon united, as is customary in children, and being only partially broken, of course all the sooner. This is the miracle. Some nurse or crank or religious enthusiast, ignorant of matters physiological and histological, evidently started the story, and unfortunately my name—for I am the party—is being circulated in circles of faith-curites, and is given the sort of notoriety I do not crave. . . .

Very respectfully yours, Carl H. Reed." [54] Conscious fraud here is not to be thought of for a moment. But all the more powerfully the lesson is driven home to us that in matters of this kind testimony to details requires the closest scrutiny. There is scarcely an item in this case which is correctly reported in the current story.

It seems to be the experience of every one who has made a serious attempt to sift the evidence for miraculous healing that this evidence melts away before his eyes. Many remarkable cures are wrought, but nothing which compels the inference of miraculous healing seems to be unambiguously established. What emerges as final result is that a sharp line is drawn between the class of cures which can be obtained and the class of cures which cannot be obtained by faith, and that this line is drawn approximately at the exact spot where the line runs which separates cures which can from those which cannot be obtained by mind-cure, mesmerism, Perkins's tractors, and other similar practices. There are classes of sickness which Faith-Healing can cure, and there are classes of sickness which it cannot cure. In particular, for example, it is powerless to heal broken bones, to renew mutilations, to do so little a thing as to restore lost teeth. Doctor Charles Cullis is reported as saying: "In no case in God's word is there a promise that we may pray over a broken bone and anoint the sufferers with oil; only the sick. A broken bone is not sickness, and should be put in the hands of a surgeon." And "he has repeatedly and publicly, in the presence of thousands at Old Orchard Beach and elsewhere, disclaimed all attempts by the prayer of faith to secure from God the restoration of an amputated hand or the setting of a broken limb." [55] This is, of course, only a confession that there is no question of miraculous action in Faith-Healing. What is the use of invoking miracle to do work equally well done without miracle, and repudiating all effects for which miracles are required? If a man asserts that he controls the motion of the sun by miraculous power, I want some better proof that he does so than his pointing to the rising and setting of the sun every day at its appointed time. And I want no better proof that he works no miracle in the case, than that the sun under his incantations moves no otherwise than it moves without them.

After the statement of the evidence from facts Gordon has nothing further to do but to draw his conclusion. This he does in a chapter called "The Verdict of Candor," while he gives a warning to his brethren not to press beyond limits in another chapter entitled "The Verdict of Caution." In both of these chapters some very good things are said, and some which are rather odd. Of the latter class is the designation of health "as the first-fruits of redemption," [56] whereas the Apostle speaks of the redemption of the body as the last thing to be looked for; and the suggestion that the reason for the fewness of instances of Faith-Healing is due to the difficulty of "an individual prayer making headway against the adverse sentiment of the great body of Christians" [57]—which sounds more like Mrs. Eddy than a Christian minister. It does not seem necessary, however, to dwell on these things. We take leave of the book with a profound conviction that its argument is inconsequent, and its contention unfounded either in Scripture or in fact.

And now let us very briefly sum up from our own point of view what it seems that we ought to think of Faith-Healing. First of all, as regards the *status quæstionis*, let it be remembered that the question is not: (1) Whether God is an answerer of prayer; nor (2) whether, in answer to prayer, He heals the sick; nor (3) whether His action in healing the sick is a supernatural act; nor (4) whether the supernaturalness of the act may be so apparent as to demonstrate God's activity in it to all right-thinking minds conversant with the facts. All this we all believe. The question at issue is distinctly whether God has pledged Himself to heal the sick miraculously, and does heal them miraculously, on the call of His children—that is to say without means—any means—and apart from means, and above means; and this so ordinarily that Christian people may be encouraged, if not required, to discard all means as either unnecessary or even a mark of lack of faith and sinful distrust, and to depend on God alone for the healing of all their sicknesses. This is the issue, even conservatively stated. For many will say that faith gives us as clear a title to the healing of our bodies as to the salvation of our souls; and this is often interpreted to mean that it is the heritage of every Christian, if a true Christian, to be free from all disease and bodily weakness, and it is a proof of special sin in a Christian if he is a special sufferer from disease.

With reference to this question it is to be said at least: (1) No promise of such miraculous action on God's part exists in Scripture. (2) No facts have been adduced which will compel the assumption that such miraculous healing takes place. (3) Such a miraculous method of action on God's part would be wholly unnecessary for the production of the effect desired; God can heal the bodily hurt of His people without miracle. (4) The employment of such a method of working would be contrary to the analogy of God's mode of working in other spheres of His activity. (5) It would be contrary to the very purpose of miracle, which would be defeated by it. If miracles are to be common, every-day occurrences, normal and not extraordinary, they cease to attract attention, and lose their very reason of existence. What is normal is according to law. If miracles are the law of the Christian life they cease to serve their chief end. (6) The contention of the Faith-Healers overlooks numerous important biblical facts. Primarily the fact that the miraculous gifts in the New Testament were the credentials of the Apostle, and were confined

to those to whom the Apostles had conveyed them—whence
a presumption arises against their continuance after the
Apostolic age. Then, again, that there are instances of
sickness in the New Testament which were not removed by
the prayer of faith. There is, for example, Paul's leaving
of Trophimus at Miletum sick, and his recommending to
Timothy, when sick, not the seeking of healing by the miraculous act of God, but the use of medicinal means—the
drinking no longer of water but of a little wine for his
stomach's sake and his often infirmities. It seems quite
clear that Paul did not share the views of our modern
Faith-Healers. (7) The Faith-Healing arguments presup-
pose or lead to many false doctrines. A desultory allusion
to some of them here may not be without its uses. (A)
Sickness and sin are often connected in an utterly unscriptural manner. That all the sicknesses which afflict our
race are a result of sin is true. But that special sicknesses
infer special sin our Saviour Himself explicitly denies.
(B) These arguments would be equally valid to commend
perfectionism. If sinfulness is not to be removed in this
life, neither is sickness. Both are the fruits of guilt, and
both are removed on the basis of the work of the guilt-
bearer; and both are removed only when the subjective
salvation is completed. (C) They are founded on a completely unscriptural view of the functions of suffering, and
the uses of sickness and pain. All sickness and suffering
are spoken of as if they were from the evil one alone; as
if they were sheerly the mark of the displeasure of God;
and as if they were a fruit of particular sin. Scripture
says: "Behold whom the Lord loveth He chasteneth, and
scourgeth every son whom He receiveth." Sickness is
often the proof of special favor from God; it always comes
to His children from His Fatherly hand, and always in
His loving pleasure works, together with all other things
which befall God's children, for good. (8) The Faith-
Healing contention leads to contempt for God's appointed

means, and this leads to the fanatical attitude of demanding from God apart from all means that for the attaining of which He has ordained appropriate means. We are not to refuse to cultivate the soil and then demand to be fed by miracle. (9) The Faith-Healing practice leads to the production of "professionals," standing between the soul and God. There is grave danger in a soul permitting an unauthorized intermediary to take up a position between it and the gracious activities of God toward it. From this germ the whole sacerdotal evil has grown. And, on the other hand, to the practitioner himself there comes inevitable temptation to spiritual pride and autocracy, which is most disastrous to his spiritual life; and sometimes even something worse.

One of the phenomena of the Faith-Healing delusion has been the production of a series of these practitioners, whose activities have not always been wholesome. From time to time an individual healer has risen to public notice and attracted the attention of the whole religious community, for a time at least attaining tremendous vogue and commanding great applause. There was, for example, to confine ourselves to recent times, Prince Alexander of Hohenlohe, who during the first half of the nineteenth century created a great stir with his miraculous healings in Austria and Germany.[58] A lesser light burned contemporaneously in Ireland in the person of Father Matthew.[59] One of the most admirable of these figures was Johann Christoph Blumhardt who, says William James, quite spontaneously developed in the early forties of the last century "an extremely pure faculty of healing," which he exerted during nearly thirty years.[60] Perhaps Doctor A. B. Simpson of New York, who has been since 1887 the president of the Christian and Missionary Alliance, founded in that year at Old Orchard, Maine, has been blamelessly in the public eye as a healer of the sick through faith for as long a period as any of our recent American healers.[61] The

fame of others has been, if more splendid, at the same time
less pure and less lasting. The name of a certain A.
Schrader, for example, was in everybody's mouth twenty
years ago. Then there was the romantic figure of Franz
Schlatter, with his meteoric career in Denver and elsewhere
in the West, as Messiah and divine healer.[62] But perhaps
the most striking of all these personages was John Alexander Dowie,[63] whose work in Chicago as general overseer
of the Christian Apostolic Catholic Church in Zion—the
product of his activities—attained gigantic proportions.
A Scotchman by birth, an Australian Congregationalist in
previous ministerial affiliation, he created, rather than
built up, in Chicago a great religious community, over
which he ruled with despotic power, and in the "divine
healing rooms" of which he wrought many a cure. No
doubt, the proportion of successful cures wrought by him
was not larger than in the case of others. If a note in one of
the issues of his newspaper—*Leaves of Healing*—may be
taken as a criterion, the work of healing in his hands can
scarcely be pronounced successful. "I pray and lay my
hands," he says, "on seventy thousand people in a year."
That would give a hundred and seventy-five thousand in
two years and a half. Yet in the two years and a half immediately preceding the date of this statement he reports
only seven hundred cures.[64] One success in every two hundred and fifty trials does not impress one as a very successful ministry of healing to the sick and sorrowing world[56]

MIND–CURE

MIND–CURE

WHEN we speak of "faith-healing" we use ambiguous language so far as we leave it undetermined whether we understand the healing in question to be effected immediately by the action of the faith itself, or by the God to whom it is committed in faith.[1] In the latter case the healing is, in the proper sense of the word, a supernatural one. In the former it is a natural healing, as natural as if it were wrought by a surgical operation or by a drug. This is, of course, not to say that God has nothing to do with the healing in this case; or, indeed, has not Himself wrought it. God has very much to do with the cures wrought by the surgeon's knife or the physician's medicaments; so much to do with them that it is He who really makes them. It is to Him that the efficacy of all means is due, in general and in particular. It is a wise man of very old time who in one breath bids us look to the physician with his remedies and to the Lord who is behind the physician and works in and through him and his remedies. "Honor a physician for the honor due unto him, for the uses which ye may have of him. . . . For of the Most High cometh healing. . . . My Son, in thy sickness be not negligent; but pray unto the Lord and He will make thee whole. . . . Then give place to the physician, for the Lord hath created him; let him not go from thee, for thou hast need of him." [2] When we think of cures wrought by means, we do not exclude God from them. But just because they are wrought by means, we do not ascribe them to God as their proximate cause. The point is that a cure wrought proximately by faith, or by any other mental act, or attitude, or state, is just as truly wrought by means as if it were wrought by a drug or a knife. And it is just as truly wrought by natural means. Our minds are ours, and all their acts and states are our acts and states; and all that is produced by them in any of their acts or states are effects of our own. Any cure supposed to be produced by faith itself is accordingly a natural cure, and that just as truly as any other natural cure whatever.

It might conduce to clearness if writers would agree to classify all such cures, the natural products of faith itself, under some such caption as mind-cures—or, if we prefer a big name, under the general designation of psychotherapy —reserving the term "faith-healing" for those cures which are ascribed not to faith itself, but to the immediate action of God sought in faith. Meanwhile this is not the universal usage. The nomenclature is far from fixed. Very frequently the term "faith-cure" is employed to express specifically cures wrought directly by faith itself. As often, it is used in a sense wide enough to embrace both of these very diverse species of cures. Naturally, this produces confusion. The confusion shows itself, for example, in the definition given to "Faith-Healing" at the head of the article printed under this title in Hastings's *Encyclopedia of Religion and Ethics*. There at least emerges from this definition, however, an express recognition of a double sense of the term "faith-cure," a strict and a wide sense. Taking so much as gain, we shall, contrary, no doubt, to this author's own meaning, discriminate these two senses in such a manner as to assign to the strict sense of the term those cures which are supposed to be immediately wrought by God on faith, and to the broader sense those which are supposed to be wrought more or less wholly by faith itself.

Having the latter of these varieties in mind, we find ourselves more in accord with our author when he remarks that "faith-healing is the oldest form of healing in the world," antedating, or at least growing up side by side with, "medical practice in its earliest and crudest form, and

as its predominant partner." [3]   We cannot, indeed, ascribe
with him the miracles of our Lord and His Apostles to this
category.[4]   But, apart from the miraculous attestation of
the special revelation of God which has been recorded for
us in the inspired Scriptures, we recognize with him a continuous stream of faith-healings in this sense, extending
from the earliest ages quite down to our own day.   The
numerous "Healing-Gods" of classical antiquity, such
practices as "temple-sleeping," and the endless narratives
of cures sought and found through it and other means, at-
test its prevalence in pre-Christian times; the Patristic and
Mediæval Ages overflow with instances; the Reformation
was far from bringing its practice to an end, and—if we
may now enlarge the category to that of mind-healing in
general—the history of such movements as those still
going on among us under the names of Animal Magnetism,
Mesmerism, Spiritualism, Mental Healing, New Thought,
Christian Science, evince the place its conscious practice
still takes in the life of the people of to-day.

In a former lecture we have sought to give some account
of the assertions which are still made that faith-healings,
in the strict sense of healings made directly by God, continue to occur among us.   For the sake of completeness it
may not be improper to proceed now to some account of
at least the more prominent varieties of faith-healing in
the wider sense—or, in a less confusing nomenclature, of
mind-cure—prevalent in our day.   No doubt, in doing so,
we overstep the limits of our formal subject.   Faith-healing
in this sense—that is to say, mind-cure—by virtue of the
very fact that some mental act or state is held to be the
producing cause at work, can make no pretense to miraculousness, and in point of fact, in the forms at least in which
it is most commonly practised, it makes no pretense to
miraculousness.   Nevertheless, its relation to faith-healing
in the stricter sense is so close, confusion with it is so common, and the lessons to be learned from it as to the real

nature of the alleged instances of faith-healing in the strict sense occurring among us are so instructive, that we should not be justified in passing it by altogether.

The variety of forms in which mind-healing is practised to-day is very great. They differ from one another less in the results obtained, or even in the means employed to obtain these results, than in the theoretical basis by which they severally attempt to explain their production. William F. Cobb, the writer of the article on "Faith-Healing" in Hastings's *Encyclopedia of Religion and Ethics*, to which we have already alluded, enumerates its principal species as Mental-healing, Magnetic-healing, Spiritualistic-healing, and Spiritual-healing, that is to say, if we may employ the popular designations of typical forms of each to symbolize the several varieties, Christian Science, Mesmerism, Spiritualism, and Faith-Healing. This enumeration is by no means exhaustive, but it will serve our present purpose. The point of importance for us is that in the action of all these varieties alike, as Cobb justly remarks, a leading part is taken by suggestion. This suggestion, when given its most scientifically developed form, is called hypnotism. But, under whatever name, and employed under the guidance of whatever underlying theory of the nature of being, or of the process of the cure established, it operates after essentially the same fashion.[5]

It is only with those forms of mind-cure which have in one way or another closely connected themselves with religion that we are for the moment particularly concerned. One of these forms, very prominent in the public eye at present, is that which is known as the Emmanuel Movement. Nothing could be further from the thought of the leaders of the Emmanuel Movement than a pretension to miraculous powers.[6] It only professes to deal, prosaically enough, and with an almost ostentatious disassociation of itself from the supernatural, with certain classes of functional or nervous diseases—by means of suggestion, of course, but also by any other forms of mental and spiritual influence which experience may commend as useful. It does not bother itself overmuch with underlying theory, although it proceeds actually on the theory—which it prefers to look upon as observed fact—of a subconscious life, the storehouse of energy capable of being tapped and drawn upon for the purposes of our daily living.[7] The common experience of the whole Christian past, it thinks, supplies it with a general support for its practice as an activity of the organized church. It quotes with particular satisfaction an entry in John Wesley's *Journal* for May 12, 1759.[8] Here Wesley remarks on the helplessness of the physicians in the presence of a woman kept ill from fretting over the death of her son. "Why," Wesley asks, "don't physicians consider how far bodily disorders are caused or influenced by the mind, and in those cases which are utterly out of their sphere, call in the assistance of a minister, as ministers, when they find the mind disordered by the body, call in the assistance of a physician?" In the intimate co-operation of the physician and the minister here desiderated, it is suggested, we have the whole principle of the Emmanuel Movement.[9] As the physician must be called in to remove the bodily disorders which inhibit right spiritual functioning, so the church may well step in to aid in correcting those bodily evils which are ultimately the result of spiritual disorders.

We confess to being chilled when we hear of such things as "religious faith and prayer" being looked upon as therapeutical agents for the cure of disease, and administered to patients as such. We are frankly shocked at the coupling together of faith and paregoric, prayer and podophyllin in a single comprehensive pharmacopœia. We are too accustomed to thinking of faith and prayer as terminating on God, and finding their response in His gracious activities, to feel comfortable when they are turned back on themselves and—while still, no doubt, addressed to God—used

as instruments for moving man.[10]   It is unfortunate, moreover, that the form of Christianity which is professed by
the leaders of the Emmanuel Movement, and the inculcation of which they rely upon to soothe troubled minds and
to inspire to effort, is rather that taught by Renan and
Harnack and Theodor Keim (the collocation of names is
not our own[11]), than that taught by John and Paul and
Jesus; so that a rationalistic veil hangs over all their religious prescriptions.   Nevertheless, although Christianity
is emphatically an "other-world" religion, and a merely
"this-world" religion is just no Christianity at all, it is
not to be denied that there is a "this-world" side to Christianity.   Undoubtedly, it has the promise of the life that
now is as well as of that which is to come, and they who
seek first the kingdom of God and His righteousness may
rightly expect all these things to be added unto them.   It
is as little to be doubted that there are valuable reflex effects
which may be confidently counted upon from the exercise,
say, of faith and prayer, as it is undeniable that these reflex effects are of infinitely less importance than their direct
working.   And of course it is unquestionable that it belongs to the Christian calling to relieve so far as it is within
our power to do so, by the use of all legitimate means,
every distress under which we find our fellow men to be
suffering.   We would not lag behind the Emmanuel Movement in zeal for service; and if we find it moved at this or
that point by extravagances of pretension, and limited
here and there by defective spiritual insight or outlook,
surely, in avoiding what is bad in it, we may not refuse to
imitate what is good, and our chief concern should be to
fashion our own conduct more, not less, completely after
the higher Christian ideal.

The particular psychological assumptions upon which
the Emmanuel Movement is at present conducted may
seem to us little assured.   No doubt, we are told that the
work "does not depend upon any theory, whether psycho-

logical or physiological, of the subconscious." [12] We are simply to act on the empirical fact that even broken men are accessible to spiritual influences, and through these spiritual influences may be brought to a better adjustment with life. To that extent we may all be believers in psychotherapy. What Christian pastor, what Christian person, has not acted on that assumption since Christianity began? But there is the organization? Well, what has the Emmanuel Movement to offer here which was not offered in the old Faith-Houses—say, Zeller's House in Mannedorf—except a very much thinner religion and a more advanced medical science? There remains the question of method. We ourselves prefer the older method of, say, the establishment of hospitals like the Presbyterian Hospitals in New York and Philadelphia, in which Christian charity provides the best medical service for human ills. We feel grave doubts as to the desirability of the minister himself becoming officially a medical practitioner, even by the method of suggestion; perhaps we would better say especially by the method of suggestion—even though that be spiritual suggestion. When Sir Clifford Allbutt declares that "notions of the priest as medicine-man" are "essentially pagan," he speaks no doubt unnecessarily harshly, but, we must admit it, essentially justly. When Doctor Charles Buttar advises the clergymen to be "content for the present to leave the untrained practice of methods of suggestion to quacks," we cannot deny that he has had some provocation for his counsel. When Stephen Paget in his gracious way remarks that "they who desire, extravagantly, to put 'spiritual healing' among the methods of the Christian ministry, seem to me to be losing sight of the fact that common sense is an essential trait of the Christian life," we cannot help feeling that he has said the right word in the right place.[13] Is it not plain common sense for each organ of the body to be content with its own functions, the eye with its seeing, the ear with its hearing? And is there not a profound warning in Paul's remark, especially to us who have a work of our own to do, that all cannot be the ear—else where were the seeing?[14]

The leaders of the Emmanuel Movement are theists. Therefore, instead of saying of an act of healing, "The forces of nature do it," they prefer to say, "God does it in and through the forces of nature." In accordance with their theistic presuppositions this is the proper account to give of any natural act of healing. No "miraculous agency" is supposed; "the forces of nature" do the work. But there is a God, and this God works in and through the forces of nature, and thus in the end it is God that does it. God does it, that is, in the same sense and after the same fashion that it is God that does everything that is done throughout this whole great universe. W. F. Cobb, to whom we have already alluded more than once, is not purely a theist; he is a mystic. In describing the varieties of what he calls broadly faith-healing, therefore, he naturally reserves the culminating place for a variety which posits behind the act of healing, as its explanation, a mystical theory. It is not quite clear whether he would give his personal adhesion to all the details of this "spiritual healing," as he calls it.[15] It is clear, however, that his sympathies go very largely with it, and that he looks upon it as, in the main at least, the true rationale of faith-healing. Its main postulate is that all physical disease, without exception, is the result, directly or indirectly, of psychical disorder, and is to be struck at, therefore, not in the body, where only symptoms manifest themselves, but in the soul, where alone lie the causes. What is sought is to procure for the soul of the sufferer an influx of spiritual life; and this life can be found, of course, only in God. "The power which alone can heal the soul," we are told, "is God." God, now, is reached by "faith"—the faith, it is to be observed, however, not of the sufferer, but of the practitioner, for in this form of theory a healer is necessary.

"This faith is defined as a quality in the spirit of the healer, . . . which enables him to render quiescent his 'mortal mind,' and so to place his spirit in a positive state of calm, poised and at peace, and a channel for the Divine Spirit to pass through to the sufferer." The state of openness and serenity thus described as faith, we are further told, is simply the normal condition for prayer. We may express the process, therefore, by saying that spiritual healing is the product of the power of God directed by faith through prayer to the soul that needs healing. Hence, it is said that it is God, and God alone, who performs the act of healing, and that all healing is obtained by the influx of spiritual life into the soul from God; although the door of ingress into the soul is opened for it by a practitioner, the soul itself being in a state of passive, not active, faith in the process. The healing is conceived thus as in a true sense supernatural: an influx into the soul from without. Accordingly, it is asserted, there can be no real failure in it. An influx of spiritual life from God, the source of all life, must bring benefit. If this benefit does not show itself on the physical plane, it is nevertheless there—the soul at least has the benefit.

From a mysticism like this it is but a single step to open pantheism, and that step is taken by the form of mind-cure which is most in vogue among us:[16] that which calls itself for some inexplicable reason by the name of Christian Science.[17] There is a sense, of course, in which—just because the fundamental elements of her thought are pantheistic—Mrs. Eddy will not allow that her Christian Science is mind-cure. It is not "mind-cure" with a small "m," she affirms, but "Mind-cure," with a capital "M."[18] But just because her fundamental thought is pantheistic, this is merely a verbal distinction. She is intensely emphatic that her Mind-cures are "not supernatural but supremely natural." [19] In its practice Christian Science does not differ greatly from other forms of mind-cure. Perceiving, or at least acknowledging, less readily than the Emmanuel Movement the limitations of mind-cure, it accepts, like the spiritual healing of which we have just been speaking, all kinds of cases—although the range of its actual cures, as Elwood Worcester dryly remarks, is not enlarged thereby.[20] Its real differentiation from its sister systems lies wholly in the pseudo-philosophical background which it has washed in with a broad brush behind its activities. This certainly is portentous enough, but it serves only for ornament, and has no effect on the practice of the mind-cure, which is the real source of the movement's vogue. It is incumbent on us before we close this series of lectures to give some account of this system of mind-healing, which has become a religion, and has in the course of a very few years overspread the earth.

The late Doctor St. John Roosa once described mind-cure as faith-cure run to seed.[21] The characterization is true as a general proposition in the history of thought. Man is a religious animal, and the religious explanation of phenomena antedates, in this department of thought also, the naturalistic. It is also, in the longer historical sequences, true of the ultimate origin of the particular species of mind-cure which Doctor Roosa had in mind, that is to say, Christian Science. For Mesmer derives from Gassner, and Christian Science is unquestionably a granddaughter —however ungrateful a granddaughter—of Mesmerism.[22] But there is no immediate affiliation of Christian Science with faith-cure, and certainly the adherents of Christian Science do not look upon themselves as its deteriorated descendants. They rather set themselves in irreducible antagonism to it.[23] Not indeed that they deny that effects are produced by it. They appear to allow even that Faith-Healers may obtain effects which they cannot themselves obtain; or at least more readily than they can obtain them. Mrs. Eddy has her characteristic way of accounting for this. "It is asked," she writes, "why are faith-cures

sometimes more speedy than some of the cures wrought
through Christian Scientists?" And she answers thus:
"Because faith is belief and not understanding; and it is
easier to believe than to understand Spiritual Truth. It
demands less cross-bearing, self-renunciation, and divine
science, to admit the claims of the personal senses, and
appeal for relief to a humanized God, than to deny these
claims and learn the divine way, drinking his cup, being
baptized with his baptism, gaining the end through persecution and purity." It must not pass without notice
that a somewhat odd admission is made here that the results obtained by Christian Science may also be obtained
without Christian Science; sometimes more speedily than by
Christian Science; by an appeal, for example, to a humanized God; by the open road of faith, that is, rather than the
difficult path of understanding. How anything can be obtained by an appeal to a humanized God is a puzzle, seeing
that it is presupposed that no such being exists. The Faith-
Healers only cry out to the void, and yet they get their results, and that sometimes more quickly and always with
less effort on their part, than the Christian Scientists.[24]
Various methods of accounting for this remarkable fact
have been suggested. Marsdon says faith-cures are really
mind-cures, wrought by "anything that will enable a sick
person to change his thought," that is to say, they are not
Mind-cures but mind-cures, wrought by our own change
of thought, which indeed is asserted scores of times by
Mrs. Eddy herself. Mrs. Kate Taylor, with much the same
implications, explaining the difference as that faith-cure
requires faith to be healed, and mind-cure does not, adds:
"Prayer to a personal God affects the sick like a drug that
has no efficacy of its own, but borrows its power from human
faith and belief. The drug does nothing because it has no
intelligence." Similarly Frances Lord represents the difference to be one of theory only, not of practice, while with
respect to the theory she remarks that there is more to be

known than the Faith-Healers admit.[25] Such statements undoubtedly show that Christian Scientists do not deny that faith-cure may be acknowledged to be an undeveloped form of their better practice. But this does not carry with it any implication of immediate historical connection.

: was out of a very different soil, in point of fact, that Christian Science actually grew. According to Mrs. Eddy's own account her previous experience had been in other forms of distinctively mind-cure. She had dabbled in homœopathy (her then husband sometimes practised this art), and had found that she could dilute the drugs until nothing of them was left, and still they cured. Then she tried—so she says—mesmerism under the guidance of "a distinguished Mesmerist," or as she elsewhere speaks of him,[26] "the magnetic doctor, Mr. P. P. Quimby." When it was subsequently pointed out that she had learned her system from him—as she certainly did—she repelled the statement thus: "The cowardly claim that I am not the originator of my own writings, but that one P. P. Quimby is, has been legally met and punished." She also toyed with Spiritualism. Her own account of the origin of her doctrine is, that having been for years a sufferer from chronic disease, she met with an injury pronounced by her physician to be necessarily fatal, and was left to die. She concluded not to do so, and got suddenly well instead. For twenty years she had been seeking to trace all physical effects to a mental cause, and now, in the early days of February, 1866—the birth-year of the new science, then, according to her account—she "gained the scientific certainty that all causation was Mind, and every effect a mental phenomenon."[27] Quimby died on January 16, 1866, and here, hard on his heels follows his successor, with, despite all denials, nothing in her hands but what she had got from him. For Quimby was not a mesmerist or magnetic healer as she represents him, but the founder of the whole school of Mental-Healers which has flourished in

America through the last half-century. And it turns out that not only was Mrs. Eddy's fundamental idea, but the characteristic language in which she expresses her idea, Quimby's before it was hers.[28]

First as openly a disciple of Quimby, and then, progressively with more and more strength and even violence of assertion of independence of him, Mrs. Eddy gradually set her doctrine afloat. She was already teaching it in 1867. Her advertisement as a teacher is found in the Spiritualistic paper, *The Banner of Light*, in 1868. In 1870 she is firmly established and greatly prospering at Lynn, in partnership with one of her pupils, Richard Kennedy, as a firm of healers on the basis of Quimby—Kennedy doing the healing while she taught.[29] Meanwhile she was writing. In 1870 her first pamphlet was copyrighted, although its issue was delayed for another six years. At length, in 1875, appeared her *magnum opus—Science and Health with Key to the Scriptures*—which, revised, and rerevised, and rerevised again—when it had reached its 440th edition in 1907 the editions ceased to be numbered—remains the sole text-book of Christian Science; or, if we prefer to think of Mrs. Eddy's followers from that point of view, the Second Bible of the Church of Christ, Scientist.[30]

Christian Science, above all other religions called book-religions, is a religion of a book. This book is, of course, represented as written under divine inspiration, and as carrying with it divine authority. "No human tongue or pen," says Mrs. Eddy in its opening pages, "taught me the Science contained in this book, *Science and Health*, and neither tongue nor pen can ever overthrow it."[31] She would blush, she tells us, to write of her book in the strain she uses toward it, "were it of human origin, and I, apart from God, its author, but as I was only a scribe echoing the harmonies of heaven, in divine Metaphysics, I cannot be supermodest of the Christian Science text-book."[32] The book is received in the spirit in which it is given.

"The Bible and the Christian Science text-book," writes
Irving C. Tomlinson, in the *Christian Science Bible Quarterly Lessons*, "are our only preachers. As the discourses
are made up wholly of passages from the Bible and the
Christian Science text-book, they contain nothing of human
opinion; they are devoid of man-made theories. They voice
the eternal fact, concerning the everlasting Truth. They
set forth the realities of being; they inform, instruct, and
enlighten concerning the verities of God and man." When
Tomlinson says that the Bible and *Science and Health* are
the only preachers which the Christian Scientists have, he
is declaring the literal fact. There are no sermons delivered
in Christian Science churches. Whenever and wherever
Christian Scientists meet together for worship the service
is the same. A passage is read from the Bible and a passage is read from *Science and Health*. Some hymns are
sung. The only prayer used is the Lord's Prayer, followed
line by line by Mrs. Eddy's adaptation of it to her system
of teaching. That is all.[33] The passage from the Bible,
it should be noted, is read by the official called the Second
Reader, and that from *Science and Health* by the First
Reader.[34] The place given to *Science and Health* in the
private life of Christian Scientists is comparable to that
given it in the public services. Every one is expected to
purchase and read it; and not only to read it but to pore
over it. It is intended that it shall dominate the whole
life.[35]

When we open the book thus sent out into the world as
divine in origin and contents, we receive a painful shock.
It is hopelessly confused and obscure whether in matter
or in style. Even Mrs. Eddy's disciples sometimes are
frank enough to admit that "the first reading of her
chief work, *Science and Health with Key to the Scriptures*,
leaves the impression, in spite of much that is strikingly
beautiful and true, that there is a prevailing tone of in-
coherence, contradiction, illogicality, and arbitrary, dic-

tatorial assertion, with no regard for evident fact either in the realm of objective nature or history." [36]   To go to the opposite extreme, a high dignitary of the Roman Catholic church, Robert Hugh Benson, declares[37] that "it is impossible to describe the confusion of mind that falls upon the student of *Science and Health*." "The quasi-philosophical phraseology of the book, the abuse of terms, the employment of ambiguous words at crucial points, the character of the exegesis, the broken-backed paradoxes, the astonishing language, the egotism—all these things and many more end by producing in the mind a symptom resembling that which neuritis produces in the body, namely the sense that an agonizing abnormality is somewhere about, whether in the writings or in the reader is uncertain." He is almost inclined to look upon the fact that Christian Science has been actually propagated by such a book as a proof of its divine origin.   This phenomenon is far more remarkable, he intimates, than any miracle of healing Mrs. Eddy claims to have performed: "for she has done more than mend broken tissues by the application of mind, she has mended minds by the application of nonsense." Another writer slyly suggests that it is by the very fact that the book is sheer nonsense that its effect is produced.[38]   If we would only say with the King in *Alice in Wonderland*, "If there's no meaning in it, that saves a world of trouble, as we needn't try to find any"—it would be all up with it.   The mischief comes from trying to find a meaning in it.   "Given the will to believe by, say, the cure of a friend, the perusal of the book, by its general unintelligibility, produces a kind of mental coma, such as is induced by staring fixedly at a single bright spot." It hypnotizes us, in short.[39]   It is barely possible, of course, that some of the obscurity of the book is intentional, designed to produce just this effect. The Unitarian clergyman, James Henry Wiggin, who served for some years as Mrs. Eddy's literary adviser, and in that capacity revised the text of the book (from 1885 on), suggests as much.[40] "As for clearness," he writes, "many Christian Science people thought her earlier editions much better, because they sounded more *like* Mrs. Eddy. The truth is that she does not care to have her paragraphs clear, and delights in so expressing herself that her words may have various readings and meanings. Really, that is one of the tricks of the trade. You know, Sibyls have always been thus oracular, to 'keep the word of promise to the ear and break it to the hope.'" Allow this theory, however, the fullest application, and the book nevertheless remains hopelessly incompetent. Wiggin puts his finger on the true cause when he adds: "Quimby had definite ideas but Mrs. Eddy has not understood them." Her ability lay in other spheres than in that of philosophic thought and literary expression.

Mrs. Eddy's pantheism deprived her, of course, of a personal God, and she insisted on the impersonality of God with the utmost vigor.[41] But she rightly found what she calls "the leading factor in Mind-Science," in the consequent proposition that "Mind" (with a capital "M") "is all, and matter is naught"; or as she otherwise expresses it, that "the only realities are the divine mind and its ideas"; [42] "nothing possesses reality and existence except God." [43] She sums up her entire teaching in four fundamental propositions which she declares to be self-evident, and so true that they are still true if they are read backwards: (1) God is all in all; (2) God is good; Good is Mind; (3) God, Spirit, being all, nothing is matter; and (4) Life, God, omnipotent good, deny death, evil, sin, disease." [44] More at large she expounds her system thus: "God is supreme; is mind; is principle, not person; includes all and is reflected by all that is real and eternal; is Spirit and Spirit is infinite; is the only substance; is the only life. Man was and is the idea of God; therefore mind can never be in man. Divine Science shows that matter and mortal body are the illusions of human belief, which seem to ap-

pear and disappear to mortal sense alone. When this belief changes as in dreams, the material body changes with
it, going wherever we wish, and becoming whatever belief
may decree. . . . Besiege sickness and death with these
principles and all will disappear."

Frances Lord says the first lesson we must learn, accordingly, is that "in the universe there is only the all and the
nothing." "God is all." "Since God is all, and God is
good, the all is the good; whatever is not good is not real
and may be proclaimed so." The power of proclamation
is so great that if we train ourselves to deny that an evil
is, and to affirm that it is not—it is not. "We could teach
ourselves Denial," she explains, "using any error to deny
away; but we deny Disease because we have set ourselves
this particular task." [45] "Mind," she says in further explanation, "in its thinking faculty is pure understanding.
Understanding casts a shadow; this shadow is Intellect.
Intellect believes things and has opinions. Intellectual
belief casts a shadow; this shadow is the human body." [46]
"If the body shows forth a bruise, the shadow is showing
forth as a defective shadow. Then the substance, or would-
be substance, must be defective. But we have just said
it is intellectual belief that plays the part of substance to
the shadow we call the body. Then the defect must be
in some intellectual belief: it must consist in some mistaken opinion or notion which the thinking mind holds. . . .
Yes, the bruise pictures out some mistaken ideas." [47]
"What is the harm of a shadow?" she continues. "There
is no harm whatever in a shadow, provided it knows it is
a shadow; the harm of error comes in when it forgets this
and claims independence. What is the proper way to
handle a shadow? Shall we argue with it, talk to it, coax
it? No." This is the essential teaching of the whole
school. Only Frances Lord goes a step further in this
shadow-dance. She believes also in Karma: that is,
shortly, in Inheritance. If the cause of illness lies further

back than this life, "it is incurable, except the patient can
be led to realize in so deep a sense the meaning of the words,
'There is no power in evil,'" that he is lifted above even
"the old shadows of former lives and thoughts." [48]

Now, if bodily disease is only "an appearance, a sensuous seeming, an empty show," an illusion only—as Mrs.
Eddy says, "You will call it neuralgia, but I call it Illusion"—all that is necessary to cure disease is to dissipate
the illusion, that is to say, to change the mind. No
knowledge of anatomy is necessary; no medicament, no
regimen, no anything except the projection of a healthy
image of body. We are sick because we think ourselves
sick; we are well whenever we change our minds and say
we are well until we believe it. There is only one possibility of failure. Suppose you are thinking yourself well,
but others persist in thinking that you are sick. This is
unfortunate: for as fast as you project yourself a well
body, they project you a sick one. You must get all
about you to think with you to insure success. Nay, you
must get the whole world to do so—unless you can persuade the world to forget you utterly, which should do
just as well.[49]

If we survey the system of Christian Science as a whole,
with an active desire to discover in it elements of value,
it is quite possible to fix upon characteristics which, viewed
in the abstract, may seem admirable. There is its un-
compromising idealism, for example; the emphasis which it
places on spirit as distinguished from matter. There is
the high value it attaches to Truth, as over against other
forms—emotional or volitional—of human activity. And
there is its constant inculcation of contentment and serenity, the quiet optimism of its outlook on life, which must
tend, one would think, to the production of a demeanor,
at least, if not a character, full of attractiveness. These
things occur in the actual system, however, not in the abstract but in very concrete forms; and the concrete forms

in which they occur in the system do not seem, upon being frankly looked in the face, very beautiful.

It is easy immediately on perceiving the idealistic presuppositions of Christian Science to go off into laudations of idealism in general, in contrast with the sordid materialism of our age. But it is our own idealism we are lauding, not Mrs. Eddy's. Her idealism is a sheer pantheism, involving a complete acosmism, which sinks, not the material universe only, but the world of individual spirits as well, in the ocean of undifferentiated Being. If it be said that Mrs. Eddy does not work her pantheistic assumption out consistently, that is true in one sense and quite untrue in another and much more important sense. It is true that she is constantly making assertions quite inconsistent with it; that in her attempts to expound it, she cannot maintain her consistency three sentences at a time, but everywhere presents us, as Miss Sturge puts it,[50] "with such a tangle of incoherent, inconsistent, confused statements, contradictory to each other, as has, perhaps, never been seriously given to the world before." But with all her inability in expounding the details of her thought to keep in view its fundamental pantheistic postulate, Mrs. Eddy does not fail to make this pantheistic postulate consistently fundamental to her system, or to press it explicitly to its extremest implications. Her system is precisely acosmic pantheism, that, all that, and nothing but that.

From another point of view also it is absurd to speak in terms of praise of Mrs. Eddy's idealism. It is but a sorry idealism at the best. It does not take its starting-point from the vision of the spiritual, from an enlarged mental outlook and a soaring sense of the value of spiritual things —but from a cringing fear of the evils of life, as life is and must be lived by creatures of sense. It makes all the difference whether we begin by affirming spirit and draw the inference thence to the relative nothingness of the material; or begin by shirking the material and inferring only thence

that spirit is all. The centre of gravity of the two attitudes, though they be described in identical language, is
antipodal; their reactions on life—expressed in thought,
feeling and doing—are so completely contrasting as to be
in point of fact directly contradictory. Mrs. Eddy's beginning lay in the denial of matter, that the suffering and
trials of life might be, if they could not be escaped, yet as
far as possible circumvented. Her attitude is that of
flight, flight from the evils of life. There is nothing heroic
about it; nothing elevated or elevating. We fear that we
must say that it looks from without rather sordid. Her
idealism is a sham idealism; merely a mechanical device
for the eluding of life, a life which must be lived in a world
of suffering (of which Mrs. Eddy has the keenest sense)
and sin (of which she appears to have no sense at all).[51]
Of course the device is as vain as it is mechanical. To
deny the evils of life, however stoutly, unfortunately does
not abolish them. Mrs. Eddy herself suffered from disease and weakness; she too grew old and died.[52] Her
idealism is as false to all the facts of experience as it is
mean in its origin. And we must add that it is as cruel
as it is false and mean. We see it in its full enormity only
when we see it at work on helpless sufferers—on those too
ill to speak for themselves, on tortured infancy. The annals of the practice of Christian Science on sick and suffering babies belongs to the history of atrocities.[53]

Similarly, when we are tempted to praise Christian
Science for the honor which it does to Truth, we are bound
to stop and ask, not only materially, what this Truth is
to which it gives honor, but also, formally, whether it can
be commended for the functions which it assigns to Truth
in its system. What it calls " Truth," when it speaks hon-
oringly of Truth, is just its pantheistic theory of Being—
that all is mind, and mind is God, and besides God there is
nothing. To this "Truth" as such—that is to say, to its
mere apprehension as true—it ascribes all healing power.

It is therefore that it calls itself "metaphysical healing," healing, that is, by metaphysics, and that it named its college, founded in Boston in 1881, the "Massachusetts Metaphysical College." This is, in point of fact, its only distinguishing feature, borrowed indeed from P. P. Quimby, but made all its own. There are other systems of mental healing abroad, seeking healing through other mental activities—faith, say, or the will. Mrs. Eddy remarks:[54] "The common custom of praying for the recovery of the sick finds help in blind belief, whereas help should come from the enlightened understanding." "Willpower is not Science," she says again.[55] "Willing the sick to recover is not the metaphysical practice of Christian Science, but sheer animal magnetism. . . . Truth and not corporeal will is the divine power which says to disease, 'Peace, be still.'" A "Christian Science Healer" explains the whole matter clearly.[56] Every man, he declares, has a "God-given right" to "spiritual, mental and bodily wholeness"; and this wholeness is "received in proportion to man's intelligent understanding of the God-nature and its operation." We pass by the mere phrases "God-given right," "spiritual, mental and bodily wholeness." The former is only a fashion of speaking with no specific meaning on a Christian Scientist's lips except as a strong way of saying, it is an inalienable right. The latter is merely rhetorical enumeration to emphasize the single idea of completeness; on Christian Science ground mind and body are both nonentities and no man can have a right to anything mental or bodily—he has only a right to be rid of all such things. What is to be noted is that everybody is affirmed to have an inalienable right to wholeness, and this wholeness to which every one has an inalienable right is affirmed to be actually enjoyed only—here is the point, note it well—in proportion as each has an intelligent understanding of "the God-nature and its operation."

Here, you see, is a truly rampant intellectualism, a pure

Gnosticism. To understand is to have and to be. In proportion as we understand, and understand intelligently, we possess. The thing to be understood and the understanding of which brings wholeness is described as "the God-nature and its operation." In this system "the God-nature" is defined as the All. "God is all," we are told, "and all is God." Understand that, and you are "whole." It is the mere understanding of it that does the work; it always does the work, and the work is not done where this understanding is not present. This is the reason why puzzled pastors sometimes complain—surely they are themselves showing little understanding—that members of their flock who are tainted with Christian Science are found to have turned away from historical Christianity. It is the first step in Christian Science that you must turn away from historical Christianity.[57] It is the "new knowledge" that does the work. Unless you have the "new knowledge" you have no Christian Science; for Christian Science is just this "new knowledge," and this "new knowledge," being just pantheistic acosmism, is the contradiction of historical Christianity. You can have a little Christian Science in your Christianity just as little as you can have a little water in your fire; and a little Christianity in your Christian Science just as little as you can have a little fire in your water. The things are mutually exclusive.

This bald intellectualism is pressed even to the absurd extreme that curative value is ascribed to the mere reading of Mrs. Eddy's writings. "The perusal of the author's publications," she tells us herself, "heals sickness constantly." [58] A palsied arm, we are told, was cured by reading a single sentence: "All is Mind." Sometimes, no doubt, appearances are against this doctrine. But Mrs. Eddy has her explanation and her encouragement to offer. "If patients sometimes seem the worse for reading this book," she says,[59]—and who can wonder, if they do?—"the change may either arise from the alarm of the physician, or may mark the crisis of the disease. Perseverance in its reading has generally healed them completely." This is healing distinctly by reading. *Tolle, lege,* is the command in a new sense.

It puzzles us greatly, therefore, to learn that healing can apparently be had nevertheless without the reading of Mrs. Eddy's book, and indeed without the understanding which we are instructed to look upon as itself the healing. Mrs. Eddy tells this story:[60] "A case of dropsy, given up by the faculty, fell into my hands. It was a terrible case. Tapping had been employed, and yet the patient looked like a barrel as she lay in her bed. I prescribed the fourth attenuation of *Argenitum nitricum*, with occasional doses of a high attenuation of *Sulphuris*. She improved perceptibly. Believing then somewhat in the ordinary theories of medical practice, and learning that her former physician had prescribed these remedies, I began to fear an aggravation of symptoms from their prolonged use, and told the patient so; but she was unwilling to give up the medicine when she was recovering. It then occurred to me to give her unmedicated pellets, and watch the result. I did so, and she continued to gain. Finally she said that she would give up her medicine for one day, and risk the effects. After trying this, she informed me that she could get along two days without globules; but on the third day she again suffered, and was relieved by taking them. She went on in this way, taking the unmedicated pellets—and receiving occasional visits from me—but employing no other means, and was cured." What had "metaphysical healing," that is, healing through understanding, to do with this cure? If understanding is healing, how was this woman, who did not understand, healed? Of course, Mrs. Eddy would say that by the deception practised on this woman she was got to project herself gradually a well-body, and so she gradually found herself with a well-body. But that is not "metaphysical" healing, in which knowing is being.

But, it seems, not only may you be healed without understanding, but you may fail to be healed even if you do
understand. If you take poison you will die; even, it
seems, if you do not know you have taken it. "If a dose
of poison is swallowed through mistake, and the patient
dies," Mrs. Eddy posits a case,[61] "even though physician
and patient are expecting favorable results, does belief,
you ask, cause this death?" "Even so," she answers,
"and as directly as if the poison had been intentionally
taken." Then follows the adjustment of the case to the
theory. "In such cases," we are told, "a few persons believe the potion swallowed by the patient to be harmless;
but the vast majority of mankind, though they know nothing of this particular case, and this special person, believe
the arsenic, the strychnine, or whatever the drug used, to
be poisonous, for it has been set down as a poison by mortal
mind. The consequence is that the result is controlled by
the majority of opinions outside, not by the infinitesimal
minority of opinions in the sick chamber." If this be true,
then it is all up with "metaphysical healing." It is not the
individual's understanding; it is the common opinion of
mankind—not as to this particular case of which few
have knowledge—but in general, which determines results.
Material things, having the ground of their being and modes
of action in the common opinion of mankind, are just as
objectively real to the individual as if they had the ground
of their being and modes of action in themselves. The individual is helpless in their presence, and all the better
understanding which he may possess as to their real nature
as illusions, can serve him in no possible way.

A pantheist has no right to a religion. He must be content with a philosophy and its postulates. As a Christian
Science Healer already quoted tells us, he understands
"the God-nature and its operation," and forthwith is
"whole" with that "spiritual, mental and bodily wholeness" which is his indefeasible right. Get into your place

as a part of that great whole which is God, and, being in your place, you have your wholeness. This is as much of a religion as a pantheist can have. It was this that the Stoic meant when he said: "Get into the stream of nature, and if you do not like the way it is flowing, at least you need not squeal." [62] And this is the reason why the religion of mystics—who are pantheizing in their fundamental thought—tends to run into what we call Quietism, which is on the passive side resignation, on the active renunciation, and in its lowest reaches becomes placid acceptance of the lot that has come to us, in its highest rises into disinterested love. Do we not have here the account also of the special type of piety which is said to be developed in Christian Science circles? Christian Science, we are told, has brought not only relief from suffering and disease, but release also from worry, anxiety, contentiousness. We will let Frank Podmore depict this self-centred piety for us. "The religion of Christian Science," says he,[63] "oils the wheels of the domestic machinery, smooths out business troubles, releases from fear, promotes happiness. But it is entirely egoistic in expression. . . . For Christian Scientists there is no recognized service to their fellows, beyond the force of their example." "There are no charities or institutions of any kind for social service in connection with the Christian Science churches." "Poverty and sin, like sickness, are illusions, errors of 'mortal mind,' and cannot be alleviated by material methods. If a man is sick, he does not need drugs; if poor, he has no need of money; if suffering, of material help or even sympathy. For the cure in all cases must be sought within. The New Religion, then, is without the enthusiasm of Humanity. It is, in fact, without enthusiasm of any kind. We shall look in vain here for spiritual rapture, for ecstatic contemplation of the divine. There is no place here for any of the passions which are associated with Christianity, nor, indeed, for any exalted emotion. There can be no remorse where there is no sin; compassion, when the suffering is unreal, can only be mischievous; friendship, as we shall see later, is a snare, and the love of man and woman a hindrance to true spirituality.   There is no mystery about this final revelation, and there is no room, therefore, for wonder and awe.   Here are no 'long-drawn aisles and fretted vaults'; the Scientist's outlook on the spiritual world is as plain and bare as the walls of his temple, shining white under the abundant radiance of the electric lamps."

The ethics of pantheism tend either to license or to asceticism.   The flesh is nothing, and all its delights and desires are nothing, and may be treated as nothing—whether in the way of careless indulgence or of stern extirpation.   We may be thankful that Mrs. Eddy's thought turns in the direction of asceticism, though, to be sure, it is to an asceticism of sufficiently mild a type.   On all matters of dietetics and hygiene she of course pours contempt, because she is thinking of them primarily as curative agents, and she can have nothing to do with curative agents; yet she manages to spice her remarks upon them with an ascetic flavor.   Eat what you please is her prescription: much or little—it is all nothing.   God gave men "dominion not only over the fish in the sea, but over the fish in the stomach." [64]   But, of course, remember[65] "that gustatory pleasure is a sensuous illusion, a phantasm of the mortal mind, diminishing as we better apprehend our spiritual existence, and ascend the ladder of Life"—Life with a capital "L," for Mrs. Eddy was not thinking of growing old.   "A metaphysician never . . . recommends or trusts in hygiene." [66]   "The daily ablutions of an infant," writes she,[67] "are no more natural or necessary, than would be the process of taking a fish out of water every day, and covering it with dirt, in order to make it thrive more vigorously thereafter in its native element.   'Cleanliness is next to godliness'; but washing should be only for the purpose of keeping the body clean, and this can be done without scrubbing the whole surface daily. Water is not the natural habitat of humanity." "Is civilization," she exclaims,[68] "only a higher form of idolatry, that man should bow down to a flesh brush, to flannels, to baths, diet, exercise, and air?" But she has a deeper feeling. "Bathing, scrubbing, to alter the secretions, or remove unhealthy exhalations from the cuticle," she declares in her earlier editions at least, received a "useful rebuke from Jesus' precept 'Take no thought . . . for the body.'" "We must beware," she adds, "of making clean only the outside of the platter." [69]

It is with respect to marriage, however, that the asceticism intrinsic to Mrs. Eddy's philosophy pushes nearest to the surface. She discourages marriage and prefers celibacy. "Is marriage more right than celibacy?" she asks, and answers,[70] "Human knowledge indicates that it is, but Science indicates that it is *not*." And so far from marriage involving children, childless marriages are the best and are to be sought after.[71] To the objection that, if every one followed this advice, the human race would soon perish, she has a ready answer. The propagation of the species, she intimates, does not depend on marriage; sex is an error of the mortal mind. "The butterfly, bee and moth," she says,[72]—we are afraid that Mrs. Eddy's knowledge of natural history was defective—even now are reproduced in an asexual manner, and this may—nay, will —be true of man when he attains more nearly to his true being. Meanwhile, these are times of ignorance; and during these times of ignorance, she counsels, let marriages continue.[73] Thus Christian Science makes its concession to "mortal mind." [74]

We observe that Mrs. Eddy has an eschatology. She is looking forward to a better time to come, when all that Christian Science dreams should be shall be. Why her dreams of the future should take the form of this golden age we do not quite understand. If all is mind and mind is God, we should think Mrs. Eddy's eschatology would point forward to a time when all the wavelets which fret the surface of the infinite deep should have sunk to rest in its depths. But no, the paradise she looks forward to is, apparently, a material paradise.[75] There are men in it, and they increase and multiply and replenish the earth—though after an asexual manner. They are in it but not of it. They tread the adder under foot; and though they drink deadly things, they will suffer no harm—for there will be no "mortal mind" then to make it harm them. They will walk on the water, it seems, and turn water into wine, and multiply loaves and fishes, as Jesus once did, but men cannot do now. At least Herman S. Hering, first reader of the church at Concord, seems to promise this to us, "eventually." "It is claimed by some opponents," he writes,[76] "that because Christian Scientists do not walk on the water, turn water into wine, multiply loaves and fishes, as did Jesus, and because they still have to do with matter at every turn, the doctrines of Christian Science, especially that of the unreality of matter, must be fallacious. Such an argument is like that which declares that, because a school-boy, who is just learning to add and subtract, cannot work out a problem in cube-root, therefore the claims of greater possibilities in the science of mathematics are fallacious, and the school-boy is badly deceived by the promise of being able eventually to solve such higher problems."

There is a good time coming, then, and we may confidently look forward to it. It contains for us, no doubt, nothing beyond what we ought to have here and now, and would have here and now were it not for the interference of "mortal mind." In enumerating the benefits which Christian Science confers on us, Frances Lord includes in the list such items as these:[77] "6. We do not need to fear any climate. . . . 7. We do not need to travel or go away for a change of air. . . . 8. We know that we do not really live by eating, and this mere knowledge—without any effort to do without food, or lessen it, or indeed interfere with our ordinary simple habits at all—has the effect of making us less dependent on our meals both as to what and when to eat. 9. And in the same way we grow less dependent upon clothing, warmth and coldness, for comfort." But she immediately adds: "Here let us say emphatically that we neither enjoin, nor encourage, any experiments about food or clothing. Experience shows us that any changes, to be worth anything, must and do come about of themselves, in persons who, having learnt the truth of life, accepted and begun to live by it, demonstrate it naturally and spontaneously." This is, of course, only a repetition of Mrs. Eddy's constant manner. For example:[78] "Food does not affect the real existence of man . . . but it would be foolish to venture beyond present understanding, foolish to stop eating until we gain more goodness, and a clearer comprehension of the living God."[79]

But what about the success, in actual healing, of this system which describes "a mental cure"—this is the way that Luther M. Marsdon puts it—as "the discovery of a sick person that he is well," and the practice of which consists simply in the transference of this thought from the practitioner to the patient? It is just as successful as any other of the many systems of mental practice; no more and no less. Its list of cures is long, and many of them are remarkable.[80] We have no reason to doubt the reality of large numbers of these cures. But by now, we surely understand that there are limitations to them which are never overpassed. These limitations are brought sharply into view by a challenge cast out by Professor L. T. Townsend.[81] He made this proposition: "If you or the president of your college, or your entire college of doctors, will put into place a real case of hip or ankle dislocation, without resorting to the ordinary manipulation or without touching it, I will give you a thousand dollars. Or if you or your president, or your entire college, will give sight to one of the inmates of the South Boston Asylum for the Blind, that sightless person having been born blind, I will give you two thousand dollars." The money was never called for. But in the *Journal of Christian Science* this reply appeared: "Will the gentleman accept my thanks due to his generosity, for if I should accept his bid he would lose his money. Why, because I performed more difficult tasks fifteen years ago. At present I am in another department of Christian work, where 'there shall be no sign given them,' for they shall be instructed in the principles of Christian Science that furnishes its own proof." We have observed that in a similar vein a Faith-Healer, Doctor Cullis, explained that "a broken bone is not sickness, and should be put into the hands of a surgeon." Mrs. Eddy does not thus curtly refuse, she only postpones, the treatment of such cases. "Until the advancing age admits the efficacy and supremacy of Mind," she writes,[82] "it is better to leave the adjustment of broken bones and dislocations to the fingers of a surgeon, while you confine yourself chiefly"—that "chiefly" is very good!—"to mental reconstruction or the prevention of inflammation or protracted confinement." Even while saying this, however, she asseverates that cures of this kind have nevertheless already been actually performed both by herself and her pupils.

It was not the magnitude of the task asked by Professor Townsend which led Mrs. Eddy to palter thus. It was the nature of it. The drawing of a tooth is not a great thing, but Mrs. Eddy's Science was not equal to it. We do indeed hear here too of "more difficult tasks" already performed. We hear, for example, of "the 'good-sized cavity' of an aching tooth filled up by mental treatment, 'not with foreign substance, but the genuine, white and perfect.'"[83] But when Mrs. Eddy herself had a troublesome tooth, she employed the good offices of a dentist to obtain relief, and even availed herself of his "painless method" to guard herself from suffering in the process.[84] The explanation she gives runs as follows: "Bishop Berkeley and I agree that all is Mind. Then, consistently with this premise, the conclusion is that if I employ a dental surgeon, and he believes that the extraction of a tooth is made easier by some application of means which he employs, and I object to the employment of this means, I have turned the dentist's mental protest against myself, he thinks I must suffer because his method is interfered with. Therefore, his mental force weighs against a painless operation, whereas it should be put into the same scale as mine, thus producing a painless operation as a logical result." This is very ingenious. The application of the anæsthetic to Mrs. Eddy's tooth was to operate not on Mrs. Eddy, directly, but on the dentist; it was not to keep the extraction of the tooth from hurting Mrs. Eddy, but to keep the dentist from thinking that its extraction would hurt Mrs. Eddy. But the real question of interest is, Why did Mrs. Eddy have recourse to a dentist at all?[85] The toothache and the tooth, Mrs. Eddy and the operator, the soothing application and the cruel forceps were one and all illusions. It is safe to say that the extraction itself—the act of a nonentity on a nonentity—did not happen.

Sir William Osler tells us in a few direct words why Mrs. Eddy went to a dentist. "Potent as is the influence of mind on body," he writes, "and many as are the miracle-like cures which may be worked, all are in functional disorders, and we know only too well that nowadays the prayer of faith neither sets a broken thigh nor checks an epidemic of typhoid fever."[86] That is to say, directly, by its own power. It may do either, indirectly, through the gracious answer of the Almighty God who has infinite resources at His disposal; who, as the old writer to whom we listened at the beginning of this lecture told us, creates physicians and medicines and gives them their skill and efficacy, that He, the Lord, may be honored in His marvellous works. But Mrs. Eddy had no Lord to pray to, and no faith in which to appear before Him, and no hope in His almighty succor. Let us be thankful that she at least had a dentist.[87]

NOTES

NOTES TO LECTURE I

THE CESSATION OF THE CHARISMATA

1. W. Yorke Fausset, for example, unduly restricts the number of our Lord's miracles, speaking of the "severe economy with which He exercised such supernatural, or extranatural, powers." (*Medicine and the Modern Church*, edited by Geoffrey Rhodes, 1910, pp. 175 ff.)

2. Χαρίσματα, or more rarely πνευματικά, I Cor. 12 : 1, or δόματα, Eph. 4 : 8.

3. Charismata: it is a distinctively Pauline term, occurring elsewhere than in Paul's writings only once in Philo (*De Alleg. Leg.*, 2 : 75) and once in the First Epistle of Peter (4 : 10), an epistle which, both in doctrine and language, is of quite Pauline character.

4. *Cf.* C. F. G. Heinrici, *Das erste Sendschreiben des Apostel Paulus an die Korinther*, 1880, p. 452: " Mosheim says that Paul sketches in this section a kind of Church Directory. That goes too far: but it at least contains the outlines of a Directory of Worship in his community, for which it was at once made clear that in all matters which concern the value and effect of the worshipping assemblages, caprice and confusion are excluded." W. Bousset, *Kyrios Christos*, 1913, p. 106, describes very vividly, though on the naturalistic hypothesis explained in note 6 below, what their assemblies were for the Christians of the Apostolic times. "Here in the assemblies of the fellowship," he writes, "there arose for the believers in Christ the consciousness of their unity and peculiar sociological individuality. Scattered during the day in pursuit of their daily callings, subject in an alien world to derision and scorn, they came together in the evening (no doubt as often as possible) for the common sacred meal. They then experienced the miracle of fellowship, the glow of the enthusiasm of a common faith and a common hope, when the Spirit flamed up and encompassed them with a miracle-filled world: prophets and tongues, visionaries and ecstatics began to speak, psalms, hymns, and spiritual songs soared through the room, the forces of brotherly charity awoke in an unsuspected fashion, an unheard of new life pulsated

through the crowd of Christians. And over this whole surging enthusiasm the Lord Jesus reigned as the head of His community, immediately present in His power with a tangibility and a certainty which takes the breath away."

5. J. H. Bernard, in an essay on "The Miraculous in Early Christian Literature," published in the volume called *The Literature of the Second Century*, by F. R. Wynne, J. H. Bernard, and S. Hemphill (New York, James Pott & Co., 1892), p. 145, gives a useful but incomplete exhibit of the references to the exercise of these gifts in the Acts and Epistles: (1) *Tongues*: Pentecost (Acts 2) and frequently alluded to by Paul in his epistles; (2) *Prophecy*: frequently called a "sign" of an Apostle, and also alluded to in the cases of Agabus (Acts 11 : 28, 21 : 10), the twelve Ephesian disciples on whom Paul laid his hands (Acts 19 : 6), and the four daughters of Philip (Acts 21 : 9); (3) *Poison*: Paul's viper (Acts 28 : 3); (4) *Exorcism*: by Paul (Acts 16 : 18); (5) *Healing*: by Paul in the case of Publius (Acts 28 : 8), by Peter in that of Æneas (Acts 9 : 33), by Peter's shadow (Acts 5 : 15), by Paul's clothing (Acts 19 : 12), by Peter and John (Acts 3 : 7); (6) *Raising the dead*: by Paul, in the case of Eutychus (Acts 20 : 9), by Peter, in the case of Dorcas (Acts 9 : 36); (7) *Punitive*: in the cases of Ananias and Sapphira (Acts 5 : 5), and Elymas (Acts 13 : 8); (8) *General references to signs and wonders*: attesting Paul and Barnabas (Acts 14 : 3), Stephen (Acts 6 : 8) and Philip (Acts 8 : 6).

6. Theologians of the "Liberal" school, of course, deny the miraculous character of the charisms on principle, and are prone to represent them as the natural manifestations of primitive enthusiasm. "We, for our part," says P. W. Schmiedel (*Encyclopedia Biblica*, col. 4776), "are constrained to" "deny the miraculous character of the charisms," "and to account for everything in the phenomena to which a miraculous character has been attributed by the known psychological laws which can be observed in crises of great mental exaltation, whether in persons who deem themselves inspired, or in persons who simply require medical treatment." From this point of view the charismata belong to the primitive church as such, to the church not merely of the Apostolic age, but of the first two centuries. This church is spoken of in contrast to the staid, organized church which succeeded it, as a Charismatic Church, that is to say, in the old sense of the word, as an Enthusiastic Church, a church swept along by an exalted state of mind and feeling which we should look upon to-day as mere fanaticism. "It is easily intelligible," says Schmiedel (col. 4775), "that the joy of enthusiasm over the possession of a new redeeming religion

should have expressed itself in an exuberant way, which, according to the ideas of the time, could only be regarded as the miraculous operation of the Holy Spirit." Or, as Adolf Harnack (*The Expansion of Christianity in the First Three Centuries*, E. T. I., pp. 250 ff.), puts it, Christianity came into being as "the religion of Spirit and power," and only lost this character and became the religion of form and order toward the end of the second century. A rather sharp expression of this view is given in an (inaugural) address delivered in 1893 by A. C. McGiffert, on *Primitive and Catholic Christianity*. "The spirit of primitive Christianity," he says (p. 19), "is the spirit of individualism, based on the felt presence of the Holy Ghost. It was the universal conviction of the primitive church that every Christian believer enjoys the immediate presence of the Holy Spirit, through whom he communes with God, and receives illumination, inspiration and strength for his daily needs. The presence of the Spirit was realized by these primitive Christians in a most vivid way. It meant the power to work miracles, to speak with tongues, to utter prophecies (*cf.* Mark 16 : 17–18, and Acts 2 : 16 ff.)." McGiffert is not describing here some Christians, but all Christians; and all Christians not of the Apostolic age, but of the first two centuries: "By the opening of the third century all these conceptions had practically disappeared." An attempt to give this general view a less naturalistic expression may be read at the close of R. Martin Pope's article, "Gifts," in Hastings's *Dictionary of the Apostolic Church*. "To sum up," he writes (vol. I, p. 451), "an examination of the passages in apostolic literature which treat of spiritual gifts inevitably brings us to the conclusion that the life of the early church was characterized by glowing enthusiasm, simple faith, and intensity of joy and wonder, all resulting from the consciousness of the power of the Holy Spirit; also that this phase of Spirit-effected ministries and service was temporary, as such 'tides of the Spirit' have since often proved, and gave way to a more rigid and disciplined Church Order, in which the official tended more and more to supersede the charismatic ministries."

It has always been the characteristic mark of a Christian that he is "led by the Spirit of God": "if any man hath not the Spirit of Christ he is none of His." It has never been the mark of a Christian that because he is "led by the Spirit of God" he is a law to himself and free from the ordinances of God's house. It is very clear from the record of the New Testament that the extraordinary charismata were not (after the very first days of the church) the possession of all Christians, but special supernatural gifts to the few; and it is equally clear from the records of the sub-Apostolic church that they did not continue in it, but only a shadow of them lingered in doubtful manifestations of which we must say, Do not even the heathen so? How little this whole representation accords with the facts the progress of the present discussion will show. For an examination of McGiffert's position, see *The Presbyterian Quarterly*, April, 1895, pp. 185-194. For a vivid popular description of conditions in the early church as reconstructed from the "Liberal" view-point, and brought into relation to the "enthusiasm" of later centuries, see *The Edinburgh Review* for January, 1903, pp. 148 ff.

7. R. Martin Pope, as cited, p. 450, speaks of modes of ministry, "in addition to the more stable and authorized modes" mentioned in I Cor. 1 : 4-12, 28, which were of "a special order, perhaps peculiar to the Corinthian Church, with its exuberant manifestations of spiritual energy, and certainly, as the evidence of later Church History shows, of a temporary character, and exhausting themselves (*cf.* H. B. Swete, *The Holy Spirit in the N. T.*, London, 1909, p. 320) in the Apostolic or sub-Apostolic age." In contrast with these special modes of ministry, he speaks of "the charisms of miracle-working as lasting down to the second century, if we may trust the evidence of Justin Martyr (*Apol.*, 2 : 6)." In the passage of Justin appealed to, as also in section 8, and in *Dial.*, 30, 76, 85, it is said only that demoniacs are exorcised by Christians; *cf.* G. T. Purves, *The Testimony of Justin Martyr to Early Christianity*, 1889, p. 159. We shall see that the evidence of the second and subsequent centuries is not such as naturally to base Pope's conclusion. When he adds of these "charisms of miracle-working" that "they never were intended, as the extreme faith-healer of to-day contends, to supersede the efforts of the skilled physician," he is of course right, since they were confined to the Apostolic age, and to a very narrow circle then. But when he goes on to say, "they represent the creative gift, the power of initiating new departures in the normal world of phenomena, which is rooted in faith (see A. G. Hogg, *Christ's Message of the Kingdom*, Edinburgh, 1911, pp. 62-70); and as such reveal a principle which holds good for all time"—he is speaking wholly without book, and relatively to the charisms of the New Testament equally wholly without meaning.

8. A. Tholuck's figure ("Ueber die Wunder der katholichen Kirche," in *Vermischte Schriften*, I, 1839, p. 28) is this: "Christ did not appear like the sun in tropical lands, which rises without a dawn and sets without a twilight, but, as millenniums of prophecy

preceded Him, so miracles followed Him, and the forces which He first awoke were active in a greater or less measure for a subsequent period. Down into the third century we have credible testimonies of the persistence of the miraculous forces which were active in the first century." A mechanical conception of the miracle-working of both Christ and His followers lurks behind such figures; Christ let loose forces which naturally required some time to exhaust their energies.

9. *Miscellaneous Works*, London, 1755, vol. I, p. xli.

10. *Works*, New York, 1856, vol. V, p. 706.

11. E. T., p. 169.

12. *Persecution and Tolerance*, pp. 55–56.

13. On the literary form of Hermas, see Kerr Duncan Macmillan in *Biblical and Theological Studies*, by the Faculty of Princeton Seminary, 1912, pp. 494–543. The Didaché tells of "prophets" who spoke "in the Spirit," as apparently a well-known phenomenon in the churches for which it speaks, and thus implies the persistence of the charism—or rather of the shadow of the charism—of "prophecy." Papias is reported by Philip of Side as having stated on the authority of the daughters of Philip that Barsabas (or Justus) drank serpent's poison inadvertently, and that the mother of Manaim was raised from the dead, as well as that those raised from the dead by Christ lived until the time of Hadrian (*cf.* Eusebius, *H. E.*, III, 39, 9; below, note 25); these events belong, in any event, to the Apostolic age.

14. *Cf.* H. M. Scott, "The Apostolic Fathers and the New Testament Revelation," in *The Presbyterian and Reformed Review*, July, 1892, vol. III, pp. 479–488.

15. J. B. Lightfoot discusses these miraculous features of the letter in *The Apostolic Fathers, Part II, S. Ignatius, S. Polycarp*, vol. I, pp. 598 ff.; *cf.* Bernard's exhibition of their natural character *op. cit.*, p. 168. H. Günter, *Legenden-Studien*, 1906, pp. 10 ff., remarks: "thus, out of the entire series of authentic Passiones there remains as an outspoken miracle-martyrdom only the Acts of Polycarp: and even they are not unquestionably such."

16. *Justin Martyr*, by the Bishop of Lincoln, ed. 3, 1853, p. 121.

17. *Cf.* Blunt, *On the Early Fathers*, p. 387.

18. Doctor Hey, in *Tertullian*, by the Bishop of Lincoln, ed. 2, 1826, p. 168.

19. *Cf.* what is said of Justin's and Irenæus's testimony by Gilles P:son Wetter, *Charis, Ein Beitrag zur Geschichte des ältesten Christentums*, 1913, p. 185: "We can still hear of χαρίσματα in the church, in Justin and Irenæus. . . . Justin and Irenæus are prob-

ably the latest witnesses of a prophetic gift of grace in the church. . . . It is generally wholly uncertain whether we can still really find 'gifts of grace' in the church in great amount in the time of Justin and Irenæus. A declaration like that in Justin, *Dial.*, 82, 1, παρὰ γὰρ ἡμῖν καὶ μέχρι νῦν προφητικὰ χαρισματά ἐστιν, testifies rather to the contrary. If both steadily speak of 'we' or of the 'church' or the like, yet it is possible that they refer by this to the great spiritual operations in the earliest period of Christianity, of which we read in the Gospels, in Acts, and perhaps in some of the Apocrypha. These were to them certainly valuable 'proofs' of the truth of the divine origin of Christianity (*cf.* for this *e. g.*, Justin, *Apol.*, I, 58; Theophilus, *ad Aut.*, III, 16 and 26; Minucius Felix, *Octavius*, 20 and 23)."

20. Bernard, as cited, p. 147, remarks that "with a few notable exceptions," "there is no trace up to the end of the second century" —and the same, we may add, is true of the third—"of any miraculous gifts still existing in the primitive church, save those of *prophecy* and *healing*, including *exorcism*, both of which are frequently mentioned." With reference to *prophecy* he adduces the warning against false prophets in Hermas (*Com.* 11) and the Didaché, together with Justin's assertion that prophetic gifts continued even —the "even" is perhaps significant—to his day (*Dial.*, 315 B). As to *healing*, he adduces the general assertions of Justin (*Dial.*, 258 A) and Origen (*Cont. Cels.*, III, 24). With respect to *exorcisms*, he appeals to repeated references by Justin (*Apol.*, 45 A; *Dial.*, 247 C, 302 A, 311 B, 350 B, 361 C) and Tertullian (*Apol.*, 23, 37, 43; *De Spect.*, 2; *De Test. Anim.*, 3; *Ad Scap.*, 2; *De Corona*, 11; *De Idol.*, 11). He remarks that these Fathers all believed in magic and betray a feeling that the miracles of their day were not quite the same kind of thing which happened in the New Testament times (Tertullian, *De Rud.*, c. 21; Origen, *Cont. Cels.*, I, 2).

21. The prominence of exorcisms in the notices of marvellous occurrences in these Fathers belongs to the circumstances of the times, and would call for no special notice except for the use which has been made of it in recent discussions (*cf.* S. McComb in *Religion and Medicine*, by Elwood Worcester, Samuel McComb, and Isador H. Coriat, 1908, pp. 295–299). In point of fact, Christianity came into a world that was demon-ridden, and, as Harnack remarks (*The Expansion of Christianity*, E. T., 1904, vol. I, p. 158), "no flight of the imagination can form any idea of what would have come over the ancient world or the Roman Empire during the third century had it not been for the church." In conflict with this gigantic evil

which dominated the whole life of the people, it is not to be won-
dered at that the Christians of the second and subsequent centuries, who were men of their time, were not always able to hold the
poise which Paul gave them in the great words: "We know that no
idol is anything in the world, and that there is no God but one."
Accordingly, as Harnack points out, "from Justin downwards,
Christian literature is crowded with allusions to exorcisms, and every large church, at any rate, had exorcists" (p. 162). But this is
no proof that miracles were wrought, except this great miracle, that,
in its struggle against the deeply rooted and absolutely pervasive
superstition—"the whole world and the circumambient atmosphere," says Harnack (p. 161), "were filled with devils; not merely
idolatry, but every phase and form of life was ruled by them:
they sat on thrones; they hovered over cradles; the earth was literally a hell"—Christianity won, and expelled the demons not only
from the tortured individuals whose imagination was held captive
by them, but from the life of the people, and from the world. The
most accessible discussion of the subject (written, of course, from
his own point of view) may be found in Harnack, *op. cit.*, vol. I,
pp. 152-180. An article really on the Christian doctrine of angels
has somehow strayed into the bounds of the comprehensive article,
"Demons and Spirits," in Hastings's *Encyclopædia of Religion and
Ethics*, and thus deprived the reader of the description which he
would naturally look for in that place of the ideas of demons and
spirits which have been prevalent among Christians.

22. Philip Schaff, *History of the Christian Church*, ed. 1884,
vol. II, 117 ff., sums up the testimony of this period as follows:
"It is remarkable that the genuine writings of the ante-Nicene
church are more free from miraculous and superstitious elements
than the annals of the Nicene age and the Middle Ages. . . . Most
of the statements of the apologists are couched in general terms,
and refer to the extraordinary cures from demoniacal possession
. . . and other diseases. . . . Justin Martyr speaks of such occurrences as frequent . . . and Origen appeals to his own personal
observation, but speaks in another place of the growing scarcity of
miracles. . . . Tertullian attributes many if not most of the con-
versions of his day to supernatural dreams and visions, as does also
Origen, although with more caution. But in such psychological
phenomena it is exceedingly difficult to draw the line of demarca-
tion between natural and supernatural causes, and between provi-
dential interpositions and miracles proper. The strongest passage
on this subject is found in Irenæus, who, in contending against the
heretics, mentions, besides the prophecies and miraculous cures of

demoniacs, even the raising of the dead among contemporary events taking place in the Catholic Church; but he specifies no particular case or name; and it should be remembered also, that his youth still bordered almost on the Johannean age."

When Schaff cites Origen as speaking of a "growing scarcity of miracles," his language is not exact. What Origen says, is: "But there were signs from the Holy Spirit at the beginning of Christ's teaching, and after His ascension He exhibited more, but subsequently fewer. Nevertheless, even now still there are traces of them with a few who have had their souls purified by the gospel." Here, there is a recognition of the facts that miracles were relatively few after the Apostolic age, and that in Origen's day there were very few indeed to be found. But there is no assertion that they had *gradually* ceased; only an assertion that they had practically ceased. "The age of miracles, therefore," comments Harnack justly, "lay for Origen in earlier days." "Eusebius is not the first (in the third book of his *History*) to look back upon the age of the Spirit and of power as the bygone heroic age of the church, for Origen had already pronounced this judgment on the past from an impoverished present." (*The Expansion of Christianity*, as cited, p. 257, and note 2.)

23. *The History of the Decline and Fall of the Roman Empire*, chap. xv, § III, ed. Smith, 1887, vol. II, pp. 178 ff.

24. These points are accordingly duly intimated by Milman in his note on Gibbon's passage. For the former of them he appeals to Middleton (*Works*, I, p. 59) as sponsor; for the latter to Douglas (*Criterion*, p. 389).

25. *H. E.*, III, 39, 9.

26. Bernard, *op. cit.*, p. 159, remarks justly that Papias "virtually implies that he himself never saw any such occurrence, his only knowledge of 'miracles' of this kind being derived from hearsay."

27. *Cf.* Bernard, as cited: "If they were frequent, if he had ever seen one himself, he would have told us of it, or to speak more accurately, Eusebius would not have selected for quotation a second-hand story, if the direct evidence of an eye-witness was on record." How did Eusebius, then, understand Irenæus? As testifying to a common occurrence in his time? Or, even to a single instance within his own knowledge? This seems unlikely.

28. *H. E.*, V, 7, 1 f.

29. I : 13: "Then, as to your denying that the dead are raised —for you say, 'Show me one who has been raised from the dead, that seeing I may believe'—first, what great thing is it if you be-

lieve when you have seen the thing done? Then, again, you believe that Hercules, who burned himself, lives; and that Æsculapius, who was struck with lightning, was raised; and do you disbelieve the things that are told you by God? But, suppose I should show you a dead man raised and alive, even this you would disbelieve. God indeed exhibits to you many proofs that you may believe Him. For, consider, if you please, the dying of seasons, and days, and nights, how these also die and rise again," etc.

30. *De Pudicitia*, 21: "And so, if it were agreed that even the blessed Apostles had granted any such indulgence, the pardon of which comes from God, not from man, it would have been competent for them to have done so, not in the exercise of discipline, but of power. For they both raised the dead, which God alone can do; and restored the debilitated to their integrity, which none but Christ can do; nay they inflicted plagues, too, which Christ would not do, for it did not beseem Him to be severe who had come to suffer. Smitten were both Ananias and Elymas—Ananias with death, Elymas with blindness—in order that by this very fact it might be proven that Christ had had the power of doing even such (miracles)."

31. *Adv. Hær.*, II, 31 : 2: Speaking of the followers of one Simon, and their inability to work miracles, Irenæus proceeds (Bernard's translation): "They can neither give sight to the blind, nor hearing to the deaf, nor put to flight all demons, except those which are sent into others by themselves, if they can, indeed, even do this. Nor can they cure the weak, or the lame, or the paralytic, or those that are troubled in any other part of the body, as often happens to be done in respect of bodily infirmity. Nor can they furnish effective remedies for those external accidents which may occur. And so far are they from raising the dead as the Lord raised them, and the Apostles did by means of prayer, and as when frequently in the brotherhood, the whole church in the locality, having made petition with much fasting and prayer, the spirit of the dead one has returned ($\epsilon\pi\epsilon\sigma\tau\rho\epsilon\psi\epsilon$), and the man has been given back ($\epsilon\chi\alpha\rho\iota\sigma\theta\eta$) to the prayers of the saints—(so far are they from doing this) that they do not believe that it can possibly be done, and they think that resurrection from the dead means a rejection of the truth of their tenets." *Adv. Hær.*, II, 32 : 4: "Those who are in truth the Lord's disciples, having received grace from Him, do in His name perform (miracles) for the benefit of other men, according to the gift which each one has received from Him. For some certainly and truly drive out demons, so that those who have been cleansed from the evil spirits frequently be-

lieve and are in the church. Others have foreknowledge of things to come, and visions, and prophetic warnings. Others heal the sick by imposition of their hands, and they are restored to health. Yea, moreover, as we said, even the dead were raised and abode with us many years (ἠγέρθησαν καὶ παρέμειναν σὺν ἡμῖν ἱκανοῖς ἔτεσι). What more shall I say? It is not possible to tell the number of the gifts which the church throughout the world has received from God in the name of Jesus Christ, who was crucified under Pontius Pilate, and which she exerts day by day for the welfare of the nations, neither deceiving any, nor taking any reward for such. For as freely as she hath received from God, so freely doth she minister." It is quite clear that in II, 32 : 4 Irenæus throws the raisings from the dead well into the past. This is made evident not only from the past tenses employed, which are markedly contrasted with the present tenses used in the rest of the passage, but also from the statement that those who were thus raised had lived after their resuscitation a considerable number of years, which shows that recent resuscitations are not in view. The passage in II, 31 : 2, ambiguous in itself, is explained by II, 32 : 4, which Irenæus himself represents as a repetition of it ("as we said"). It appears, then, that in neither passage has Irenæus recent instances in view—and there is no reason why the cases he has in mind may not have occurred during the lifetime of the Apostles or of Apostolic men.

32. As cited, p. 164. *Cf.* Douglas, as cited in note 24.

33. Th. Trede, *Wunderglaube im Heidentum und in der alten Kirche*, 1901, pp. 83–88, brings together the instances from the literature. No doubt the heathen did not really believe in these resuscitations, at least when they were instructed men. It did not require a Lucian to scoff at them: Minucius Felix (*Octavius*, chap. 11 *ad fin.*) makes his Cæcilius remark that despite the long time that has passed away, the innumerable ages that have flowed by, no single individual has returned from the dead, either by the fate of Protesilaus, with permission to sojourn even a few hours, or to serve as an example to men. The Christians, he asserts, in teaching a resurrection from the dead, have but revamped the figments of an unwholesome belief with which deceiving poets have trifled in sweet verses.

34. *Cf.* Erwin Rohde, *Der griechische Roman und seine Vorläufer*, 1900, p. 287, note 1. Also Origen, *Contra Celsum*, 2 : 16, 48–58. The famous physician Asclepiades is said to have met a funeral procession and detected that the corpse was still living (Pliny, *Nat. Hist.*, 7 : 124; *cf.* Weinreich, p. 173). Apuleius, *Flor.*, 19, re-

lates this as an actual resuscitation. The texts may be conveniently consulted in Paul Fiebig, *Antike Wundergeschichten*, etc., 1911.

35. *Cf.* F. C. Baur, *Apollonius von Tyana und Christus*, p. 140.

36. *Antike Heilungswunder*, 1909, pp. 171–174.

37. Weinreich, as cited, p. 171, note 1; R. Reitzenstein, *Hellenistische Wundererzählungen*, 1906, p. 41, note 3.

38. Philostratus, *The Life of Apollonius of Tyana*, etc., with an English translation by F. C. Conybeare (The Loeb Classical Library), vol. I, 1912, pp. 457 ff.

39. *Cf.* E. von Dobschütz, "Der Roman in der Altchristlichen Literatur," in the *Deutsche Rundschau*, vol. CXI, April, 1902, p. 105. He remarks: "To that we owe it that so many of these legends have been preserved."

40. Von Dobschütz, as cited, p. 88. "I think that I may venture to say," says Reitzenstein, *op. cit.*, p. 55, "that the literary model of the Christian Acts of the Apostles was supplied by the Aretalogies of prophets and philosophers. We should not think merely of the few which accident has preserved for us—and that exclusively in literary reworkings or parodies; a certain importance attaches to the connection of one of these essentially anonymous miracle-stories already with Athenodorus, the Stoic teacher of Augustus."

41. Perhaps we may roughly represent these two things by "romance" and "fable."

42. *Op. cit.*, p. 97.

43. As cited, p. 100.

44. As cited, pp. 100 ff.

45. On Greek and Latin fiction, the short article by Louis H. Gray in Hastings's *Encyclopædia of Religion and Ethics*, vol. VI, pp. 6–8, may be consulted, and the work on which Gray chiefly depends, F. M. Warren, *History of the Novel Previous to the Seventeenth Century*, 1890, pp. 21 ff. A good brief account of Greek and early Christian novels is given by T. R. Glover, in the last chapter of his *Life and Letters in the Fourth Century*, 1901, pp. 357–386. The German replica of this is Von Dobschütz's essay already mentioned. The great work on the Greek romances is Erwin Rohde's, already mentioned, by the side of which should be placed E. Schwartz, *Fünf Vorträge über den Griechen Roman*, 1896, and A. Chassang, *Histoire du Roman dans l'Antiquité Grecque et Latine*, 1862. Reitzenstein, in the book already mentioned, seeks to introduce more precision into the treatment of literary forms. See also the concluding chapter on *Die Bekenner-vitæ* in E. Günter's *Legenden-Studien*,

1906 (*cf.* also his *Die christliche Legende des Abendlandes*, 1910), and *cf.* G. H. Gerould, *Saints' Legends*, 1916, pp. 33 f.

46. The use to which this opinion, become traditional, is put, may be illustrated by its employment by Charles Herman Lea, *A Plea . . . for Christian Science*, 1915, p. 58, and its similar employment by Samuel McComb, *Religion and Medicine*, 1908, pp. 295 ff. The former writes: "In the early years of the Christian Church, this command to heal the sick appears to have been fulfilled to a considerable degree, and history records that Christian healing was practiced until the end of the third century. Then it appears to have been gradually discontinued, as the spiritual life of the church declined, until the power was entirely lost sight of in the gross materialism that culminated in the union of Church and State. That the power to heal is not generally possessed by the 'Christian' Church to-day is certain; nor could anything be more misleading than the idea, sometimes propounded from the pulpits, that the ability to heal was withdrawn because it became no longer necessary for the church to give such evidence of God's power, and of their understanding of Him. For this very power was the evidence that Jesus Christ himself gave as proof of the truth of his teaching. Hence, one of the questions that the churches of Christendom need to face to-day is, 'Why are we unable to fulfil our Lord's clear and express command?' Is it because they do not correctly understand his teaching, or because they do not consider obedience to him, in this respect, necessary? Or has the church not yet risen above the materialism that marked its decadence in the early centuries of its history?" "Perhaps nowhere in history," writes McComb, "can we find the power of faith to heal disorders of a semi-moral and semi-nervous character so strikingly illustrated as in the early centuries of the church's existence. The literature of the ante-Nicene period is permeated with a sense of conquest over sickness, disease, and moral ills of every kind. . . . Gibbon, in his famous fifteenth chapter, mentions as the third cause of the spread of Christianity, 'the miraculous powers of the primitive church,' among which he names the expulsion of demons, but he dismisses the whole matter with a scoff as a product of superstition. Wider knowledge now shows that the historian's skepticism was quite unjustified. There is abundant testimony that one of the most important factors of the early propaganda of the Christian faith was an especial power which Christians seemed to have over various psychical disturbances. . . . Even so late as the time of Augustine, we find a belief in the healing power of faith still existent. In his *City of God* he describes various healing-wonders of

which he was an eye-witness, and which were done in the name of Christ." The entire angle of vision here is unhistorical.

47. John Lightfoot (*Works*, Pittman's 8 vol. ed., vol. III, p. 204) suggests as the reason for these two exceptions: "The Holy Ghost at this its first bestowing upon the Gentiles is given in the like manner as it was at its first bestowing on the Jewish nation,— namely, by immediate infusion; at all other times you find mention of it, you find mention of imposition of hands used for it."

48. Acts 9 : 12–17 is no exception, as is sometimes said; Ananias worked a miracle on Paul but did not confer miracle-working powers. Paul's own power of miracle-working was original with him as an Apostle, and not conferred by any one.

49. Schaff-Herzog, *Encyclopedia of Religious Knowledge*, 1st edition, vol. II, p. 873.

50. The connection of the "signs and wonders and manifold powers of the Holy Ghost" in some particular fashion with the first generation of Christians—"them that heard" the Lord, that is to say, at least the Apostolic generation, possibly specifically the Apostles—seems to be implied in Heb. 2 : 4. That Paul regards the charismata as "credentials of the Apostolic mission" (possibly even Rom. 1 : 11 may be cited here) is clear even to J. A. MacCulloch (Hastings's *E R E.*, VIII, p. 683 b), although he himself doubts the soundness of this view. A. Schlatter (Hastings's *Dictionary of the Apostolic Church*, I, 577 a) says with great distinctness: "The Gospels, the Book of Acts, and the utterances of St. Paul regarding his 'signs' (II Cor. 12 : 12), all show distinctly that miracles were intimately related to the Apostolic function."

51. *The Ecclesiastical History of the Second and Third Centuries, Illustrated from the Writings of Tertullian*, 1825; 2d ed., 1826; 3d ed., 1845, pp. 98 ff.

52. Bernard, as cited, p. 130, gives his acceptance to Kaye's view, speaking of "that power which in the days of the Apostles was confined to them and those on whom they had laid their hands." B. F. Manire, in an article on the "Work of the Holy Spirit," in *The New Christian Quarterly*, IV, 2, p. 38 (April, 1895), gives exceptionally clear expression to the facts: "The matter of imparting the Holy Ghost through the laying on of their hands, belonged exclusively, as it appears to me, to the Apostles, and therefore passed away with them. . . . Others besides the Apostles could preach the Gospel 'with the Holy Spirit sent down from heaven,' and could work miracles in confirmation of their testimony; but only the Apostles by the imposition of their own hands could impart the Holy Spirit to others in its wonder-working power.

To me it appears that the bestowal of this power on the Apostles was the highest testimonial of their official character and authority." Paton J. Gloag comments on Acts 8 : 15–16 thus: "By the Holy Ghost here is not to be understood the ordinary or sanctifying influences of the Spirit. The Samaritans, in the act of believing the gospel, received the Holy Ghost in this sense. . . . The miraculous influences of the Spirit, which are manifested by speaking with tongues and prophesyings, are here meant. As Calvin remarks, 'He speaks not in this place of the common grace of the Spirit, whereby God regenerates us that we may be His children, but of those singular gifts whereby God would have certain endowed, at the beginning of the Gospel, to beautify the Kingdom of Christ.' But the question arises, Why could not Philip bestow the Holy Ghost? . . . The common opinion appears to be the correct one —namely, that Philip could not bestow the Holy Ghost because he was not an Apostle. This, though not expressly stated, yet seems implied in the narrative. So Chrysostom and Epiphanius among the fathers, and Grotius, Lightfoot, DeWette, Baumgarten, Meyer, Olshausen, and Wordsworth among the moderns." John Lightfoot holds that the charismata were not conferred indiscriminately on all but only on a select few, to endow them (a plurality in each church) for the office of "minister." But that these gifts were conferred only by laying on the Apostles' hands he is clear. Cf. Works, ed. Pittman, vol. III, p. 30: "To give the Holy Ghost was a peculiar prerogative of the Apostles"; vol. III, p. 194, commenting on Acts 8: "Philip baptized Samaritans and did great wonders among them, but could not bestow the Holy Ghost upon them: that power belonged only to the Apostles; therefore Peter and John are sent thither for that purpose."

53. *Encyclopedia of Sacred Theology*, E. T., 1898, p. 368; cf. pp. 355 ff.

54. *Institutes of the Christian Religion*, E. T., by John Allen; ed. Philadelphia, 1909, vol. I, pp. 26 ff.: "Their requiring miracles of us is altogether unreasonable; for we forge no new Gospel, but retain the very same whose truth was confirmed by all the miracles ever wrought by Christ and the Apostles"—and so forth.

55. *Gereformeerde Dogmatiek²*, I, pp. 363 f.

56. On Wesley's relations with Middleton, see F. J. Snell, *Wesley and Methodism*, 1900, pp. 151 ff.

57. *Free Answer to Dr. Middleton's Free Inquiry*, etc., 1749.

58. *A Vindication of the Miraculous Powers which Subsisted in the Three First Centuries of the Christian Church*, 1750. Chapman's *Miraculous Powers of the Primitive Church*, 1752 (following up his

Discovery of the Miraculous Powers of the Primitive Church, 1747) came too late to be included in Middleton's *Vindication*.

59. The literature of the subject has been intimated in the course of the lecture. By the side of Middleton's *Free Inquiry* may be placed J. Douglas, *The Criterion; or rules by which the True Miracles recorded in the New Testament are distinguished from the Spurious miracles of Pagans and Papists*, 1752, new edd. 1857, etc., 1867; and Isaac Taylor, *Ancient Christianity*, 1839; ed. 4, 1844, vol. II, pp. 233–365. *Cf.* also Lecture VIII in J. B. Mozley, *Eight Lectures on Miracles*, 1865. Of J. H. Newman's *Two Essays on Scripture Miracles and on Ecclesiastical*, some account will be given in the next lecture. By its side should be placed Horace Bushnell's eloquent argument for the continuation of miracles in the church in the fourteenth chapter of his *Nature and the Supernatural* (1858; ed. 4, 1859, pp. 446–492).

NOTES TO LECTURE II

PATRISTIC AND MEDIÆVAL MARVELS

1. *Horæ Sabbaticæ*, vol. II, pp. 413 ff.
2. Gregory's Panegyric on Gregory Thaumaturgus is described and characterized, and its true character shown, by Th. Trede, *Wunderglaube im Heidentum und in der alten Kirche*, 1900, pp. 144 ff.: "Our declaimer attains the climax of rhetorical fire-works in his Christian Panegyric on Gregory Thaumaturgus." In this connection Trede makes some very illuminating remarks on the transference into the church of the bad traditions of the heathen rhetorical schools in which so many of the Christian leaders had their training.
3. Cap. 8.
4. The confidence which Augustine reposed in these narratives is perhaps most strongly shown in such an incidental remark as meets us in the *City of God*, 22 : 28. He is speaking of Plato and Cornelius Labeo, and reporting what they say of resuscitations. He remarks: "But the resurrection which these writers instance resembles that of those persons whom we have ourselves known to rise again, and who came back indeed to this life, but not so as never to die again." Augustine supposes himself to have actually known people once dead to have come back to this life; he has no doubt of it at all.
5. Raising the dead, so common an occurrence in Augustine's day, seems later to have passed somewhat out of fashion. John of Salisbury, at all events, when speaking of the miracles wrought at

the tomb of Thomas à Becket († 1170), includes this among them, but speaks of it as something new to experience: "And (a thing unheard of from the days of our fathers) the dead are raised" (E. A. Abbott, *St. Thomas of Canterbury*, 1898, I, p. 227, *cf.* II, p. 17, and, in general, the Index *sub voc.*, "Death, Restoration from"). Later, however, this miracle recovered its popularity. No less than fourteen instances of it are attributed to Francis Xavier—although he himself, unfortunately, died without knowledge of them. Andrew D. White (*The Warfare of Science with Theology in Christendom*, ed. 1896, vol. II, p. 17) sums up the facts thus: "Although during the lifetime of Xavier there is neither in his own writings, nor in any contemporary account any assertion of a resurrection from the dead wrought by him, we find that shortly after his death such stories began to appear. A simple statement of the growth of these may throw some light on the evolution of miraculous accounts generally. At first it was affirmed that some people at Cape Comorin said that he had raised one person; then it was said that he had raised two persons; then in various authors—Emmanuel Acosta, in his commentaries written as an afterthought nearly twenty years after Xavier's death, De Quadros and others—the story wavers between one and two cases; finally in the time of Tursellinus, four cases had been developed. In 1622, at the canonization proceedings, three were mentioned; but by the time of Father Bonhours there were fourteen, all raised from the dead by Xavier himself during his lifetime, and the name, place, and circumstances are given with much detail in each case." The references to Bonhours are given thus: *The Life of St. Francis Xavier*, by Father Dominic Bonhours, translated by James Dryden, Dublin, 1838, pp. 69, 82, 93, 111, 218, 307, 316, 321. For the repeated occurrence of raisings of the dead in mediæval legend, see H. Günter, *Die christliche Legende des Abendlandes*, 1910, pp. 25, 32, 43, 47, 191; it is, in spite of John of Salisbury's ignorance of it, of common occurrence in the legends. An instructive instance is repeated to us by H. Delehaye, *Les Légendes Hagiographiques*, 1905, p. 101: "When St. Bernard was preaching the crusade in the diocese of Constance, an archer in the following of the Duke of Zähringen jeered at his preaching and at the preacher himself, saying, 'He cannot work miracles any more than I can.' When the saint proceeded to lay his hands on the sick, the mocker saw it, and suddenly fell over as if dead; he remained a considerable time without consciousness. Alexander of Cologne adds: 'I was close to him when the thing happened. . . . We called the Abbé, and this poor man could not get up until Bernard came, made a prayer and lifted him up.' No single eye-witness says a word which can make us think of a resuscitation of a dead man. Yet, a century later, Herbert, author of a collection of the miracles of St. Bernard, Conrad, author of the *Exordium*, and Cesar of Heisterbach, affirm that the archer was dead and the saint restored him to life." Delehaye refers to G. Hüffer, *Der heilige Bernard von Clairvaux*, vol. I (Münster, 1886), pp. 92, 182.

6. 25 : 47.

7. § 34: *Nicene and Post-Nicene Fathers*, vol. III, p. 364.

8. I, 14, 5.

9. I, 13, 7.

10. *Ibid.*

11. *Nicene and Post-Nicene Fathers*, vol. I, p. 346.

12. *Tract. in Joh.*, 13, (15): *Nicene and Post-Nicene Fathers*, vol. VII, p. 93. When he says: "Contra istos, ut sic loquar, mirabiliarios cautum me fecit Deus meus, he is obviously using a contemptuous term.

13. *City of God*, 22, 10, at the end.

14. On Augustine's doctrine of miracles, see especially, Friedrich Nitzsch, *Augustinus' Lehre vom Wunder*, 1865; especially pp. 32–35 on the "Continuance of Miracles in the Church," and pp. 35–37, "Miracles outside the limits of the Revelation-history and the Church."

15. *City of God*, 22, 8.

16. *Cf.* T. R. Glover, *Life and Letters in the Fourth Century*, 1901, pp. 40, 287.

17. How little the abounding miracles of the lives of the saints were noted—or we should better say, known—in mediæval times, we may learn from a remark of H. Günter's (*Legenden-Studien*, 1906, pp. 176 f.): "For the proper estimate of these things we must bear in mind that contemporary profane history very essentially corrects the literature of the *Lives:* the very names which here seem to move the world, scarcely receive bare mention there: of the flood of miracles in the *Lives* there is not even a trace. The Chronicles and Annalists were nevertheless children of those times, and receptive enough for everything that was miraculous. The notion which might occur to one, that the Chronicles, the newspapers of the day, purposely left the domain of the saints to biography and romance, is clearly untenable. He who reads Widukind's *History of the Saxons*, the *Continuatio Regionis*, the *Chronicle* of Thietmar of Merceberg, will not fail to learn of the saints of the Saxon period. Thietmar's description of the saint-bishop and ascetic Eido of Meissen (VIII, c. 25) is a true classic. But saints in the same sense of the legend, these figures are not."

18. *Dial.*, III, 5.

19. *Dial.*, I, 26.

20. *Cf.* T. R. Glover, as cited, p. 289: "Sulpicius says, and it is not improbable that he is presenting Martin's view, as well as his own, that to doubt these marvels of healing, etc., is to diminish the credibility of the gospel, 'for when the Lord Himself testified that such works as Martin did were to be done by all the faithful, he who does not believe Martin did them, does not believe Christ said so.' Perhaps the logic is not above suspicion, but it is clear that it was held Martin's miracles were proven no less by the words of the gospel than by ocular evidence." J. H. Newman had already made much the same remark, *Two Essays on Scripture Miracles and on Ecclesiastical*, p. 209: "Sulpicius almost grounds his defence of St. Martin's miracles on the antecedent force of this text." It would be a curious and not unprofitable study to ascertain how large a part this spurious text has had in producing spurious miracles in all ages of the church.

21. Ep. 22 : 9; *Nicene and Post-Nicene Fathers*, p. 438.

22. *Hom. on I Cor.* 6 : 2, 3 (Hom. 6, vol. X, p. 45).

23. *Hom.* 8, *in Col.* No. 5 (vol. XI, p. 387).

24. *Cf. e. 'g. Hom. 24 in Joan.* (vol. VIII, p. 138); *Hom. in Iscr. Act.* (vol. III, p. 60).

25. *De. Sacerd.*, lib. 4; *Opera*, ed. Sav., vol. VI, p. 35.

26. Ep. 4 : 80.

27. *In Evang.*, 2, 29.

28. Isid. Hispal. *Sententiarum* lib. 1, cap. 27; ed. Col. Agripp., 1617, p. 424.

29. *Serm. i. de Ascens.*, 2.

30. The Patristic citations in this paragraph have been taken largely, without verification, from Newman, *op. cit.*, pp. 135 ff., 208, and W. Goode, *The Modern Claims to the Possession of the Extraordinary Gifts of the Spirit*, 1834, pp. 4 ff., 275 ff. *Cf.* also A. Tholuck, *Vermischte Schriften*, I, pp. 35 ff. Such passages abound. H. Günter, *Legenden-Studien*, 1906, pp. 77 ff., very naturally raises the question whether the legends of the Middle Ages really wished to be believed, and whether they were believed. His conclusion is that there can be no doubt that they were put forth as literal facts, but that the credit accorded to them by men of independent mind left certainly something to be desired. "No one of the theologians of importance," he remarks (p. 82), "ever made an attempt to support scientific speculations by appeals to legendary tales as historical evidence, no matter how near at hand an illustration from them lay." *Cf.* what he says in *Legenden-Studien*, 1906, p. 132: "I think it is not by accident, when Cassian observes that the

monks of his time—he died in 435—were no longer subjected to the power of the demons as the 'Fathers' were. Similarly Gregory the Great later finds that miracles do not manifest themselves now as in the past (*Dial.*, I, c. 12). And the same reflection is repeated dozens of times in the literature of the Middle Ages. Is there not a sufficient suggestion in this?"

31. *The History of the Decline and Fall of the Roman Empire*, ed. Smith, 1887, vol. II, p. 180, note 81.

32. *Op. cit.*, p. 220.

33. Among the many anomalies of the legends of the saints, the question asks itself why the saints, many of whom had severe sufferings to undergo, many of whom were lifelong invalids, never rescued or healed themselves by the exercise of their miraculous powers? Bernard of Clairvaux, for example, when in extremities, needed to be saved from without—by the intervention of Mary, who gave him her breast. Christina Mirabilis, it is true, nourished herself with her own virgin milk; but this is an exception to the general rule. It is a proverb, "Physician, heal thyself"; yet even the most diseased of the saints did not do it—and all of them apparently died. That the Martyr-heroes of the Martyr-aretalogies ultimately succeeded in dying is a standing wonder. They are delivered apparently from every imaginable, and often unimaginable, peril, at the cost of every imaginable, and often unimaginable, miracle; fire will not burn them, nor steel cut their flesh; the sea will not drown them, nor will chains bind them. They bear a charmed life and walk unscathed through every conceivable danger. And then suddenly their heads are simply chopped off as if it were the most natural thing in the world—and they are dead. The reader catches his breath and cannot believe his eyes: the exceeding *sang-froid* with which the author kills at the end those whom nothing can harm in the meantime produces nothing less than an enormous anticlimax. Has the miracle-power of the martyr given suddenly out—been all used up in its wonderful action hitherto? Or is it merely that the invention of the author has been exhausted, and he has to close thus lamely because he can think of nothing else to say? We have something of the same feeling when we contemplate sick saints healing others with wonderful facility, while apparently wholly without power to heal themselves. Is it adequate to say with Percy Dearmer (*Body and Soul*, p. 133): "And often, when they healed others they did not spare the strength to heal themselves; often they endured without thinking of themselves the infirmities which they could not bear to see unhelped in others. They thought so much of One of whom it is said, 'He saved others;

Himself He cannot save.'" The suggested comparison with Christ is, of course, offensive. The sufferings of the saints are not expiatory sacrifices offered to God in behalf of a sinful world—although it must be sadly acknowledged that many of them (e. g., the Stigmatics) fancied they were. Christ could not save Himself, not because He lacked the power to do so, but because the work which He came to do was precisely suffering—to give His life a ransom for many. There was no more reason in the nature of things, on the other hand, why the saints should suffer than others. And the description which Dearmer gives of the saints is not true to life, in many instances at least. They do not seem to have borne their sufferings without thinking of them; they apparently thought a great deal of them, either to bewail them or, by a spiritual perversion, to glory in them as a mark of spiritual distinction. And how does it do to say in one sentence, "The saints have always seemed to regard their healing works as easy things, done by the way and out of compassion"; and then in the next, "They did not spare the strength to heal themselves"? If it cost them nothing to heal —if they did it with a passing wave of the hand—why should they have not healed themselves? The sicknesses of the saints is a standing puzzle.

34. Horstman, *Richard Rolle of Hampole*, vol. II, p. xxviii.

35. *Cf.* H. Günter, *Die christliche Legende des Abendlandes*, 1910, p. 187, who cites the Vita of St. Gongolf at the end of the ninth century, and Gislebert of Sens, about 1150, as declaring that in the absence of good merit miracles are nothing, since they are performed by many evil men; as also the archdeacon Robert of Ostrevand in his life of Aybert, of the same age, who remarks that the virtue of love which belongs to the good alone is of far more worth than the virtue of miracles which belongs alike to good and evil. *Cf.* also the like citation from Thomas of Reuil. Günter refers on the general matter to L. Zöpf, *Das Heiligen-Leben in 10 Jahrh.* in "Beiträge z. Kulturgesch. des Mittelalters u. des Renaissance," herausgegeben von W. Götz, Heft 1 (1908), pp. 62 f., pp. 181 ff.

36. This is of course the established doctrine; *cf. The Catholic Encyclopedia*, vol. X, 1911, p. 351, where Benedict XIV is quoted (on *Heroic Virtue*, 1851, III, p. 130) to the effect that, since the gift of miracle-working is a grace *gratis data*, it is independent of the merit of the recipient; even bad men might be granted it (for God's own purposes) and good men denied it. It forms no ground of inference then to saintliness. But do not difficulties arise then with reference to the customs of "canonization"?

37. Vol. II, p. 2049. On miracles connected with the host, see

very especially Yrjö Hirn, *The Sacred Shrine*, 1912, pp. 120 ff., with the literature given on pp. 502 ff.

38. Newman, as cited, p. 134.

39. Middleton, as cited, vol. I, p. li.

40. Smith and Cheatham, as cited.

41. *Dict. des Prophéties et des Miracles* (Migne), vol. I, p. 370. For the miracle of Bolsena and its significance in the historical development of the legends, see H. Günter, *Legenden-Studien*, 1906, pp. 174 ff.; *cf.* Yrjö Hirn, *The Sacred Shrine*, 1912, pp. 103 f.

42. Deut. 13 : 1 ff.

43. *Biblical Repertory and Princeton Review*, April, 1856, pp. 255–285, article on "Miracles and their Counterfeits."

44. As cited, p. 99.

45. Pp. 115 ff.

46. Pp. 150 f.

47. This portion of Fleury's great *Histoire Ecclésiastique* (Paris, 1691–1720, 20 vols., quarto), from 381 to 400 A. D., translated by Herbert (London, 1828), was republished in three volumes, Oxford, 1842, in a text carefully revised by Newman, and supplied with this introduction.

48. P. 188.

49. Nor indeed can John T. Driscoll writing as late as 1911 (*The Catholic Encyclopedia*, X, p. 346). If we may judge from reports of cases in the public press, modern surgery provides numerous similar instances. We have happened to clip the following two examples. The New York *Tribune* for May 6, 1901: "William H. Crampton, the lecturer, who some time ago had the greater part of his tongue cut out on account of a cancerous growth, is now able to articulate slowly so that he can make himself understood. . . . Crampton, who for some years has made his living by lecturing, just before the operation was performed, spent two days in delivering his lectures into a phonograph. His idea was that when he left the hospital, bereft of speech, as he anticipated, he would still be able to earn a living by giving phonograph lectures. . . . Doctor L. S. Pitcher, of the staff of the Seney Hospital, who performed the operation, has asked Mr. Crampton to appear before the next meeting of the Brooklyn Surgical Society in order that its members may get a thorough understanding of the case. Mr. Crampton will have his phonograph records with him to show the effects of the operation upon his speech." The Lexington (Ky.) *Leader*, January 11, 1906 (Associated Press Telegram): "Chicago, Jan'y 10.—Frederick Power, actor and stage-manager, who had his tongue cut from his mouth in an operation for cancer five weeks

ago, is again able to talk so as to be understood. The case is said by physicians to be a remarkable triumph for surgery. All of Mr. Power's tongue and part of the root had to be removed in the operation. With his tongue gone, he is able to articulate, uttering some words quite distinctly. For several days Mr. Power has been attempting to sing, and the hospital attendants say that while the efforts were not entirely successful, they have encouraged the patient and made him quite hopeful. There is still some paralysis in Mr. Power's lower lip, due to the operation, and there is a heavy gold bridge in his mouth. His jaw is still held in a heavy plaster cast, and when these impediments are removed it is believed he will be able to articulate fairly well."

50. *Philomythus : An Antidote against Credulity. A Discussion of Cardinal Newman's Essay on Ecclesiastical Miracles.* By Edwin A. Abbott, 1891. Second edition, 1891.

51. *St. Thomas of Canterbury: His Death and Miracles.* By Edwin A. Abbott, M.A., D.D., 2 vols., 1898.

52. P. 189.

53. *Loc. cit.*, p. 105, note 2.

54. *Op. cit.*, p. 55; *cf.* pp. 82 ff.

55. Pp. 54 ff.

56. *Loc. cit.*, p. 384.

57. Pp. 81 f. On the integrity of the present text of the *Life of Hilarion*, see H. Günter, *Legenden-Studien*, 1906, p. 130, note 3.

58. Th. Trede, in the chapter on "Mönchtum," in his *Wunderglaube im Heidentum und in der alten Kirche*, 1901, has some very useful remarks (pp. 213 ff.) on Athanasius's *Life of Antony* and its relation to the miracle-love of the times. "As apostle of Monasticism," he says, "Athanasius becomes a rhetorician, with reference to whom we ask, Where does fancy stop and where does reality begin? When the great doctor of the church assures us that he has throughout looked only to the truth, his idea of the truth was not different from that which we have found among other leaders of the church and permitted him such means to reach his purpose as were looked upon as self-evident in the heathen notions of the time." With an appeal, then, to Lucian's exposition of the different laws which govern history and panegyrics (*The Way to Write History*, 7 and 8: "The panegyrist has only one concern—to commend and gratify his living theme some way or other; if misrepresentation will serve his purpose, he has no objection to that. History, on the other hand, abhors the intrusion of any least scruple of falsehood . . ."), he continues: "The *Life of Antony* by Athanasius is a panegyric, just such as Gregory of Nyssa wrote about Gregory

Thaumaturgus. . . ." When Gregory of Nazianzus describes Athanasius as setting forth in this book "ἐν πλάσματι of a narrative, the laws of the monastic life" (*Oration* XXI, 5, *Post-Nicene Fathers*, p. 270), does he not really suggest that it is fiction, in part at least? Trede discusses in a similar spirit Jerome's *Lives of Paul* and *Hilarion*. On the *Vita Pauli*, see Weingarten, *PRE²*, X, 760, and Grützmacher *PRE³*, XIII, 217. The reality of Paul's existence is defended by Butler, *The Lausiac History*, I, 231, and Workman, *The Evolution of the Monastic Ideal*, 1913, p. 96, both of whom defend also the historicity of the *Life of Antony*, I, 178 and 354 respectively. *The Lausiac History* is interpreted as a mere romance also by Lucius and Amélineau, but defended as history by Butler, I, 257 ff. There is a good brief statement of Athanasius's relation to miracle-working in the *Vita Antonii* and elsewhere, in A. Robertson's preface to the English translation of the *Vita Antonii* printed in the *Nicene and Post-Nicene Fathers*, II, II, p. 192.

59. *Das Mönchthum, seine Ideale und seine Geschichte*,[1] 1881, p. 21; ed. 3, 1886, p. 27; *cf.* G. Grützmacher, *Hieronymus*, I, p. 162.

60. *Op. cit.*, pp. 1 f.

61. See *Acts of Peter and Andrew*, in the *Ante-Nicene Fathers*, Am. ed., vol. VIII, p. 527: "Peter says to him: One thing I say unto thee: it is easier for a camel to go through the eye of a needle, than for a rich man to go into the kingdom of heaven. When Onesiphorus heard this, he was still more filled with rage and anger, . . . saying, . . . If thou wilt show me this miracle, I will believe in thy God, . . . but if not thou shalt be grievously punished. . . . The Saviour appeared . . . and he says to them, Be courageous and tremble not, my chosen disciples, for I am with you always: let the needle and camel be brought. . . . And there was a certain merchant in the city, who had believed in the Lord, . . . and, . . . he ran and searched for a needle with a big eye, to do a favour to the Apostles. When Peter learned this, he said, My son, do not search for a big needle, for nothing is impossible with God: rather bring us a small needle. And after the needle had been brought . . . Peter looked up and saw a camel coming. . . . Then he fixed the needle in the ground, and cried out with a loud voice, saying, In the name of Jesus Christ, who was crucified under Pontius Pilate, I order thee, O camel, to go through the eye of the needle. Then the eye of the needle was opened like a gate, and the camel went through it, and all the multitude saw it. And Peter says to the camel: Go again through the needle. And the camel went through the second time." Even this is not enough. Onesiphorus now provides a needle and a camel of his own, and

sets a woman on the camel—and the same thing is done. Is not the conception here, mere magic?

62. *The Ancient Catholic Church*, 1902, pp. 302 f.

63. *Cäsarius von Arelate*, 1894, p. 165.

64. P. 166, note 545 (see Migne, *Pat. Lat.*, XXXIX, 2257, 3).

65. E. T., pp. 33 f. His reference is Cesar of Heisterbach, *Dialogus miraculorum* (Strange's ed., Cologne, 1851, 2 vols., 8vo; vol. II, pp. 255 and 125).

66. Sabatier, *op. cit.*, p. 192. His references are: Egbert von Schönau's *Contra Catharos*, Serm. I, cap. 2 (Migne, *Pat. Lat.*, vol. CXCV), *cf.* Heisterbach, *loc. cit.*, 5 : 18; Luc de Tuy's *De altera Vita*, lib. 2 : 9; 3 : 9, 18 (Migne, *Pat. Lat.*, vol. CCVIII).

67. *Inquisit. in verit. Miraculor. F. de Paris*, sec. 1, as cited by Newman, *op. cit.*, p. 90, note l. On the Jansenist miracles *cf.* the excellent criticism of A. Tholuck, *Vermischte Schriften*, 1839, I, pp. 133–148; he mentions the chief sources of information, among which *cf.* especially Carré de Montgeron, *La Verité des Miracles Operés par l'Intercession de M. de Paris et Autres Appelans*, Cologne, 1747, with the comments on it by J. M. Charcot in *The New Review*, January, 1893, vol. VIII, pp. 25 ff., and the comment on Charcot's use of this book by G. Bertrin, *Lourdes*, E. T., 1908, pp. 138 ff. On the use made of these miracles by Hume, see James Orr, *Hume*, p. 215, who refers us for the real facts to Campbell and Leland.

68. *Cf.* Middleton, as cited, I, p. 357; Newman, as cited, p. 45; Hastings's *Encyclopædia of Religion and Ethics*, vol. VII, p. 480.

69. The first of the ten miracles which Montgeron discusses at large was wrought on a young Spaniard, who was stone blind in one eye and saw but dimly with the other. Only the better eye was healed, and the famous oculist Gendron told him that he ought to be content with that, since the restoration of the other eye, in which many parts were absolutely destroyed, would require a miracle of creation comparable to giving a cripple two new legs, and no one ever heard of such a miracle. Yet Charlotte Laborde, we are told, who on the certificate of two surgeons had no legs at all, recovered a serviceable pair by one of these Jansenist miracles. Here is a miracle which overtops all other miracles—even that of the famous Pierre de Rudder at Lourdes, who only had an old fracture of the leg mended. Compare pp. 118 ff.

70. The literature of the subject is sufficiently intimated in the course of the lecture. The following may be profitably consulted: E. Lucius (ed. G. Anrich), *Die Anfänge des Heiligenkults in der christlichen Kirche*, 1904; H. Achelis, "Die Martyrologien, ihre Ge-

schichte und ihr Wert," in the *Abhandlungen d. kaiserl. Gesellschaft des Wissensch. zu Göttingen*, N. F. III, 1900; P. Allard, *Dix leçons sur le martyre*[3], 1907 (E. T. by L. Cappadelta, *Ten Lectures on the Martyrs*); L. Leclercq, *Les Martyrs*, 1902–1906; A. van Gennep, *La Formation des Légendes*, 1910; H. Delehaye, *Les Légendes Hagiographiques*, 1905 (E. T. by N. M. Crawford, *The Legends of the Saints*); H. Günter, *Legenden-Studien*, 1906, *Die christliche Legende des Abendlandes*, 1910, article "Legends of the Saints" in the *Catholic Encyclopedia;* E. von Dobschütz, article "Legende" in Haupt-Herzog[3]; G. H. Gerould, *Saints' Legends*, 1916.

Naturally the same infection from heathenism which produced the Christian miracles of these ages, showed itself also among the Jews. For the earliest period, see P. Fiebig, *Jüdische Wunder-geschichten des neutestamentl. Zeitalters*, 1911 (original texts in same author's *Rabbinische Wunderges. d. N. T. Zeitalters*, 1911). S. Schechter (*Jewish Quarterly Review*, April, 1900, pp. 431–432) writes: "Again our knowledge of the spiritual history of the Jews during the first centuries of our era might be enriched by a chapter on Miracles. Starting from the principle that miracles can only be explained by more miracles, an attempt was made some years ago by a student to draw up a list of the wonder-workings of the Rabbis recorded in the Talmud and the Midrashim. He applied himself to the reading of these works, but his reading was only cursory. The list, therefore, is not complete. Still it yielded a harvest of not less than two hundred and fifty miracles. They cover all classes of supernatural workings recorded in the Bible, but occur with much greater frequency." As the Christians did not think of denying the reality of the heathen miracles, but had their own way of accounting for their occurrence (see the interesting discussion in Augustine, *City of God*, X, 16), so the Jews. P. J. Hershon (*Genesis with a Talmudic Commentary*, E. T., p. 284) quotes from the *Avoda-zarah*, fol. 51, col. 1, as follows: "Zonan once said to Rabbi Akiva: Both I and thou know that an idol has nothing in it, and yet we see men who go to it lame and return sound; how dost thou account for it? He replied: I will tell thee a parable. There was a faithful man with whom his townspeople deposited their goods, without the presence of witnesses. One man did so likewise, but was careful to bring witnesses with him. Once, however, he de-posited something with him when no one else was present. Oh, said his wife, after his departure, let us keep that deposit for our-selves. What! replied the husband, because the fool acted im-properly shall we forfeit our faith? So also when chastisements are sent on men, they (the chastisements) are adjured not to leave them before a certain day, a certain hour, and then only by a certain medicament. It happens that the heathen man repairs to the heathen temple at that very time. The chastisements then say: By right we should not depart just now; but, on reflection, they add: Because that fool acts improperly, shall we violate our oath?" Where the Christians invoked demons, Akiva fell back on coincidence.

NOTES TO LECTURE III

ROMAN CATHOLIC MIRACLES

1. *Mysticism and the Creed*, 1914, p. ix.
2. *The Sacred Shrine*, 1912, p. xi.
3. The sense of this continuity is very strong among Romanist writers; *e. g.*, R. H. Benson, *Lourdes*, 1914, p. 59: "'These signs shall follow them that believe,' He said Himself; and the history of the Catholic Church is an exact fulfillment of the words. It was so, St. Augustine tells us, at the tombs of the martyrs; five hundred miracles were reported at Canterbury within a few years of St. Thomas' martyrdom. And now here is Lourdes, as it has been for fifty years, in this little corner of France."
4. The same general point of view finds expression sometimes in non-Romanist quarters. For example, J. Arthur Hill, *The Hibbert Journal*, October, 1906, vol. V, p. 118, writes as follows: "Christ's miracles and resurrection were objective phenomena, and Christianity was based upon them. . . . But belief in Christianity has gradually crumbled away because there has been no continuance of well-attested cognate facts. The Catholic miracles and ecstasies make belief easier for one section of Christianity; but Protestantism—which cuts off miracles at the end of the Apostolic Times—has committed suicide; by making unique events of its basic phenomena it has made continued belief in them impossible." On this view no man can believe in miracles who has not himself witnessed miracles. Testimony is discredited out of hand; man believes only what he has seen. Must we not go further on this ground? Can a man continue to believe in miracles unless he continues to see them? Is not memory itself a kind of testimony? Must not there be a continuous miracle in order to support continuous faith? We cannot thus chop up the continuity of life, whether of the individual or of the race, in the interests of continuous miracle. Granted that one or the other must be continuous, life or miracle; but both need not be.

5. Above, pp. 17 ff., 61 ff.
6. *Römische Geschichte*, I, p. 181.
7. *Wunderglaube im Heidentum und in der alten Kirche*, 1901, p. 101.
8. *Op. cit.*, pp. 56–57.
9. *Loc. cit.*
10. *Monasticism and the Confessions of Augustine*, E. T., p. 123.
11. *History of Dogma*, E. T., vol. V, p. 172, note 1.
12. *The City of God*, book XXI, chap. IV (*Post-Nicene Fathers*, vol. II, p. 458).
13. *De cura pro mortuis gerenda*, c. 12 : 15 (Migne, vol. VI, pp. 602 f.).
14. *Dialog.*, IV, 36 (Migne, vol. III, p. 384 A).
15. *Philopseudes*, 25 (*The Works of Lucian of Samosata*, translated by H. W. Fowler and F. G. Fowler, vol. III, 1905, p. 244).
16. *Die christliche Legende des Abendlandes*, 1910, p. 111.
17. *The Catholic Encyclopedia*, vol. X, 1911, p. 130.
18. *Les Légendes Hagiographiques*, 1905, p. 210.
19. *Hellenistische Wundererzählungen*, 1906, p. 6.
20. Eusebius, *The Preparation for the Gospel*, 11 : 37 (E. T. by E. H. Gifford, vol. III, pp. 610 f.), quotes it from Plutarch's treatise *On the Soul*. Plutarch is speaking of his friend Antyllus. He writes: "For he was ill not long ago, and the physician thought that he could not live; but having recovered a little from a slight collapse, though he neither did nor said anything else showing derangement, he declared that he had died and had been set free again, and was not going to die at all of that present illness, but that those who had carried him away were seriously reproved by their Lord; for, having been sent for Nicandas, they had brought him back instead of the other. Now, Nicandas was a shoe-maker, besides being one of those who frequent the palustræ, and familiar and well-known to many. Wherefore the young men used to come and mock him, as having run away from his fate, and as having bribed the officers sent from the other world. It was evident, however, that he was himself at first a little disturbed and disquieted; and at last he was attacked by a fever and died suddenly the third day. But this Antyllus came to life again, and is alive and well, and one of our most agreeable friends."
21. *Psyche²*, 1898, vol. II, p. 364, note.
22. *Festschrift Theodor Gomperz dargebracht*, usw., 1902.
23. *Loc. cit.*
23a. Erasmus has some very sensible remarks on the matter

(*Epistle* 475) which J. A. Froude (*Life and Letters of Erasmus*, 1894, p. 301) reproduces in a condensed form thus: "This Dialogue [Lucian's *Philopseudes*] teaches us the folly of superstition, which creeps in under the name of religion. When lies are told us Lucian bids us not disturb ourselves, however complete the authority which may be produced for them. Even Augustine, an honest old man and a lover of truth, can repeat a tale as authentic which Lucian had ridiculed under other names so many years before Augustine was born. What wonder, therefore, that fools can be found to listen to the legends of the saints or to stories about hell, such as frighten cowards or old women. There is not a martyr, there is not a virgin, whose biographies have not been disfigured by these monstrous absurdities. Augustine says that lies when exposed always injure the truth. One might fancy they were invented by knaves or unbelievers to destroy the credibility of Christianity itself." Miracles, according to Erasmus, did not happen in his time—though they were said to happen. "I have spoken of miracles," he writes (Froude, p. 351). "The Christian religion nowadays does not require miracles, and there are none; but you know that lying stories are set about by crafty knaves." He describes with his biting satire what happened (and did not happen) when the Protestants took over Basle. "Smiths and carpenters were sent to remove the images from the churches. The roods and the unfortunate saints were cruelly handled. Strange that none of them worked a miracle to avenge their dignity, when before they had worked so many at the slightest provocation" (p. 359). "No blood was shed; but there was a cruel assault on altars, images, and pictures. We are told that St. Francis used to resent light remarks about his five wounds, and several other saints are said to have shown displeasure on similar occasions. It was strange that at Basle not a saint stirred a finger. I am not so much surprised at the patience of Christ and the Virgin Mary" (p. 360). As to relics and relic-worship: "What would Jerome say could he see the Virgin's milk exhibited for money; with as much honor paid to it as to the consecrated body of Christ; the miraculous oil; the portions of the true cross, enough if they were collected to freight a large ship? Here we have the head of St. Francis, there our Lady's petticoat or St. Anne's cowl, or St. Thomas of Canterbury's shoes; not presented as innocent aids to religion, but as the substance of religion itself—and all through the avarice of priests and the hypocrisy of monks playing on the credulity of the people. Even bishops play their parts in these fantastic shows, and approve and dwell on them in their rescripts" (pp. 121 f.).

24. *Legenden-Studien*, 1906; *Die christliche Legende des Abend-landes*, 1910.

25. *Die christliche Legende*, usw., p. 69.

26. Pp. 3, 4.

27. P. 117.

28. *Op. cit.*, p. 8; cf. *Legenden-Studien*, p. 70.

29. *Die christliche Legende*, usw., p. 118.

30. On the miracles, especially of healing, of classical antiquity, see E. Thräner, art., "Health and Gods of Healing," in Hastings's *ERE*, vol. VI, pp. 540–566; Otto Weinreich, *Antike Heilungswunder*, 1909; R. Lembert, *Die Wunderglaube der Römer und Griechen*, 1905; and *Antike Wunderkuren*, 1911; G. von Rittersheim, *Der medizin. Wunderglauben und die Incubation im Altertum*, 1878; L. Deubner, *De Incubatione*, 1900; M. Hamilton, *Incubation*, 1906. On the transference of the heathen customs to Christianity, see Deubner and Hamilton, and especially E. Lucius, *Die Anfänge des Heiligenkults in der christliche Kirche*, 1904; Th. Trede, *Wunderglaube im Heidentum und in der alten Kirche*, 1901, and *Das Heidentum in der Römishen Kirche*, 4 vols., 1889–1891; P. Saintyves, *Les Saints successeurs des Dieux*, 1907. With respect to the mediæval miracles, see especially P. Toldo of Turin, who began in 1901 in the *Studien der vergleichenden Literaturgeschichte* a "scientific classification" of the mediæval miracles, in a series of articles entitled, "Lives and Miracles of the Saints in the Middle Ages"; see also Koch's *Zeitschrift für vergleichende Literaturgeschichte*, vol. XIV (1901), pp. 267 ff., where Toldo prints the Introduction to these studies. The bizarre character of these miracles is fairly illustrated by a brief but brightly written review of them in R. A. Vaughan's *Hours with the Mystics*,[6] 1903, vol. II, pp. 218–222.

31. Heinrich Günter, *The Catholic Encyclopedia*, vol. X, 1911, p. 229, singles the stigmata out from other miraculous manifestations as "an especially Christian manifestation"; all the rest have heathen parallels.

32. Consult, however, A. M. Königer, in Schiele and Zscharnack's *Die Religion in Geschichte und Gegenwart*, vol. V, 1913, col. 924: "In the absolute sense in which it has been until recently thought to be such, Francis of Assisi does not begin the long list. It is, on the contrary, possible to show that at the least the idea of imitating the stigmata, as a consequence of longing after the sufferings of the Lord, was active for the period of the opening thirteenth century when not only was reverence for the sufferings of Christ fostered by the crusades, but more still self-mortifications of all sorts were set on foot by the growing call to repentance and

amendment. Consult the self-mutilations of the Belgian Beguine
Marie of Oignies († 1213), of the religious fanatic condemned by
the Oxford Synod of 1222, further of the Marquis Robert of Mont-
ferrand, about 1226, of the Dutch hermit Dodon von Hasha
(† 1231)."

Francis was not only the first of the stigmatics in both time and
importance, but presented the stigmata in a form which has remained peculiar to himself. The contemporary accounts agree in
describing the marks on his hands and feet as blackish, fleshy ex-
crescences, recalling in form and color the nails with which the
hands and feet of Jesus were pierced. Only the mark in the side
was a wound, whence at times exuded a little blood. No bloody
exudation took place except at the side. (*Cf.* Paul Sabatier, *Life
of Francis of Assisi*, E. T., 1894, p. 296, note, and p. 435). Francis's stigmatization consisted, then, not of five bleeding wounds
but of the imitation of the four nails and the spear thrust in the
side. The description given of them by Brother Elias (Sabatier,
p. 436) in his letters as Vicar of the Order to the brothers, sent out
after Francis's death, describes them as follows: "For (or Not) a
long time before his death our Brother and Father appeared as
crucified, having in his body five wounds, which are truly the stigmata of Christ, for his hands and his feet bore marks as of nails
without and within, forming a sort of scars; while at the side he
was as if pierced with a lance, and often a little blood oozed from
it." Joseph von Görres, *Die christliche Mystik*, ed. of 1836, vol.
II, p. 422, puts together a very detailed description of the wounds
on the hands and the feet: "The wounds of notable extent opened
in the centre of the extremities. In the middle of them had grown
out of the flesh and cellular tissue nails like iron; black, hard,
fixed, with heads above, below pointed and as if clinched, so that
a finger could be inserted between them and the skin. They were
movable from side to side, and if drawn out to one side, were cor-
respondingly drawn in on the other but could not be extracted;
as St. Clara discovered when she tried to extract them after his
death, and could not do it. The fingers remained, moreover,
flexible as before, and the hands performed their service; neither
did the feet fail, although walking had become more difficult to
him, and he therefore rode thereafter in his journeying through
the neighborhood." A. Tholuck, *Vermischte Schriften*, 1839, I, pp.
105 f., points out the defects in the testimony: "In the case of all
other saints the legend speaks only of wound scars, and the por-
traits of Francis present him only with the scars; the old reporters
nevertheless describe them in a peculiar way as if there had grown

nails of flesh, with the color of fresh iron and with clinched points. Nevertheless perfect clearness is lacking in the reports. The report of the *tres socii* says: nails of flesh were seen *et ferri quoque nigredinem*. Celano says: *Non clavorum quidem puncturas, sed ipsos clavos in eis impositos, ex ferri recenti nigredine;* the last words yield no sense, and the editors conjecture: *ex ferri recentis nigredinem*. The matter is spoken of still less clearly in a letter of Francis's immediate successor in the generalship of the Minorites (in Wadding, *ad annum* 1226, no. 45). Here we read: *Nam manus ejus et pedes, quasi puncturas clavorum habuerunt ex utraque parte confixas, reservantes cicatrices, et clavorum nigredinem ostendentes*. According to this also nails were present." For recent discussions see the works mentioned at the close of the article on the "Stigmatics" in Schiele and Zscharnack, as cited, pp. 433–443.

33. Görres, as cited, pp. 426–428: *cf*. Margaret Roberts, *Saint Catherine of Sienna and Her Times*[2], 1907, p. 103: "Catherine spent long hours in the Church of St. Cristina, and it was there that to her inner consciousness she received the stigmata, invisible to human eyes, but to her awfully real." On her bloody sweat and weeping with bloody tears, see Augusta T. Drane, *The History of St. Catherine of Siena*[3], 1899, vol. I, p. 52.

34. Germano di Stanislao, *Gemma Galgati*, German version by P. Leo Schlegel, 1913; W. F. Ludwig, *Gemma Galgati, eine Studie aus jüngste Zeit*, 1912. The most well-known instance of stigmatization of the later years of the nineteenth century was probably Louise Lateau. Her case is discussed by William A. Hammond, *Spiritualism and Allied Causes and Conditions of Nervous Derangement*, 1876, pp. 350–362; on page 350 an extended bibliography is given which may be supplemented from that at the end of the article, "Stigmatization," in the New Schaff-Herzog *Encyclopedia of Religious Knowledge*, vol. XI, pp. 96–97. A. Rohling's *Louise Lateau, nach authentischen medizinischen und theologischen Documenten*, 1874, was translated and printed in *The Catholic Review*, and afterward in a pamphlet entitled *Louise Lateau, Her Stigmas and Ecstasy*, New York, Hickey & Co., 1891. The following account is drawn from this pamphlet.

Louise Lateau was born a peasant girl, in a Belgian village, on the 30th of January, 1850. Her early life was passed in poverty and sickness. In the spring of 1867 she fell into a violent illness, and remained in a dying condition for a year, suffering from abscesses and hemorrhages, until she was miraculously cured, arising at once from her bed, on the 20th of April, 1868. "Three days later," says Rohling, "Louise received the stigmas of our

Saviour, Jesus Christ" (p. 8). Here is the account given by Doctor Rohling:

"We have seen that she was suddenly restored to health on the 20 April, 1868. During the two following days she continued perfectly well, the thought of receiving the stigmas of the Passion never of course entering her mind. Indeed at that time, she had never even heard of God's having bestowed this wonderful favor either on St. Francis, or upon any other of his faithful servants. On the 24th of April, however, she experienced a return of those excruciating pains, from which she had been enduring a martyrdom of suffering since the beginning of the preceding year. And on the same day, which was Friday, the first trace of the stigmas appeared. On that occasion, however, blood flowed only from the left side. Next day the bleeding had entirely ceased, and all the pain had disappeared. Louise, thinking that it was some transient form of her late illness, remained silent about what had occurred. But on the following Friday, the 1st of May, the stigmas again appeared; and the blood now flowed not only from the side, as in the previous week, but also from the upper surface of both feet. Filled with anxiety and embarrassment, Louise still kept the matter a profound secret, speaking of it only to her confessor . . . (who) . . . made nothing of what had occurred. . . . On the next Friday, the 8th of May, blood came as in the previous weeks, and, in addition, about nine o'clock in the morning it began to flow copiously from the palms and backs of both hands." . . . "Since then the bleeding is accustomed to return on Fridays." "On the 25th September, 1868, blood flowed for the first time from the forehead and from a number of points around the head—a striking memorial of our Lord's crown of thorns—and this has also occurred regularly ever since. On the 26th April, 1873, an additional wound of large dimensions appeared on Louise's right shoulder, such as our Lord received in carrying the cross to Calvary. The blood usually begins to flow from the stigmas about midnight on Thursdays; occasionally the bleeding from the left side does not begin until somewhat later. Sometimes blood flows only from either the upper or lower surface of the feet, and from either the palms or backs of the hands; but frequently the bleeding takes place from both. Nor is the time uniform, during which the bleeding continues . . . but invariably the blood ceases to flow before midnight Friday. The first symptom of the commencement of the bleeding is the formation of blisters on the hands and feet. . . . When they are fully developed, the blisters burst, the watery liquid passes off, and blood immediately begins to flow from the true skin beneath. . . . During the rest of the week, the position of the stigmas can be discerned by a reddish tinge, and a glassy appearance of the skin, the epidermis is intact, exhibiting no trace of wound or scar, and beneath it with the aid of a good lens (with a magnifying power of 20) the skin may be observed in its normal condition. . . . During the ecstasy Louise has no consciousness of material occurrences around her. . . . The stigmas are the seat of acute pain."

35. *Les Stigmatisées, Louise Lateau,* etc., Paris, 1873; *La Stigmatization, l'ecstasie divine, et les miracles de Lourdes,* Paris, 1894. We are drawing, however, directly from *The Catholic Encyclopedia,* vol. XIV, p. 294. Two American cases are described incidentally in the *Proceedings of the Society for Psychical Research,* vol. VII (1891–1892), pp. 341 and 345.

36. Migne, *Dictionnaire des Prophéties et des Miracles,* p. 1069.

37. *Op. cit.,* pp. 1068 f.; cf. *Revue des Deux Mondes,* May 1, 1907, p. 207.

38. G. Dumas, *Revue des Deux Mondes,* May 1, 1907, p. 207, quoting Ribadeneira, *Vie d'Ignace de Loyola,* book V, chap. x.

39. Pp. 1066 ff.

40. P. 1070.

41. Pp. 1080 f.

42. A. Poulain, *The Catholic Encyclopedia,* vol. XIV, p. 295: "It seems historically certain that ecstatics alone have the stigmata."

43. It is the judgment of a sympathetic critic that "trances, losses of consciousness, automatisms, visions of lights, audition of voices, 'stigmata,' and such like experiences, are evidences of hysteria, and they are not in themselves evidences of divine influence or of divine presence."—Rufus M. Jones, *Studies in Mystical Religion,* 1909, p. xxviii. Compare what he says more at large, when speaking of Francis of Assisi (p. 165): "The modern interpreter, unlike the mediæval disciple, finds this event, if it is admitted, a point of weakness rather than a point of strength. Instead of proving to be the marks of a saint, the stigmata are the marks of emotional and physical abnormality." In a like spirit, Baron von Hügel, *The Mystical Element of Religion,* vol. II, p. 42, declares generally that "the downright ecstatics and hearers of voices and seers of visions have all, wherever we are able to trace their temperamental and normal constitution and history, possessed and developed a definitely peculiar psycho-physical organization." On the Stigmata and Stigmatics, see especially F. W. H. Myers, *Personality, Human and Divine,* vol. I, pp. 492 ff.

44. *Die christliche Mystik*, new ed., 1836, vol. II, pp. 407–468: "Die Ecstase im unterem Leben, und die durch sie gewirkte Transformation der Leiblichkeit." English translation of this section under the title of *The Stigmata: A History of Various Cases*, London, 1883.

45. A. M. Königer, in Schiele and Zscharnack, as cited, col. 924: "Their bearers are predominantly women and simple people. In the immaturity of their understanding they have not yet reached stability. . . ."

46. *The Catholic Encyclopedia*, vol. XIV, p. 294. The italics are ours.

47. Pp. 205 ff.

48. Görres, *op. cit.*, vol. II, p. 189.

49. J. K. Huysmans, *Sainte Lydwine*, p. 101.

50. We are reminded by Mrs. E. Herman, however (*The Meaning and Value of Mysticism*, 1915, p. 159), that in one element of the faith of those "moderns" whom she represents, there is a return to this desire to help Christ save the world.   Commenting on some remarks of Angela de Foligno, she says: "To those unacquainted with mediæval religious literature this seems curiously modern in its implied insistence upon our obligation to ask a humble share in the atoning suffering, instead of acquiescing in a doctrine which would make a passive acceptance of Christ's sufferings on our behalf sufficient for the remission of sins." No sharing in Christ's *atoning* sufferings can be described as humble. It is not the "acceptance of Christ's sufferings" which is represented by the Scriptures and understood from them by evangelicals as "sufficient for the remission of sins." It is Christ's sufferings themselves which are all-sufficient, and the trail of the serpent is seen in any suggestions that they need or admit of supplementing.

51. For example, A. Poulain, as cited; *cf.* A. M. Königer, as cited: "The analogous cases of suggestion from without (local congestion of blood, slight blood-sweating, formation of blisters, and marks of burning) lie so far from the real stigmata, connected with lesion of the walls of the blood vessels (hemorrhages), that medical science knows as yet nothing else to do but to class this among the 'obscure neuropathic bleedings.'"

52. *The Principles of Psychology*, ed. 1908, vol. II, p. 612. Compare the statement quoted by A. T. Schofield, *The Force of Mind*, 1908, pp. 61 f., from Professor Barrett, of Trinity College, Dublin, *Humanitarian*, 1905: "It is not so well known but it is nevertheless a fact, that utterly startling physiological changes can be produced in a hypnotized subject merely by conscious or uncon-

scious mental suggestion. Thus a red scar or a painful burn, or even a figure of definite shape, such as a cross or an initial, can be caused to appear on the body of the entranced subject solely through suggesting the idea. By creating some local disturbance of the blood-vessels in the skin, the unconscious self has done what it would be impossible for the conscious self to perform. And so in the well-attested cases of stigmata, where a close resemblance to the wounds on the body of the crucified Saviour appears on the body of the ecstatic. This is a case of unconscious *self*-suggestion, arising from the intent and adoring gaze of the ecstatic upon the bleeding figure on the crucifix. With the abeyance of the conscious self the hidden powers emerge, whilst the trance and mimicry of the wounds are strictly parallel to the experimental cases previously referred to."

53. These cases, with others of the same kind, are cited by F. W. A. Myers, *Proceedings of the Society for Psychical Research*, vol. VII (1891–1892), pp. 337 ff., who introduces them with the following remarks: "The subliminal consciousness, it will be seen, was able to turn out to order the most complicated novelty in the way of hysterical freaks of circulation. Let us turn to an equally marked disturbance of the inflammatory type, the production namely, of suppurating blisters by a word of command. This phenomenon has a peculiar interest, since, from the accident of a strong emotional association with the idea of the stigmata in the hands and feet, this special organic effect has been anticipated by the introverted broodings of a line of mystics from St. Francis of Assisi to Louise Lateau." *Cf.* the similar cases cited by G. Dumas, as cited, pp. 215 ff.

54. Myers, as cited, p. 333.

55. Letter to Thomas de Gardo, a Florentine physician, printed in the Eighth Book of his Correspondence—as cited by Dumas, as cited, p. 213.

56. *Traité de l'Amour de Dieu.* Book IV, chap. xv (E. T. in Methuen's "Library of Devotion," *On the Love of God*, 1902, p. 196). *Cf.* Dumas, as cited, who, however, quotes more at large, including certain phrases (not found in the E. T.) which withdraw somewhat from the purity of the naturalistic explanation.

57. The literature of Stigmatization is very large and varied; a guide to it may be found in the bibliographies attached to the appropriate articles in Herzog-Hauck, the New Schaff-Herzog, Schiele and Zscharnack and *The Catholic Encyclopedia*. The essay by Dumas in the *Revue des Deux Mondes* for May 1, 1907, is exceptionally instructive. With it may be consulted the older discus-

sions by A. Maury, in the *Revue des Deux Mondes*, 1854, vol. IV, and in the *Annales Medico-Psychologiques* (edited by Baillarger, Cerise, and Longet), 1855; and the more recent studies by R. Virchow, "Ueber Wunder und Medizin," in the *Deutsche Zeitschrift für practische Medizin*, 1872, pp. 335–339; Paul Janet, "Une Ecstatique," in the *Bulletin de l'Institute psychologique* for July, 1901, and *The Mental State of Hystericals : A Study of Mental Stigmata*, New York, 1901; and Maurice Apte, *Les Stigmatisés*, 1903; *cf.* also W. A. Hammond, *Spiritualism and Allied Causes and Conditions of Nervous Derangement*, 1876, pp. 329–362, and the short note in W. B. Carpenter, *Principles of Mental Physiology*, 1874, pp. 689–690. No general description is better than Görres's, as cited; and no general discussion supersedes Tholuck's, as cited. O. Stoll, *Suggestion und Hypnotismus in der Völker-psychologie*[2], 1904, pp. 520 ff., is chiefly useful for the setting in which the subject is placed.

58. *Les Légendes Hagiographiques*, 1905, p. 187. *Cf.* what is said by G. H. Gerould, *Saints' Legends*, 1916, p. 42.

59. L. Deubner, *De Incubatione :* "The religion of Christians had and has its own demi-gods and heroes; that is to say, its saints and martyrs"; G. Wobbermin, *Religionsgeschichtliche Studien*, 1896, p. 18: "The saints of the Christian Churches, and especially those of the Greek Church, present a straightforward development of the Greek hero-cult. The saints are the heroes of the Ancients." *Cf.* P. Saintyves, *Les Saints successeurs des Dieux*, 1907, and especially Lucius, as cited; also M. Hamilton, as cited.

60. *Cf.* Friedrich Pfister, *Der Reliquienkult im Altertum*, 1902, pp. 429 ff.; E. Lucius, *Die Anfänge des Heiligenkults in der christliche Kirche*, 1904.

61. *Cf.* the account by Pfister, as cited, p. 323, and especially 430ff.

62. *Cf.* Saintyves, as cited, pp. 33 ff. We are told that many of the bones of the eleven thousand virgin martyrs displayed at the Church of St. Ursula at Cologne are bones of men (A. D. White, *Warfare*, etc., vol. II, p. 29).

63. A. D. White records that Frank Buckland noted that the relics of St. Rosalia at Palermo are really the bones of a goat (Gordon's *Life of Buckland*, pp. 94–96); and yet they cure diseases and ward off epidemics.

64. Harbey, *Supplément aux Acta Sanctorum*, vol. I, 1899, p. 203 (cited by Günter). *Cf.* in general Saintyves, as cited, pp. 44 ff.

65. H. Günter, *Legenden-Studien*, 1906, p. 109, note 6, citing the *Vita S. Maximini*, c. 9 (*Scriptores rerum Merov.*, III, 78).

66. Pausanias, III, 16, 1 (Pfister, p. 325); also Delehaye, p. 186, with references given there.

67. Henri Etienne, *Apologie pour Hérodote, ou Traité de la Conformité des Merveilles anciennes avec les modernes,* ed. le Duchat, 1735, chaps. XXIX–XXVIII, as cited by P. Saintyves, as cited, p. 46, who may be consulted (pp. 44–48) on the general subject.

68. *Cf.* Paul Parfait, *La Foire aux Reliques,* pp. 137–138.

69. On Mary's milk, see the whole chapter on "Le Saint Lait d'Evron," in Paul Parfait, as cited, pp. 135–144. On what may lie in the background of this whole series of legends, see article "Milk," in Hastings's *ERE,* vol. VIII, pp. 633–637.

70. *The Sacred Shrine,* 1912, p. 363.

71. These words are Mechthild's; and Hirn adds: "The idea that the Madonna gives milk to all believers appears finely in a poem in the Swedish collection of Latin hymns, *Piæ Cantiones,* p. 161:

> 'Super vinum et unguentum
> the mamme dant fomentum,
> fove, lacta parvulos.'"

72. P. 365.

73. He gives a series of references to instances.

74. *Deutsche Schriften,* I, p. 74.

75. *Acta Sanctorum,* 38, pp. 207–208.

76. *Legenden-Studien,* 1906, pp. 165 f. Compare *Die christliche Legende des Abendlandes,* 1910, p. 43: "That the legend [of Mary] praises the Mother of Pity also as the succorer of the sick is a matter of course. But the mysticism of the Mary-legend brought a new means of healing, in that it makes Mary give her breast to the sick." *Cf.* the curious details on p. 85. In the notes accompanying the passage quoted from the *Legenden-Studien,* Günter shows how wide-spread and how full of variants such legends were. In one MS. the motive is varied in a threefold way: a cleric in his illness had bitten off his tongue and lips, and was suddenly healed by Mary's milk; a monk thought already dead was healed; another monk had his experience only in a dream, but with the same effect. Noting that the milk with which Fulbert, bishop of Chartres, was sprinkled and healed, is said in one MS. to have been gathered up and saved as a relic, Günter infers that the milk-relics date from this epoch. This is how the story of Fulbert is told in Sablon, *Histoire et Description de la Cathédrale de Chartres :* "St. Fulbert, Bishop and Restorer of this Church, having been visited by God with an incurable fire which parched him and consumed his tongue, and seized with an insupportable pain

which permitted him no rest through the night, saw as it were a noble lady who commanded him to open his mouth, and when he had obeyed her she at once ejected from her sacred breasts a flood of celestial and savory milk which quenched the fire at once and made his tongue more well than ever. Some drops had fallen on his cheeks, and these were afterwards put into a vial and kept in the treasury."

77. Günter, *Legenden-Studien*, p. 178; *Die christliche Legende*, pp. 85, 162.

78. Günter, *Legenden-Studien*, p. 59.

79. *Ibid.*, p. 208.

80. *Ibid.*, p. 107; *cf.* the list of others of similar character in Th. Trede, *Das Heidentum in der Römischen Kirche*, I, 1889, pp. 158 ff.

81. *Ibid.*

81a. *Op. cit.*, p. 610.

82. *Legenden-Studien*, p. 106.

83. J. B. Heinrich, *Dogmatische Theologie*, vol. X, p. 797, makes much of this: "A miracle which belongs peculiarly to them, wrought not by but *on* the holy bodies, is their incorruptibility through the centuries. No doubt this incorruptibility can in many cases be explained by purely natural causes; but in many cases the miracle is obvious. It is especially evident when a portion only of the holy body remains uncorrupted, particularly that portion which was peculiarly placed at the service of God during life, as the tongue of St. John of Neponac, the arm of St. Stephen of Hungary, the heart of St. Teresa, etc. And especially when, with the preservation of the body there is connected a pleasant fragrance instead of the necessarily following penetrating corpse-odor, or when everything was done, as there was done with the body of St. Francis Xavier, to bring about a speedy corruption." It is astonishing what stress is laid on this incorruptibility of the body of the saints. Thus Herbert Thurston (Hastings's *ERE*, VIII, 149) thinks it worth while, in a very condensed article on *Lourdes*, to record, of Bernadette Soubirous: "It is noteworthy that, though her body at the time of death (1879) was covered with tumors and sores, it was found, when the remains were officially examined in 1909, thirty years afterwards, entire and free from corruption (see Carrière, *Histoire de Notre-Dame de Lourdes*, p. 243)." On this matter see A. D. White, *A History of the Warfare of Science with Theology*, 1896, II, pp. 10, 11, who sets it in its right light, and mentions similar instances—of those who were not saints.

84. Accordingly, Percy Dearmer, *Body and Soul*[9], 1912, p. 262,

says: "For the greater part of Christian history faith-healing was mainly centered in relics, so that probably more people have benefited in this way than in any other." Speaking particularly no doubt of the ancient church, but in terms which would apply to every age, Heinrich (*op. cit.*, X, p. 796) observes: "Now, however, these miracles are regularly wrought at the graves, in the churches, and often precisely by the relics of the saints," and he is led to add two pages further on (p. 798): "There is scarcely another doctrine of the church which has been so approved, established by God Himself, as the veneration of the saints and relics"—that is to say by miraculous attestation.

85. For the literature of pilgrimages, see the bibliography attached to the article "Wallfahrt und Wallfahrtsorten," in Schiele and Zscharnack's *Religion*.

86. Hastings's *ERE*, vol. VIII, pp. 684 f. It is a refreshing note that Meister Eckhard strikes, proving that common sense was not quite dead even in the opening years of the fourteenth century, when he asks, "What is the good of the dead bones of saints? The dead can neither give nor take."

87. W. R. Inge, *Christian Mysticism*, 1889, p. 262 and note 2, is prepared to maintain that "a degraded form" of fetichism is exhibited in much else in modern Roman Catholicism than its relic-worship. He finds it exhibited, for example, "by the so-called neo-mystical school of modern France, and in the baser types of Roman Catholicism everywhere." He adduces in illustration Huysmans two "mystical" novels, *En Route* and *La Cathédrale*, and comments as follows: "The naked fetichism of the latter book almost passes belief. We have a Madonna who is good-natured at Lourdes and cross-grained at La Salette; who likes 'pretty speeches and little coaxing ways' in 'paying court' to her, and who at the end is apostrophised as 'our Lady of the Pillar,' 'our Lady of the Crypt.' It may, perhaps, be excusable to resort to such expedients as these in the conversion of savages" (Query: Is it?); "but there is something singularly repulsive in the picture (drawn apparently from life) of a profligate man of letters seeking salvation in a Christianity which has lowered itself far beneath educated paganism." "Our Lady of the Pillar," "Our Lady of the Crypt," are two images of Mary venerated at the cathedral at Chartres, information concerning which is given in the article entitled "The oldest of our Lady's Shrines: St. Mary's Under-Earth," in *The Dolphin*, vol. VI (July–December, 1904), pp. 377–399. On Mary's shrines in general, see below. Those who have read Huysmans's *La Cathédrale* should read also Blasco Ibañes's *La Catedral*, and

perhaps Evelyn Underhill's *The Lost Word*, that the lascinations of cathedral symbolism may be viewed from several angles.

88.   *Op. cit.*, vol. X, p. 799. Yet it is not merely God who is venerated in the saints, he says; there is an honor due to the saints in themselves, and accordingly Alexander VIII condemned the proposition: The honor that is offered to Mary as Mary is vain. On the other hand it is said that it is merely the saint and through him God that is venerated in the relic, according to the explanation of Thomas Aquinas: "We do not adore the sensible body on its own account, but on account of the soul which was united with it, which is now in the enjoyment of God, and on account of God, whose ministers they were." Why then continue to adore the body when it is no longer united with the soul, on account of its union with which alone it is adored?

89.   P. 794.

90.   P. 794.

91.   What Pfister says, p. 610, although not free from exaggerations, is in its main assertion true.   In the Christian religion, he says, the presence in the relics of a supernatural, in a certain degree magical, power is accustomed to be emphasized even more than it is in the heathen.   For, according to the Greek belief, the graves were thought of chiefly as the protection of the heroes, without the bones themselves being thought able to work miracles—for they rest in the grave; the miracle, the help, comes in general from the hero himself, not from an anonymous, impersonal, magical power which dwells in the relics.   According to the Christian belief the relics themselves, on the other hand, can perform miracles, and the power residing in them can by contact be directly transferred and produce effects.   Thus artificial relics can be produced by contact with genuine ones.   The habit of relic-partition is connected with this: a part of the object filled with magical power may act like the whole.   Compare Hirn, p. 490, note 2: "We deliberately leave out of consideration here the assertion of educated Catholics that in the relics was really worshipped the saint in the same way that God is worshipped in a picture or a symbol (*cf.* Esser, art., 'Reliquien,' in Wetzer-Welte, *Kirchenlexicon*). It cannot be doubted that relic worship—for the earlier Christians as for the mass of believers to-day—was based on utilitarian ideas of the help that might be had from the sacred remains."

92.   See the characterization of the Catholic world-view, by E. Schmidt in Schiele and Zscharnack's *Religion*, etc., vol. V, col. 1736.

93.   Baumgarten, in Schiele and Zscharnack's *Religion*, etc., vol. V, col. 2162.

94. *The Sacred Shrine*, chaps. I–IV.

95. Compare Smith and Cheatham, *Dictionary of Christian Archæology*, I, pp. 62, 429; II, p. 1775, and especially I, p. 431: "As churches built over the tombs of martyrs came to be regarded with peculiar sanctity, the possession of the relics of some saint came to be looked upon as absolutely essential to the sacredness of the building, and the deposition of such relics in or below the altar henceforward formed the central portion of the consecration rite." The succeeding account of the ritual of the consecration should be read.

96. The literature of relics and relic-veneration is sufficiently indicated in the bibliographies attached to the articles on the subject in the encyclopedias: Herzog-Hauck, New Schaff-Herzog, Schiele-Zscharnack. The exhibition of the Holy Coat at Trèves from August 20 to October 3, 1891, with the immense crowd of pilgrims which it brought to Trèves, created an equally immense literature, a catalogue of which may be derived from the *Theologischer Jahresbericht* of the time, and a survey of which will give an insight into the whole subject of the veneration of relics in the nineteenth century.

97. The recent history of relic-miracles in the United States is chiefly connected with the veneration of relics of St. Ann. Certain relics of St. Anthony venerated in the Troy Hill Church at Allegheny, Pa., have indeed won large fame for the miracles of healing wrought by their means, and doubtless the additional relic of the same saint deposited in the Italian Church of St. Peter, on Webster Avenue, Pittsburgh, has taken its share in these works. But St. Ann seems to promise to be the peculiar wonder-worker of the United States. The Church of St. Anne de Beaupré has, within recent years, become the most popular place of pilgrimage in Canada; until 1875 not over 12,000 annually visited this shrine, but now they are counted by the hundred thousand; in 1905 the number was 168,000. A large relic of St. Ann's finger-bone has been in the possession of this shrine since 1670; three other fragments of her arm have been acquired since, and it was in connection with the acquisition of one of these, in 1892, that the cult and its accompanying miracles of healing were transferred to New York. St. Ann seems to be one of those numerous saints too much of whom has been preserved in the form of relics. Her body is said to have been brought from the Holy Land to Constantinople, in 710; and it is said to have been still in the Church of St. Sophia in 1333. It was also, it is said, brought by Lazarus to Gaul, during the persecution of the Jewish Christians in Palestine under Herod Agrippa, and finally found a

resting-place at Apt. Lost to sight through many years, it was rediscovered there in the eighth century, and has been in continuous possession of the church at Apt ever since. Yet the head of St. Ann was at Mainz up to 1516, when it was stolen and carried to Düren in the Rhineland, and her head, "almost complete"— doubtless derived from Apt—is preserved also at Chiry, the heir of the Abbey of Ourscamp. Churches in Italy, Germany, Hungary, and in several towns in France "flatter themselves that they possess more or less considerable portions of the same head, or the entire head" (Paul Parfait, *Le Foire aux Reliques*, p. 94, in an essay on "The Head of St. Ann at Chiry"). Despite all this European history, a relic of St. Ann was again brought from Palestine in the thirteenth century, and it was this that was given to St. Anne d'Auray in Brittany in the early half of the seventeenth century by Ann of Austria and Louis XIII. The origin of the pilgrimages and healings at St. Anne d'Auray was not in this relic, however, but antedated its possession, taking their start from apparitions of St. Ann (1624-1626). The relics which have been recently brought to this country are said to derive ultimately from Apt. Thence the Pope obtained an arm of the saint which was intrusted to the keeping of the Benedictine monks of St. Paul-outside-the-Wall, Rome. From them, through the kind offices of Leo XIII, Cardinal Taschereau obtained the "great relic" which was presented to St. Anne de Beaupré in 1892; and from thence also came the relic, obtained by Prince Cardinal Odeschalchi, and presented to the Church of St. Jean Baptiste in East Seventy-sixth Street, New York, the same year (July 15, 1892). Another fragment was received by the Church of St. Jean Baptiste on August 6, 1893; and some years later still another fragment was deposited in the Church of St. Ann in Fall River, Mass., whence it was stolen on the night of December 1, 1901.

The "Great Relic"—a piece of the wrist-bone of St. Ann, four inches in length—was brought from Rome by Monsignor Marquis; and, on his way to Quebec, he stopped in New York with it. Monsignor O'Reilly has given us an enthusiastic account of the effect of its exposition at the Church of St. Jean Baptiste during the first twenty days of May of that year (see the *Ave Maria* of August 6, 1892; and *The Catholic Review* of the same date). Something like two or three hundred thousand people venerated the relic; cures were wrought, though apparently not very many. When Monsignor Marquis returned on July 15 with the fragment which was to remain at St. Jean Baptiste, the enthusiasm was redoubled, and St. Ann did not let her feast-day (July 26) pass "without giving some signal proof of her love to her children." Since then a novena and an exposition of the relics are held during the latter part of each July, in conjunction with St. Ann's feast-day, and many miracles have been wrought. In 1901 a new marble crypt was completed at the church, and used for the first time for this novena and exposition, and public attention was very particularly called to it. The public press was filled with letters pointing out abuses, or defending the quality of the cures, which were numerous and striking (see a short summary note in *The Presbyterian Banner*, August 8, 1901). On the whole Monsignor O'Reilly's hope that the depositing of the relics of St. Ann in the Church of St. Jean Baptiste will result in "the founding here in New York of what will become a great national shrine of St. Anne"—to be signalized, the editor of the *Ave Maria* adds, "by such marvels as have rendered the sanctuaries of St. Anne de Beaupré and St. Anne d'Auray famous throughout Christendom"—seems in a fair way to be fulfilled. The following is a typical instance of what is happening there. It was reported in *The Catholic Telegraph*. It is the case of a young man aged nineteen, of New Haven, Conn.: "Two years ago young Maloney, who was working at the time in a New Haven factory, fell and injured his hip. Every doctor consulted said he would be a cripple for life. When he walked he was obliged to use crutches. Until recently he has been under the care of the ablest physicians in the city, yet all declared him incurable. Hearing of several cures wrought at St. Anne's shrine, New York, he started thither, making a retreat on arriving. After several days spent in prayer, he visited the shrine of St. Anne. The morning of his visit he received holy communion, and then the relic of the saint was applied, and the sufferer anointed with consecrated oil. Almost instantly he felt better. Another visit and he was able to walk without crutches, leaving the latter before the shrine in which the relics are kept. He was well, quite well, and thus returned to New Haven, to the astonishment of all who knew him." It is worth noting that the Cincinnati *Enquirer* of July 28 and the Lexington (Ky.) *Leader* of July 29, 1902, record the sudden cure of a deaf woman in St. Anne's Church, West Covington, Ky., on St. Ann's feast-day. "She said she had heard the key in the tabernacle, which contains a relic of St. Ann, click as the priest turned it"—and after that she heard everything.

The following extract from *The New York Tribune* for August 13, 1906, will be not uninteresting in this connection: "Two thousand quarts of water from the shrine of Our Lady of Lourdes, in France, arrived here in huge sealed casks on Saturday, consigned to the Fathers of Mercy, who have charge of the American shrine of that name, at Broadway and Aberdeen Street, Brooklyn. The water will be distributed to thousands of physically afflicted men, women and children from all parts of the country next Wednesday afternoon and the following Sunday. Next Wednesday in the Catholic calendar is known as the Feast of the Assumption. It is the titular day of the French shrine, and is kept with equal solemnity by the Fathers of Mercy at the American shrine. The water comes to this country under the seal of the clergy in charge of the French shrine, who guarantee it to be undiluted. Father Porcile, rector of the Brooklyn church, said yesterday that only two ounces would be given to each person applying. The celebration of the festival will begin at [blurred] o'clock on Wednesday morning with a solemn mass. In the afternoon at 3.30 o'clock the pilgrimage to the shrine, which has stood for years on the grounds of the church, will take place. Father Porcile, who has been at the French shrine several times, says the French Government will not attempt to carry out the threatened abandonment of Lourdes on the charge that it is a menace to public health. 'I read about French pathologists holding that the piscina in which the afflicted bathe is unhealthy,' he said. 'Anybody who has seen the piscina knows better. It is not a pool, but a cavity, which is filled with running water. If the pool were stagnant, it might be argued, with some show of truth, that it was unhealthful.'" It is only right to suppose that the reporter misunderstood his collocutor with regard to the piscinas—whether their formation or their filth. Their filth is not glossed by, say, Robert Hugh Benson (*Lourdes*, 1914, pp. 51 ff.), who bathed in one of them: "That water," says he, "had better not be described."

98. *Cf.* Günter, *Legenden-Studien*, p. 177, and especially *Die christliche Legende des Abendlandes*, pp. 35 ff.

99. This string of epithets is taken from the Roman Breviary, Antiphon to the Magnificat. If we wish to know the extravagances to which the prevalent Mariolatry can carry people, we may go to Liguori's *Le Glorie di Maria*, a book which a J. H. Newman could defend (*Letter to Pusey on the Eirenicon*, 1866, pp. 105 ff.). "The way of salvation is open to none otherwise than through Mary." "Whoever expects to obtain graces otherwise than through Mary, endeavors to fly without wings." "Go to Mary, for God has decreed that He will grant no grace otherwise than by the hands of Mary." "All power is granted to thee (Mary) in heaven and on earth, and nothing is impossible to thee." "You, oh Holy Virgin, have over God the authority of a Mother, and hence can ob-

tain pardon for the most obdurate of sinners." Here is the way J. K. Huysmans represents her as thought of by her votaries, doubt-less drawing from the life (*La Cathédrale*, ed. 1903, p. 9): "He meditated on the Virgin whose watchful attentions had so often preserved him from unforeseen danger, easy mistakes, great falls. Was she not"—but we must preserve the French here—"le Puits de la Bonté sans fond, la Collatrice des dons de la bonne Patience, la Tourière des cœurs secs et clos; was she not above all the active and beneficent Mother?"

100. Compare Lachenmann in Schiele and Zscharnack's *Religion*, etc., vol. V, col. 1837: "Belief in miracles is the chief motive of the favorite places of pilgrimage and the climax is reached in the innumerable localities where the grace of Mary is sought. The origin of these lies not in the region of veneration of relics since the Catholic church knows neither the grave of Mary nor relics of her body, but goes back to stories of visible appearances or of inner revelations of the Mother of God at particular localities which she herself has thus indicated for her special worship, or as places of grace (La Salette, Lourdes); or else to vows made to Mary by individuals, or by whole communities, in times of need; or finally to the miraculous activities of an image of Mary."

101. A full account of it is given by Léon Marillier in *The Proceedings of the Society of Psychical Research*, vol. VII (1891–1892), pp. 100–110.

102. "Our Lady of Pellevoisin," reprinted in *The Catholic Review* (New York) for July 30, 1892, from the Liverpool *Catholic Times*.

103. In J. K. Huysmans's *La Cathédrale* we are given a highly picturesque meditation on the several manners in which Mary has revealed herself. She owes something to sinners, it seems, for had it not been for their sin she could never have been the immaculate mother of God. She has tried hard, however, to pay her debt, and has appeared in the most diverse places and in the most diverse fashions—though of late it looks as if she had deserted all her old haunts for Lourdes. She appeared at La Salette as the Madonna of Tears. Twelve years later, when people had got tired of climbing to La Salette (the greatest miracle about which was that people could be got to go there), she appeared at Lourdes, no longer as Our Lady of the Seven Sorrows, but as the Madonna of Smiles, the Tenant of the glorious Joys. How everything has been changed! The special aspect in which Mary is worshipped at Chartres, it is added, is under the traits of a child or a young mother, much more as the Virgin of the Nativity than as Our Lady of the Seven Sorrows.

The old artists of the Middle Ages, working here, have taken care not to sadden her by recalling too many painful memories, and have wished to show, by this discretion, their gratitude to her who has constantly shown herself in their sanctuary the Dispensatrice of benefits, the Chatelaine of graces.

104. *The Catholic Encyclopedia*, vol. XV, p. 464.

105. See *The Catholic Encyclopedia*, vol. X, p. 115; vol. XV, p. 115; also B. M. Aladel, *The Miraculous Medal: Its Origin, History*, etc. Translated from the French by P. S. Baltimore, 1880.

106. Doctor Rouby, *La Vérité sur Lourdes*, 1910, pp. 318 f.

107. A sufficient outline of these scandals is given in the article on La Salette in *The Catholic Encyclopedia*, which also mentions the chief literature. It was said that "the beautiful lady" seen by the children was a young woman named Lamerlière; suits for slander were brought; and A. D. White is able to say (*Warfare*, etc., II, pp. 21-22, note) that the shrine "preserves its healing powers in spite of the fact that the miracle which gave rise to them has twice been pronounced fraudulent by the French courts." The whole matter is involved in inextricable confusion. A sympathetic account of La Salette may be read in J. S. Northcote, *Celebrated Sanctuaries of the Madonna*, 1868, pp. 178 ff. Gustave Droz's first novel, *Autour d'une Source*, 1869, seems to have drawn part of its inspiration from the story of La Salette; it is extravagantly praised by A. D. White (*Warfare*, II, p. 44) as "one of the most exquisitely wrought works of modern fiction"; and not quite accurately described as "showing perfectly the recent evolution of miraculous powers at a fashionable spring in France." It does show how easily such things may be even innocently invented. On the question whether the visions of Bernadette may not have been the result of ecclesiastical arrangement, see J. de Bonnefon, *Lourdes et ses Tenanciers*, Paris, without date, and, on the other side, G. Bertrin, *Lourdes, un document apocryphe*, in the *Revue pratique d'Apologétique*, April 15, 1908, pp. 125-133.

108. See Marillier, as cited, and *cf.* H. Thurston's remarks in Hastings's *ERE*, vol. VIII, p. 149.

109. J. K. Huysmans, in his *La Cathédrale*, suggests that two rules seem to govern the appearances of Mary. First, she manifests herself only to the poor and humble. Secondly, she accommodates herself to their intelligence and shows herself under the poor images which these lowly people love. "She accepts the white and blue robes, the crowns and garlands of roses, the jewels and chaplets, the appointments of the first communion, the ugliest of attire. The peasants who have seen her, in a word, have had no

other examples by which to describe her (except under the appearance of a 'fine lady') but the traits of an altar Virgin of the village, of a Madonna of the Saint-Sulpice quarter, of a Queen of the street-corner."

110. We are quoting A. T. Myers and F. W. H. Myers, *Proceedings of the Society of Psychical Research*, vol. IX, 1894, p. 177.

111. *Legenden-Studien*, p. 126.

112. *Lourdes*, 1891, p. 31, as cited by Myers, as cited, p. 178.

113. Myers, as cited, pp. 178, 179.

114. In the contrast which he draws between La Salette and Lourdes, in his *La Cathédrale*, J. K. Huysmans does not neglect this one. "And God who imposed La Salette, without having recourse to the methods of worldly publicity, has changed His tactics and, with Lourdes, puffing comes into play. This is very confounding—Jesus resigning Himself to employ the miserable artifices of human commerce, accepting the repulsive stratagems of which we make use in pushing a product or a business!"

115. *Lourdes* (the first of the triad on "the cities," Lourdes, Rome, Paris) was published in 1894; E. T. same year, by Vizetelly, and often since. *Cf.* a critical article on it in *The Edinburgh Review*, 1903, No. 103. The secret of Lourdes, says Zola, is that it offers to suffering humanity "the delicious bread of hope, for which humanity ever hungers with a hunger that nothing will ever appease"; it proposes to meet "humanity's insatiable yearning for happiness." Since its publication Catholic writers on Lourdes have, as is natural, concerned themselves very much with Zola's book; G. Bertrin's work (*Histoire critique des événements de Lourdes*) which reached its 37th edition in 1913, and which Herbert Thurston pronounces "undoubtedly the best general work on Lourdes" (Hastings's *ERE*, vol. VIII, p. 150), would not be unfairly described as a formal reply to Zola.

116. Edward Berdoe, "A Medical View of the Miracles at Lourdes," in *The Nineteenth Century*, October, 1895, pp. 614 ff. Doctor Berdoe was a liberal-minded Catholic in faith; see Herbert Thurston's remarks in *The Month* for November, 1895, and his citation of Doctor Berdoe's own representations in *The Spectator*, July, 1895. (*Cf. Public Opinion*, November 28, 1895, p. 108.)

117. *Lourdes*, 1914, p. 29.

118. The details are given by Benson, p. 32.

119. A curious fact emerges from Bertrin's tables in his appendix (E. T., p. 292); more physicians visit Lourdes every year to look on at the cures than there are cures made for them to observe. For the fourteen years from 1890 to 1903, inclusive, 2,530 physicians

visited the Medical Office there, an average of 180 yearly. During these fourteen years 2,130 cures were registered at that office, an average of 152 yearly.

120. A. D. White, *Warfare*, etc.,[2] vol. II, p. 24: E. Berdoe, as cited, p. 615. Other estimates of the proportion of the cured to patients may be found in Dearmer, *Body and Soul*,[9] 1912, p. 315, and in Rouby, *La Vérité sur Lourdes*, 1910, p. 272. Rouby thinks that about five out of every thousand patients are cured, that is, about one-half of one per cent; Dearmer can arrive at no more than one per cent from the figures given, and remarks that even if five per cent be allowed, as is asserted by some, the proportion is much smaller than under regular psychotherapeutical treatment.

121. *The Catholic Encyclopedia*, vol. X, 1911, p. 390; *cf.* the earlier estimates in his *Lourdes, A History of its Apparitions and Cures*, E. T., 1908, p. 91.

122. A rather favorable opportunity for estimating the proportion of cures to patients seems to be afforded by the figures given concerning the patients from Villepinte, a private asylum for consumptive girls, near Paris. Bertrin (E. T., pp. 98 ff.) tells us that for the three years 1896–1898 inclusive, 58 of these girls were sent to Lourdes, of whom 20 were cured. Rouby (pp. 163 ff.) derives from Boissarie a report also for three years (apparently just preceding those given by Bertrin, but not explicitly identified) during which 58 girls were sent to Lourdes, of whom 24 were cured or ameliorated, the cure being maintained with two or three exceptions. Rouby says he investigated the facts for one of these years, 1894, in which out of 24 girls who were sent, 14 were reported cured or ameliorated; he found that 10 of those so reported afterwards relapsed, leaving only 4 benefited. He went to Villepinte, he says, and investigated personally the facts for 1902, finding that 30 girls had been sent, and all 30 had come back unbenefited; and he quotes Ludovic Naudeau as having investigated the facts for 1901 with the same result—none were benefited. We gather from Bertrin, p. 101, that the same thing was true for 1903. Here, apparently, then, are three consecutive years, 1901–1903, in which no cures at all were wrought in the Villepinte delegation.

123. Benson, as cited, pp. 25–26.

124. We find Doctor E. Mackey, *Dublin Review*, October, 1880, pp. 396 f., very properly dissenting when Père Bonniot (*Le Miracle*, etc., p. 89) lays stress thus on suddenness as a proof of miraculousness in a cure. "Mere suddenness of cure," he says, "is not decisive . . . the power of imagination is very great." Cures just as remarkable and just as sudden as those of Lourdes constantly

occur in the ordinary experience of physicians. Doctor J. Burney Yeo quite incidentally records two such sudden cases, in an article on a subject remote from Lourdes, in *The Nineteenth Century* for August, 1888, vol. XXIV, pp. 196–197—one of blindness and the other of lameness. "A gentleman," says he, "the subject of serious disease, who had shown a tendency to the development of somewhat startling subjective symptoms, suddenly declared that he was blind. He was carefully examined by the writer and by an eminent oculist, and although no particular optical defect could be found in his eyes, to all the tests it was possible to apply, he appeared to be blind. A few days afterwards, and without any apparent or sufficient cause or reason for the change, and almost without comment, he asked for the *Times* newspaper, which he proceeded to read in bed without any difficulty!" "The next instance," he continues, "is perhaps still more remarkable. A young woman presented herself at a London Hospital, supporting herself on crutches, and declared she was losing the use of her legs. After one or two questions, and after noticing the awkward manner in which the crutches were used, the writer took from her both crutches, and ordered her, in a firm manner, to walk away without them, which she did! Some years afterwards he was sent for into a distant suburb to see this person's father, having himself quite forgotten the preceding incident, when this same young woman came forward and reminded him that he 'had cured her of lameness' many years ago! Now, although no curative agency whatever, in the ordinary sense, was introduced or applied, in either of these instances, yet one of them might have said, 'whereas I was blind, now I see,' and the other, 'whereas I was lame, now I walk.'" Professor Charles (or George?) Buchanan, "a distinguished Professor of Surgery in Glasgow" "visited Lourdes in the autumn of 1883, and was much interested in the undoubted benefit that some of the pilgrims received." He published some notes in the *Lancet* of June 25, 1885, from which Doctor A. T. Myers and F. W. H. Myers extract the following account of an instantaneous cure in which he was an actor (*Proceedings of the Society for Psychical Research*, vol. IX, 1893–1894, pp. 191 ff.). "With regard," he writes, "to persons who have been lame and decrepit and known as such to their friends, the fact of their leaving their crutches and walking away without help does seem astonishing and miraculous, and it is cases such as these which make the greatest impression." "I believe that the simple visit to the grotto by persons who believe in it, and the whole surroundings of the place, might have such an effect on the mind that a sudden change in the nerve condition might result in immediate improvement in cases where there is no real change of structure, but where the malady is a functional imitation of organic disease. Such cases are frequent and familiar to all medical men, and are the most intractable they have to deal with, the disorder being in the imagination and not in the part. . . . It is rather a remarkable coincidence that on October 2, 1883, within three weeks of my visit to Lourdes, I received a letter from Mrs. F., reminding me that some years before I had performed in her case a cure, instantaneous, and to all appearances miraculous, and which she properly attributed to undoubting faith in my word. It is a very good illustration of the kind of case to which I have been alluding, and of the power of mind over mind, and of the effect of imagination in simulating real disease. Mr. F. called on me in October, 1875, and requested me to visit his wife, who had been confined to bed for many months with a painful affection of the spine. When I went into the house I found Mrs. F., a woman of about thirty-one years of age, lying in bed on her left side, and her knees crouched up, that being the position that afforded most relief. She was thin and weak-looking,. with a countenance indicative of great suffering. I was informed that for many months she had been in the same condition. She was unable to move her limbs, any attempt being attended with pain, and practically she was paralytic. She was not able to alter her position in bed without help, and this always gave so much trouble that she would have remained constantly in the same position if the attendants had not insisted on moving her to allow of the bed-clothes being changed and arranged. She had altogether lost appetite, and had become dreadfully emaciated, and only took what was almost forced on her by her husband and friends. She had given up all hope of recovery, but had expressed a strong desire to be visited by me in consequence of something she had heard from her husband in connection with a health lecture he had been present at many years before. When I entered her bedroom something in the way she earnestly looked at me suggested the idea that I might have some influence over her supposing it to be a case of hysterical spine simulating real spine irritation and sympathetic paralysis. The story I got was not that of real disease of spine or cord or limbs, and I at once resolved to act on the supposition that it was subjective or functional, and not dependent on actual molecular change or disintegration. I went to her bedside and said suddenly: 'I cannot do you any good unless you allow me to examine your back.' In an instant she moved slightly round, and I examined her spine, running my finger over it at first lightly, then very firmly, without her wincing at all. I then said:

'Get out of bed at once.' She declared she could not move. I
said: 'You can move quite well; come out of bed,' and gave her
my hand, when, to the surprise of her husband and sister, who
looked perfectly thunderstruck, she came out of bed almost with
no help at all, and stood alone. I said: 'Walk across the floor
now,' and without demur, she walked without assistance, saying:
'I can walk quite well; I knew you would cure me; my pains are
gone.' She then went to bed with very little assistance, lay on her
back, and declared she was perfectly comfortable. She was given
a glass of milk which she took with relish, and I left the house
having performed a cure which to the bystanders looked nothing
short of a miracle. For many years I heard nothing of Mrs. F.,
when on October 2, 1883, I got her letter referred to, and shortly
after the patient herself called at my house. In February, 1885,
she again called on me. She is at present in fair health, not robust,
but cheerful and contented. She says she never altogether re-
gained her full strength; but as an evidence that she is not feeble
or unable for a good deal of exertion, I may state that she now
lives about five miles from my house, and she made her way alone,
partly by omnibus, partly by tramway, and the rest on foot.''
Compare the curiously parallel case, happening half a century
earlier, described in note 26 to Lecture IV, on the "Irvingite Gifts."

125. Benson, as cited, p. 24.
126. Bertrin, as cited, p. 280.
127. Pp. 256, 262.
128. P. 280.
129. P. 256.
130. P. 280.
131. P. 262.
132. On the case of Frau Ruchel, see the report in the *Deutsch-
evangelische Korrespondenz* for August 11, 1908. The facts are
brought out in the brochure of Doctor Aigner of Munich, *Die
Wahrheit über eine Wunderheilung in Lourdes*.
133. Pp. 197–198.
134. Zola, wishing to express these limitations in a word, said
he would not ask very much—only let some one take a knife and cut
his finger and immerse it in the water, and if it came out cured he
would say nothing more. Charcot puts it in a higher form: "Faith-
cure has never availed to restore an amputated limb" (as cited, p.
19). Percy Dearmer, having theories of his own, makes merry
over such statements. There is no such thing as the supernatural,
he says; all that God does is natural. But that carries with it
that it is not unnatural. The only limit to such cures as we see at

Lourdes, then, is that nothing unnatural can happen there. Of course, then, faith cannot grow a new leg. But that is only because we are men and not crabs, and cannot be expected to act in a crustacean manner. Grace can turn a sick man into a well one, but it cannot turn a man into an apple-tree or a cactus. God must act on the lines of nature; the supernatural is not the unnatural (*Body and Soul*,[9] pp. 90 ff.). All this is, of course, pure absurdity. It is to be noted, not obscured, that there are limitations to such cures; that a lost member cannot be restored by them, not even a lost tooth. It is only to dodge the question to say that such things are out of the question; they are not out of the question but very much in it—when it is a question of miracle. It is easy to say, "Better far to hop about on crutches than to have the soul of a crab," but it is better simply to acknowledge that there are physical disabilities which Lourdes cannot repair, and that the reason is that they are above the power of nature to repair. It should be noted in passing that Lourdes does not admit that there are any physical disabilities which she cannot repair, and that the reason is that she, unlike Dearmer, believes in the supernatural, and believes that she wields it.

135. Ed. 7, 1905, p. 55. (E. T., *Medicine and Mind*.)

136. *The New Review*, January, 1893, p. 31: "I have seen patients return from the shrines now in vogue who had been sent thither with my consent, owing to my own inability to inspire the operation of the faith-cure. I have examined the limbs affected with paralysis or contraction some days before, and have seen the gradual disappearance of the local sensitive spots which always remain for some time after the cure of the actual disease—paralysis or contraction."

137. *The Psychic Treatment of Nervous Disorders*, E. T., 1908, p. 72: A patient, "whose neck and jaw had been immobilized for years, and who had undergone unsuccessfully medical and surgical treatment from the most renowned clinicians, found sudden cure in the piscina at Lourdes." Yet Dubois does not think well of Lourdes (p. 211); that is to say, after experience with it. His expectations had been good, and he was disillusioned only by experience. "The cures there," he says, "are in fact rare." Superstition goes all lengths, and—well, "Lourdes is not very far from Tarascon."

138. As cited, p. 271.

139. Jean de Bonnefon has accumulated at the end of his trenchant pamphlet, *Faut-il fermer Lourdes?* 1906—in which he argues that Lourdes should be abolished by the state—a number of

opinions from French physicians to whom a *questionnaire* was sent, asking whether they thought the enterprise of Lourdes useful or injurious to the sick, whether they thought the piscinas were dangerous, on account of the chill or the filth, whether the long pilgrimages of the sick across France were or were not a menace to the country, and whether they thought the laws of hygiene were observed at Lourdes. The opinions of the physicians vary greatly: many are thoroughly hostile, a few are wholly favorable. What is noticeable is that a considerable number believe it is useful and ought to be sustained, although they have no belief whatever in the supernaturalness of the cures wrought there. One physician, for example, writes: "For a great number of sick people, and particularly women, Lourdes is a benefit. . . . Free from all religious opinions, I never hesitate to send to Lourdes sick people who are in the particular mental condition to receive benefit from it, and I have often had occasion to congratulate myself on having done so" (p. 51). Another writes in a less genial spirit (p. 51): "The enterprise of Lourdes is useful for feeble-minded people, and there are legions of these in our fine land of France. . . . I know Lourdes, and it seems to me that they are as filthy there—in the medical sense of the word—as they are everywhere else in France."

140. W. B. Carpenter, *Principles of Mental Physiology*, 1824, p. 684, is engaged in pointing out the physical effects which may be wrought by "expectant attention." He says: "That the *confident expectation of a cure* is the most potent means of bringing it about, doing that which no medical treatment can accomplish, may be affirmed as the generalized result of experiences of the most varied kind, extending through a long series of ages. For it is this which is common to methods of the most diverse character; some of them —as the Metallic Tractors, Mesmerism, and Homœopathy—pretending to some physical power; whilst to others, as to the invocations of Prince Hohenlohe, and the commands of Doctor Vernon, or the Zouave Jacob, some miraculous influence was attributed. It has been customary, on the part of those who do not accept the 'physical' or the 'miraculous' hypothesis as to the interpretation of these facts, to refer the effects either to the 'imagination' or to 'faith'—two mental states apparently incongruous, and neither of them rightly expressing the condition on which they depend. For although there can be no doubt that in a great number of cases the patients have *believed themselves* to be cured, when *no real amelioration* of their condition had taken place, yet there is a large body of testimony and evidence that permanent amendment of a kind perfectly obvious to others has shown itself in a great variety of

local maladies, when the patients have been sufficiently possessed by the *expectation* of benefit, and by *faith* in the efficacy of the means employed."

141. *The New Review*, January, 1893, p. 23.

142. A writer in *The Edinburgh Review* for January, 1903, p. 154, has this to say of the use of "suggestion" at Lourdes: "What is so painful and so repulsive in Lourdes and similar centres of popular devotion, is not so much the fanaticism of the pilgrims, the commercial element inseparable from the necessity of providing transport and lodging for the multitude of strangers, or even the incongruous emergence of those lower passions never wholly absent when men are met together, and separated by so small an interval from overwrought emotion, whatever its source, as the deliberate organization of hysteria, the training of suggestion, the exploitation of disease. Everything in the pilgrimage is calculated to disturb the equilibrium of the faculties, to stimulate, to excite, to strain. The unsanitary condition under which the journey is made, the hurry, the crowding, the insufficient food and sleep, the incessant religious exercises, the acute tension of every sense and power, all work up to a calculated climax."

143. *Op. cit.*, E. T., pp. 118 ff.

144. *Lourdes*, pp. 42 ff.

145. *Ibid.*, p. 56.

146. *Ibid.*, p. v, *cf.* also Herbert Thurston, Hastings's *ERE*, vol. VIII, p. 150. This is apparently also what J. A. MacCulloch means when he says (Hastings's *ERE*, vol. VIII, p. 682): "Occasionally miracles at Lourdes are also wrought on more than neurotic diseases," and "they suggest an influx of healing power from without."

147. *Op. cit.*, pp. 150 ff. *Cf.* John Rickaby, "Explanation of Miracles by Unknown Natural Forces," in *The Month* for January, 1877.

148. October, 1880, pp. 386–398.

149. P. 398.

150. *La Vérité sur Lourdes*, pp. 123 ff.

151. We take the account as given by A. Tholuck, *Vermischte Schriften*, I, p. 139.

152. The shortcomings of the authorities at Lourdes in their reports of the cures may be read in *The Dublin Review*, October, 1908, pp. 416 ff., *apropos* of Doctor Boissarie's *L'Œuvre de Lourdes*, new ed., 1908. *Cf.* Paul Dubois, *The Psychic Treatment of Nervous Disorders*, p. 211: "I have detected in the physicians of the bureau of statistics, in spite of their evident good faith, a mentality of such a nature that their observations lose all value in my eyes."

153. Sir Francis Champneys, M.D., F.R.C.P., in *The Church Quarterly Review*, April, 1917, p. 44, says justly: "It is not safe to define a Miracle as something which cannot be understood; for, at that rate, what can be understood?"

154. *Systematic Theology*, vol. I, p. 52.

155. Deut. 13 : 2.

156. *Paris*, p. 195.

157. *Lourdes*, p. 39.

158. See above, p. 59.

159. *Lourdes*, p. 82.

160. P. Saintyves, *Les Saints successeurs des Dieux*, p. 11, note 1.

161. The bibliography at the end of Herbert Thurston's article "Lourdes," in Hastings's *ERE*, is a model list, and contains all that the student need concern himself about. The English reader has at his disposal: H. Lasserre, *Miraculous Episodes of Lourdes*, 1884; R. F. Clarke, *Lourdes, and its Miracles*, 1888; G. Bertrin, *Lourdes; a History of its Apparitions and Cures*, 1908; R. H. Benson, *Lourdes*, 1914; together with such illuminating articles as that of Professor George Buchanan in the *Lancet* of June 25, 1885; of a series of British physicians and surgeons in the *British Medical Journal* for June 18, 1910; of J. M. Charcot ("The Faith Cure") in *The New Review*, January, 1893, vol. VIII, pp. 18–31; and of Doctor A. T. Myers, and F. W. H. Myers ("Mind Cure, Faith Cure and the Miracles of Lourdes") in the *Proceedings of the Society for Psychical Research*, vol. IX, 1893–1894, pp. 160–209. There are also three excellent articles by Catholic physicians accessible: Doctor E. Mackey, *Dublin Review*, October, 1880, pp. 386–398; Doctor J. R. Gasquet, *Dublin Review*, October, 1894, pp. 342–357; Doctor E. Berdoe, *Nineteenth Century*, October, 1895, pp. 614–618.

NOTES TO LECTURE IV

IRVINGITE GIFTS

1. *Edinburgh Review*, vol. LIII, p. 302.

2. F. J. Snell, *Wesley and Methodism*, 1900, p. 157.

3. "The Principles of a Methodist Farther Explained," etc., in *Works*, New York, 1856, vol. V, p. 328.

4. "I acknowledge," he says, "that I have seen with my eyes, and heard with my ears, several things which, to the best of my judgment, cannot be accounted for by an ordinary course of natural causes; and which I therefore believe ought to be 'ascribed to the extraordinary interposition of God.' If any man choose to style them *miracles*, I reclaim not. I have diligently inquired into the

facts, I have weighed the preceding and following circumstances. I have strove to account for them in a natural way. . . . I cannot account for (them) . . . in a natural way. Therefore, I believe they were . . . supernatural." (*Op. cit.*, p. 325.) On Wesley's ingrained superstition and wonder-craving proclivities, see the remarks by L. Tyerman, *The Life and Times of the Rev. John Wesley*,[5] 1880, I, pp. 220 ff.; and Isaac Taylor, there referred to.

5. "A Letter to the Rev. Dr. Conyers Middleton; occasioned by his late 'Free Inquiry,'" in *Works*, as cited, vol. V, p. 746.

6. Snell, as cited, pp. 153 f.

7. *Works*, 1811, vol. VIII, pp. 322, 329. *Cf. The Edinburgh Review*, January, 1831, p. 272, note. On Wesley's views on extraordinary exercises, see Richard Watson, "Life of Rev. John Wesley," in Watson's *Works*, 1835, pp. 89 ff.; also Watson's observations on Southey's *Life*, pp. 385 ff., 421 ff.

8. *John Lacy's Prophetical Warnings*, 1707, pp. 3, 31, 32, as cited by William Goode, *The Modern Claims to the Possession of the Extraordinary Gifts of the Spirit, Stated and Examined*, etc., second edition, 1834, p. 194. *Cf.* pp. 188–189. Goode's account of "The French Prophets" and similar phenomena is very instructive.

9. An interesting account of present-day "Irvingism" will be found in an article by Erskine N. White in *The Presbyterian and Reformed Review*, October, 1899, vol. X, pp. 624–635; see also the article by Samuel J. Andrews, "Catholic Apostolic Church," in *The New Schaff-Herzog Encyclopedia of Religious Knowledge*, with its supplement by Th. Kolde, and the added bibliography.

10. *The Collected Writings of Edward Irving*, edited by his nephew, the Reverend G. Carlyle, M.A. In five volumes, London and New York, 1866, vol. V, pp. 499 ff., 532 ff.

11. Chalmers himself says: "When Irving was associated with me at Glasgow he did not attract a large congregation, but he completely attached to himself and his ministry a limited number of persons with whose minds his own was in affinity. I have often," he adds, "observed this effect produced by men whose habits of thinking and feeling are peculiar or eccentric. They possess a *magnetic* attraction for minds assimilated to their own." (William Hanna, *Memoirs of the Life and Writings of Thomas Chalmers*, New York, 1855, vol. III, pp. 275–276.) C. Kegan Paul (*Biographical Sketches*, 1883, p. 8) puts it thus: "Though his labors from house to house were unceasing, though all brought face to face with him loved him, in the pulpit he was unrecognized. . . . A few looked on him with exceeding admiration, but neither the congregation nor Chalmers himself gave him cordial acceptance." In Glasgow,

says Mrs. Oliphant (*The Life of Edward Irving*, New York, 1862, p. 98), "Irving lived in the shade." "It was then a kind of deliverance," says Th. Kolde (*Herzog-Hauck*, vol. IX, 1901, p. 425, lines 14 f), "when by the intermediation of Chalmers, he was chosen in 1822 as minister to the little (it had then about fifty members) Scottish (so-called Caledonian) congregation which was connected with a small Scotch Hospital in Hatton Garden, London."

12. See *sub. nom.* in the *Dictionary of National Biography.*

13. From 1829 to 1833 they published a periodical, *The Morning Watch, a Journal of Prophecy.*

14. J. A. Froude, *Life of Carlyle*, 1795–1835, vol. II, p. 177.

15. See Mrs. Oliphant's *Life*, p. 302.

16. *Ibid.*, pp. 312, 362.

17. The writer of the sketch of Scott in the *Dictionary of National Biography* thinks Mrs. Oliphant does him injustice. There seems to be no good reason for so thinking. *Cf.* what David Brown says of him, *The Expositor*, III, VI, pp. 219, 266.

18. *Fraser's Magazine*, January, 1832, quoted by Mrs. Oliphant, p. 363.

19. *Ibid.*, p. 363.

20. *Ibid.*, p. 365.

21. *Ibid.*, p. 378.

22. *Ibid.*, p. 379.

23. *Ibid.*, p. 363.

24. *Ibid.*, p. 379.

25. *Ibid.*, p. 381. It is perhaps worth mentioning that neither of these young women was bedridden. The miracle did not consist in their literally rising up from their beds.

26. Samuel J. Andrews, *The New Schaff-Herzog Encyclopedia of Religious Knowledge*, vol. II, 457, thinks it worth while, in the interest of the genuineness of the "gifts," to insist on their first occurrence in England apart from Irving's congregation. The deputation to Scotland, he writes, "returned fully convinced that the utterances were divine. In May, 1831, like utterances were heard in London, the first in a congregation of the Church of England. This being reported to the bishop, he forbade them in the future as interfering with the service. Their occurrence in several dissenting congregations brought forth similar prohibitions, and this led to the utterances being made chiefly in the church of Edward Irving, he being a believer in their divine origin. But they were not confined to London. At Bristol and other places the same spiritual phenomena appeared." The entire drift of Andrews's account is to represent the "gifts" as thrust upon, rather than

earnestly wooed, by Irving and his fellows. This is wholly unhistorical. On Miss Fancourt's case, see Mrs. Oliphant, *Life*, etc., pp. 416, 561; it was the subject of a controversy between *The Morning Watch* and *The Christian Observer*, some account of which may be read in *The Edinburgh Review*, June, 1831 (vol. LIII, pp. 263 ff.). The opinion of the medical attendants was that there was nothing miraculous in the cure. One of their opinions (Mr. Travers's) is so modern, and a parallel case which is inserted in it is so instructive, that we transcribe the latter part of it. "A volume, and not an uninteresting one," we read, "might be compiled of histories resembling Miss Fancourt's. The truth is, these are the cases upon which, beyond all others, the empiric thrives. Credulity, the foible of a weakened though vivacious intellect, is the pioneer of an unqualified and overweening confidence, and thus prepared, the patient is in the most hopeful state of mind for the credit as well as the craft of the pretender. This, however, I mention only by the way, for the sake of illustration. I need not exemplify the sudden and remarkable effects of joy, terror, anger, and other passions of the mind upon the nervous systems of confirmed invalids, in restoring to them the use of weakened limbs, etc. They are as much matters of notoriety as any of the properties and powers of direct remedial agents recorded in the history of medicine. To cite one. A case lately fell under my notice of a young lady, who, from inability to stand or walk without acute pain in her loins, lay for near a twelvemonth upon her couch, subjected to a variety of treatment by approved and not inexperienced members of the profession. A single visit from a surgeon of great fame in the management of such cases set the patient upon her feet, and his prescription amounted simply to an assurance, in the most confident terms, that she must disregard the pain, and that nothing else was required for her recovery, adding, that if she did not do so she would become an incurable cripple. She followed his directions immediately, and with perfect success. But such and similar examples every medical man of experience could contribute in partial confirmation of the old adage, 'Foi est tout.' Of all moral energies, I conceive that faith which is inspired by a religious creed to be the most powerful; and Miss Fancourt's case, there can be no doubt, was one of the many instances of sudden recovery from a passive form of nervous ailment, brought about by the powerful excitement of this extraordinary stimulus, compared to which, in her predisposed state of mind, ammonia and quinine would have been mere trifling." A curiously similar instance to that given by Mr. Travers is adduced by a distinguished recent surgeon, Mr. George Buchanan, in illustrating what he saw done at Lourdes. It is recorded by the Messrs. Myers, in the *Proceedings of the Society for Psychical Research*, vol. IX (1893–1894), pp. 191 ff., and we have cited it thence on a previous occasion. See above, pp. 218 ff. Doctor W. B. Carpenter, in an article in *The Quarterly Review*, vol. XCIII (1853), p. 513, directly refers to Miss Fancourt's case, and pronounces it a case of "hysterical" paralysis, such as is well known to be curable by mental means.

27. Mrs. Oliphant, *Life*, p. 420.

28. *Ibid.*, p. 417.

29. *Ibid.*, p. 418.

30. *The Expositor*, Third Series, vol. VI (October, 1887), 268.

31. *Cf.* what Irving says, in Mrs. Oliphant's *Life*, p. 418.

32. For example, Mr. Pilkington's, printed in Mrs. Oliphant's *Life*, p. 424.

33. *Cf.* Mrs. Oliphant's *Life*, pp. 448 ff.

34. Robert Baxter, *Narrative of Facts, Characterizing the Supernatural Manifestations in Members of Mr. Irving's Congregation, and other Individuals in England and Scotland, and formerly in the Writer Himself*, second edition, 1893 (April; the first edition had been published in February of the same year). Mrs. Oliphant prints extracts from Baxter's *Narrative* in her Appendix B, pp. 562 ff.

35. Baxter, *op. cit.*, p. 118.

36. As cited, p. 272.

37. "Though Irving was the 'angel' of the church," writes Theo. Kolde (*The New Schaff-Herzog Encyclopedia of Religious Knowledge*, vol. VI, p. 34), "the voices of the prophets left him little hearing. Cardale, Drummond, and the prophet Taplin took the lead of the movement, and the new organization proceeded rapidly, new functionaries were created as the Spirit bade, on the analogy of the New Testament indications, and presently there were six other congregations in London, forming with Irving's the counterpart of the seven churches of the Apocalypse. Irving accepted the whole development in faith, although he had conceived the Apostolic office as something different which should not interfere with the independence of himself as the 'angel.' But he had lost control of the movement, and those who now led it lost no opportunity of humiliating the man to whose personality they had owed so much. When the sentence of deposition was confirmed by the Presbytery of Annan, and then by the Scottish General Synod, and he returned to London strong in the consciousness of his call of God to the office of angel and pastor of the church, he was not allowed to baptize a child, but was told to wait until, on the bidding of the prophets, he should be again ordained by an apostle. His

health was now failing, and his physician ordered him, in the autumn of 1834, to winter in the South. He went, however, to Scotland, where the prophets had promised him great success in the power of the Spirit, and died in Glasgow, where he is buried in the crypt of the Cathedral." There are obvious slips in this account, due apparently to the translator, but we transcribe it as it stands. On the matter, *cf.* Mrs. Oliphant's *Life*, pp. 527 ff.

38. Mrs. Oliphant's *Life*, p. 505.

39. C. Kegan Paul, as cited, pp. 29 ff., strongly protests against this representation, citing Mrs. Oliphant's account, and controverting it. "The congregation," he writes, "after some wanderings, found refuge in a picture-gallery in Newman Street, their home for many years. Here it was that the organization and ceremonies began to set aside the old Presbyterian forms, and gain somewhat of Catholic magnificence. Here it was that by the voice of prophecy six apostles were called out to rule the church before Mr. Irving's death. Mr. Irving was not called as an apostle, nor was he a prophet, nor did he speak with tongues; but he remained as he had ever been, the chief pastor of the congregation, the Angel, as the minister in charge of each church began to be called. He was not shelved in any degree, nor slighted, and though the details which took place were ordered by others in prophecy, yet the whole was what he had prayed for and foreseen, as necessary in his estimation to the perfection of the church. So in ordering and building up his people under, as it seemed to him, the immediate direction of the Holy Spirit, passed the rest of that year." There is nothing here inconsistent with Mrs. Oliphant's representation; it is the same thing looked at from a different angle. Paul, however, by adducing the dates, does show, that, as he puts it, "there was no period of mournful silence during which he waited to speak, nor was his recognition for a moment doubtful." For the rest, he only shows that Irving kissed the rod.

40. *The Brazen Serpent*, p. 253, quoted in William Hanna, *Letters of Thomas Erskine of Linlathen from 1800 till 1840*, 1877, p. 183. Compare these passages quoted on the same page from *On the Gifts of the Spirit:* "Whilst I see nothing in the Scripture against the reappearance, or rather the continuance of miraculous gifts in the church, but a great deal for it, I must further say that I see a great deal of internal evidence in the west country to prove their genuine miraculous character, especially in the speaking with tongues. . . . After witnessing what I have witnessed among those people, I cannot think of any person decidedly condemning them as impostors, without a feeling of great alarm. It certainly is not a thing

to be lightly or rashly believed, but neither is it a thing to be lightly or rashly rejected. I believe that it is of God."

41. Hanna, as cited, p. 218; *cf.* p. 220.

42. Hanna, as cited, p. 209: "I think that I mentioned to Lady Matilda at Cadder the circumstance that shook me with regard to the Macdonalds at Port Glasgow, that in two instances when James Macdonald spoke with remarkable power, a power acknowledged by all the other gifted people there, I discovered the seed of his utterances in the newspapers. . . . And I put it to him; and although he had spoken in perfect integrity (of that I have no doubt) yet he was satisfied that my conjecture as to its origin was correct. . . . I thus see how things may come into the mind and remain there, and then come forth as supernatural utterances, although their origin be quite natural. James Macdonald could not say that he was conscious of anything in these two utterances distinguishing them from all the others; but only said that he believed these two were of the flesh. Taplin made a similar confession on being reproved by Miss Emily Cardale for having rebuked Mr. Irving in an utterance. He acknowledged that he was wrong; and yet he could not say where the difference lay between that utterance and any other."

43. Hanna, as cited, p. 204. He adds: "This does not change my mind as to what the endowment of the church is, if she had faith, but it changes me as to the present estimate that I form of her condition."

44. In March, 1834, after hearing in Edinburgh "the utterances" through Cardale and Drummond, he speaks of his scepticism regarding them, despite his agreement (except in two instances) with the matter delivered in them, and the pleasingness of their form. "The shake which I have received on this matter," he writes (Hanna, as cited, p. 209), "is, I find very deep; or rather it would be a truer expression of my feelings to say that I am now convinced that I never did actually believe it." He adds: "My conviction that the gifts ought to be in the church is not in the least degree touched, but a faith in any one instance of manifestation which I have witnessed, like the faith which I have in the righteousness and faithfullness of God, I am sure I have not and never have had, as far as I can judge on looking back—that is, the only true faith, even 'the substance of things hoped for.'"

45. Hanna, as cited, p. 233: "James Macdonald is to be buried to-day at one o'clock. . . . This event has recalled many things to my remembrance. I lived in the house with them for six weeks, I believe, and I found them a family united to God and to each,

other. James especially was an amiable and clean character, perfectly true. And those manifestations which I have so often witnessed in him were indeed most wonderful things and most mighty, and yet—I am thoroughly persuaded—delusive." This was written February 6, 1835. George Macdonald died the year following—both of consumption, the disease which carried off Isabella Campbell, and from which both Mary Campbell and Margaret Macdonald were supposed to be suffering when they were "healed."

46. P. 279.

47. P. 304.

48. *Life of Story of Rosneath*, by his son, p. 23ː, note, quoted by Henry F. Henderson, *The Religious Controversies of Scotland*, 1905, p. 126.

49. *Scottish Divines 1505–1872*, etc., 1883, being a series of "St. Giles Lectures," Lecture VII, *Edward Irving*, by R. Herbert Story, p. 254.

50. Henderson, as cited, p. 126. "Story concluded by confessing," continues Henderson, "that he had greatly sinned in not exposing her earlier, but he had been restrained from doing this by feelings of affection. What change this letter might have wrought on Irving had he received it we cannot tell. Probably not even Story's voice could have now recalled him." Mary Campbell had in 1831 married a young clerk in a writer's office in Edinburgh, of the name of W. R. Caird, and was residing at Albury (not without interruptions for journeys) as the guest of Henry Drummond; she died in 1840 (see Edward Miller, *The History and Doctrines of Irvingism*, 1878, vol. I, pp. 58 ff.). Caird, who was acting as a lay-evangelist, undertook in 1841 an Irvingist mission in south Germany, and in 1860 was raised to the "apostolic" office. On the 27th of January, 1832, Irving wrote to Story announcing the new developments which had been introduced by Baxter, and concluding with the remarkable appeal: "Oh, Story, thou hast grievously sinned in standing afar off from the work of the Lord, scanning it like a skeptic instead of proving it like a spiritual man! Ah! brother, repent, and the Lord will forgive thee!" To this letter, as a postscript, he adds this single unprepared-for line: "Mrs. Caird is a saint of God, and hath the gift of prophecy." We cannot miss the air of defiant assertion, or fail to read behind it a feeling of the need of something in Mrs. Caird's defense. Mrs. Oliphant (p. 450) justly comments: "The sentence of approval pronounced with so much decision and brevity at the conclusion of this letter addressed to him was Irving's manner of avoiding controversy, and making his friend aware that, highly as he esteemed himself,

he could hear nothing against the other, whose character had received the highest of all guarantees to his unquestioning faith." The cause of Irvingite gifts was indeed bound up in one bundle with the trustworthiness of Mary Campbell's manifestations. Thomas Bayne, writing on Robert Story, in the *Dictionary of National Biography* (vol. LIV, p. 430), condenses the story thus: "In 1830 his parishioner, Mary Campbell, professed to have received the 'gift of tongues,' and though Story exposed her imposture, she found disciples in London, and was credited by Edward Irving, then in the maelstrom of his impassioned fanaticism. On the basis of her predictions arose the 'Holy Catholic Apostolic Church' (see Carlyle, *Life*, II, 204)."

51. Hanna, as cited, p. 209.

52. P. 213.

53. The nearest he came to it seems to be expressed in the sentence (p. 208): "I have a witness within me which, I am conscious, tries truth; but I do not know a witness within me which tries power." With this inner infallible sense compare Mrs. Eddy's assertion (*Christian Science History*, ed. 1, p. 16): "I possess a spiritual sense of what the malicious mental practitioner is mentally arguing which cannot be deceived; I can discern in the human mind thoughts, motives, and purposes; and neither mental arguments nor psychic power can affect this spiritual insight." An infallible spiritual insight is a dangerous thing to lay claim to, and what we take to be its deliverance a still more dangerous thing to follow.

54. Pp. 507 ff.

55. Erskine in his tract, *On the Gifts of the Holy Spirit*, 1830, writes: "For the languages are distinct, well-inflected, well-compacted languages; they are not random collections of sounds, they are composed of words of various lengths, with the natural variety, and yet possessing that commonness of character which marks them to be one distinct language. I have heard many people speak gibberish, but this is not gibberish, it is decidedly well-compacted language."—(Quoted in Hanna, *Chalmers*, vol. III, p. 253; *Erskine*, p. 392.)

56. As quoted in *The Edinburgh Review*, June, 1831, p. 275: "The tongues spoken by all the several persons who have received the gift are perfectly distinct in themselves, and from each other. J. Macdonald speaks two tongues, both easily discernible from each other. I easily perceived when he was speaking in the one, and when in the other tongue. J. Macdonald exercises his gift more frequently than any of the others; and I have heard him speak for twenty minutes together, with all the energy of action and voice

of an orator addressing his audience. The language which he then, and indeed generally, uttered is very full and harmonious, containing many Greek and Latin radicals, and with inflections also much resembling those of the Greek language. I also frequently noticed that he employed the same radical with different inflections; but I do not remember to have noticed his employing two words together, both of which, as to root and inflection, I could pronounce to belong to any language with which I am acquainted. G. Macdonald's tongue is harsher in its syllables, but more grand in general expression. The only time I ever had a serious doubt whether the unknown sounds which I heard on these occasions were parts of a language, was when the Macdonalds' servant spoke during the first evening. When she spoke on subsequent occasions, it was invariably in one tongue, which not only was perfectly distinct from the sounds she uttered at the first meeting, but was satisfactorily established to my conviction, to be a language." "One of the persons thus gifted, we employed as our servant while at Port Glasgow. She is a remarkably quiet, steady, phlegmatic person, entirely devoid of forwardness or of enthusiasm, and with very little to say for herself in the ordinary way. The language which she spoke was as distinct as the others; and in her case, as in the others (with the exceptions I have before mentioned), it was quite evident to a hearer that the language spoken at one time was identical with that spoken at another time." Perhaps it ought to be added that when Mary Campbell's written-tongue (for she wrote as well as spoke) was submitted to the examination of Sir George Staunton and Samuel Lee, they pronounced it no tongue at all (Hanna, *Chalmers*, vol. III, p. 266).

57. Mrs. Oliphant, *Life*, p. 430.

58. *Ibid.*

59. *Ibid.*, p. 431.

60. *Ibid.*

61. *Reminiscences*, p. 252.

62. *The British Weekly*, January 18, 1889. We have purposely drawn these descriptions from the more sympathetic sources. We must add, however, that the more competent the observer was the less favorable was the impression made upon him. J. G. Lockhart writes to "Christopher North," in 1824 (*Christopher North, A Memoir of John Wilson*, by his daughter, Mrs. Gordon. Am. ed., New York, 1863, p. 271): "Irving, you may depend upon it, is a pure humbug. He has about three good attitudes, and the lower notes of his voice are superb, with a fine manly tremulation that sets women mad, as the roar of a noble bull does a field of kine;

but beyond this he is nothing, really nothing. He has no sort of
real earnestness; feeble, pumped-up, boisterous, overlaid stuff is
his staple; he is no more a Chalmers than —— is a Jeffrey." That
is a vignette from a competent hand of Irving as a preacher, in the
first flush of his popularity in London—before the arrival of the
"gifts." And here, now, is a full-length portrait, from an equally
competent hand, of a service ten years afterwards (spring of 1833), at
Newman Street. It is taken from the intimate journal of Joseph
Addison Alexander (*The Life of Joseph Addison Alexander, D.D.*,
by Henry Carrington Alexander, New York, 1870, vol. I, pp. 289 ff.):

"After breakfast, having learned that Edward Irving was to
hold a meeting at half-past eleven, we resolved to go; but without
expecting to hear the tongues, as they have not been audible of
late. Mr. Nott, who had called before breakfast, conducted us
to Newman Street, where Irving is established since he left the
house in Regent Square. As we walked along we saw a lady before
us arm in arm with a tall man in black breeches, a broad-brimmed
hat, and black hair hanging down his shoulders. This, Mr. Nott
informed us, was Irving himself with his *cara sposa*. We followed
them to the door of the chapel in Newman Street, where Mr. Nott
left us, and we went in. The chapel is a room of moderate size,
seated with plain wooden benches, like our recitation rooms. The
end opposite the entrance is semicircular, and filled with amphi-
theatrical seats. In front of these there is a large arch, and immediately beneath it a reading-desk in the shape of an altar, with a large
arm-chair beside it. From this point there are several steps de-
scending toward the body of the house, on which are chairs for the
elders of the church. I mention these particulars because I think
the pulpit and its appendages extremely well contrived for scenic
effects. . . .

"Soon after we were seated, the chairs below the pulpit were
occupied by several respectable men, one of them quite handsome
and well dressed. Another man and a woman took their seats
upon the benches behind. While we were gazing at these, we heard
a heavy tramp along the aisle, and the next moment Irving walked
up to the altar, opened the Bible, and began at once to read. He
has a noble figure, and his features are not ugly, with the exception of an awful squint. His hair is parted right and left, and
hangs down on his shoulders in affected disorder. His dress is
laboriously old-fashioned—a black quaker coat and small clothes.
His voice is harsh, but like a trumpet; it takes hold of one, and
cannot be forgotten. His great aim appeared to be to vary his attitudes and appear at ease. He began to read in a standing posture,

but had scarcely finished half a dozen verses when he dropped into
the chair and sat while he read the remainder. He then stepped
forward to the point of his stage, dropped on his knees and began
to pray in a voice of thunder; most of the people kneeling fairly
down. At the end of the prayer he read the Sixty-sixth Psalm,
and I now perceived that his selections were designed to have a
bearing on the persecutions of his people and himself. The chapter
from Samuel was that relating to Shimei. He then gave out the
Sixty-sixth Psalm in verse; which was sung standing, very well,
Irving himself joining in with a mighty bass. He then began to
read the Thirty-ninth of Exodus, with an allegorical exposition,
after a short prayer for divine assistance. The ouches of the breast-
plate he explained to mean the rulers of the church. While he was
dealing this out, he was interrupted in a manner rather startling.
I had observed that the elders who sat near him kept their eyes
raised to the skylight overhead, as if wooing inspiration. One in
particular looked very wild. His face was flushed, and he occasionally turned up the white of his eyes in an ominous style. For
the most part, however, his eyes were shut. Just as Irving reached
the point I have mentioned and was explaining the ouches, this
elder . . . burst out in a sort of wild ejaculation, thus, 'Taranti-
hoiti-faragmi-santi' (I do not pretend to recollect the words); 'O
ye people—ye people of the Lord, ye have not the ouches—ye have
not the ouches—ha-a-a; ye must have them—ye must have them
—ha-a-a; ye cannot hear—ye cannot hear.' This last was spoken
in a pretty loud whisper, as the inspiration died away within him.
When he began, Irving suspended his exposition and covered his
face with his hands. As soon as the voice ceased, he resumed the
thread of his discourse, till the 'tongue' broke out again 'in unknown strains.' After these had again come to an end, Irving knelt
and prayed, thanking God for looking upon the poverty and deso-
lation of his church amidst her persecutions. After he had finished
and arisen from his knees, he dropped down again, saying, 'one
supplication more,' or 'one thanksgiving more.' He now proceeded
to implore the Divine blessing on the servant who had been ordained as a prophet in the sight of the people. After this supple-
mentary prayer, he stood up, asked a blessing in a few words, and
began to read in the sixth John about feeding on Christ's flesh. In
the course of his remarks he said: 'The priests and churches in
our day have denied the Saviour's flesh, and therefore cannot feed
upon him.' He then prayed again (with genuflexion), after which
he dropped into his chair, covered his face with his hands, and said,
'Hear now what the elders have to say to you.' No sooner was

this signal given than the 'tongue' began anew, and for several minutes uttered a flat and silly rhapsody, charging the church with unfaithfulness and rebuking it therefor. The 'tongue' having finished, an elder who sat above him rose, with Bible in hand, and made a dry but sober speech about faith, in which there was nothing, I believe, *outré*. The handsome, well-dressed man, whom I have mentioned, at Irving's left hand, now rose and came forward with his Bible. His first words were, 'Your sins which are many are forgiven you.' His discourse was incoherent, though not wild, and had reference to the persecution of the church. The last preacher on the occasion was a decent, ministerial-looking man in black, who discoursed on oneness with Christ. A paper was now handed to Irving, which he looked at, and then fell upon his knees. In the midst of his prayer he took the paper and read it to the Lord, as he would have read a notice. It was a thanksgiving by Harriet Palmer for the privilege of attending on these services to-day. After the prayer, they sang a Psalm, and then the meeting was dismissed by benediction. The impression made on my mind was one of unmingled contempt. Everything which fell from Irving's lips was purely flat and stupid, without a single flash of genius, or the slightest indication of strength or even vivacity of mind. I was confirmed in my former low opinion of him, founded on his writings. . . . Dr. Cox and I flattered ourselves that he observed us, and preached at us. I saw him peeping through his fingers several times, and I suppose he was not gratified to see us gazing steadfastly at him all the time, for he took occasion to tell the people that it would profit them nothing without the circumcision of the ear. This he defined to be the putting away of all impertinent curiosity and profane inquisitiveness—all gazing and prying into the mysteries of God, and all malicious reporting of his doings in the church."

63. Robert Baxter, *Narrative of Facts*, ed. 2, 1833, p. xxviii; *cf.* C. Kegan Paul, *op. cit.*, p. 29, as above in note 39.

64. Baxter, as cited.

65. Baxter, *op. cit.*, p. 133.

66. Baxter, *op. cit.*, p. 95.

67. Can the mind help going back to the vivid description which Irenæus gives us of how Marcus the Magician made his women prophesy (Irenæus, *Adv. Hær.*, I, 13, 3)? "Behold," he would say after rites and ceremonies had been performed fitted to arouse to great expectations, "grace has descended upon thee; open thy mouth and prophesy!" "But when the woman would reply, 'I have never prophesied and do not know how!' he would begin afresh

with his incantations so as to astonish the deluded victim, and command her again, 'Open thy mouth, and speak whatever occurs to thee and thou shalt prophesy.' She then, vainly puffed up and elated by these words and greatly excited by the expectation of prophesying, her heart beating violently, reaches the requisite pitch of audacity, and idly as well as impudently utters some nonsense as it happens to occur to her, such as might be expected from one heated by an empty spirit. And then she reckons herself a prophetess."

68. Henderson, *op. cit.*, p. 125.

69. The literature on Edward Irving and Irvingism will be found noted with sufficient fulness in *The New Schaff-Herzog Encyclopedia of Religious Knowledge*, vol. II, p. 459, and vol. VI, p. 34; and at the head of the article on Irving in *Herzog-Hauck*. The primary literature on the Scotch movement is given in the footnotes to the brief account of it inserted by William Hanna at pp. 175-183 of his *Letters of Thomas Erskine of Linlathen from 1800 till 1845*, 1877. For an almost world-wide recent recurrence of phenomena similar to the Irvingite "gifts," especially "speaking with tongues," see the informing article of Frederick G. Henke, "The Gift of Tongues and Related Phenomena at the Present Day," in *The American Journal of Theology*, April, 1909, XIII, 2, pp. 193-206. Henke gives references to the primary literature. For a first-hand account of some related phenomena in connection with a great revival in Kentucky in 1801-1803, see the letter of Thomas Cleland on "Bodily Affections produced by Religious Excitement," printed in *The Biblical Repertory and Princeton Review* for 1834, vol. VI, pp. 336 ff.; references to further first-hand accounts of the Kentucky phenomena are given by William A. Hammond, M.D., *Spiritualism and Allied Causes and Conditions of Nervous Derangement*, 1876, pp. 232 ff. See also Catherine C. Cleaveland, *The Great Revival in the West, 1795-1805*, 1916. The judicious remarks of Charles Hodge on "The Disorders Attending the Great Revival of 1740-1745," in his *The Constitutional History of the Presbyterian Church in the United States of America*, 1857, vol. II, pp. 65 ff., should be read along with the account of them given by Jonathan Edwards. On the physical accompaniments of John Wesley's preaching at Bristol, chiefly in 1739, see an account in Tyerman, *The Life and Times of the Rev. John Wesley*,[5] 1880, vol. I, pp. 255-270. Compare note 7, on p. 288.

NOTES TO LECTURE V

FAITH-HEALING

1. *The Natural History of Immortality*, by Joseph William Reynolds, M.A., rector of St. Anne and St. Agnes with St. John Zachary, Gresham St., London, and prebendary of St. Paul's Cathedral, 1891, p. 286.

2. These facts are taken from a paper by R. Keiso Carter, *The Century Magazine*, March, 1887, vol. XI, p. 780.

3. P. 13.

4. January, 1884; vol. V, p. 49.

5. How natural this attitude is, in the circumstances, is interestingly illustrated by its appearance even among the pre-Christian Jews. A. Schlatter, in his *Der Glaube im Neuen Testament*, 1885, when discussing the conception of faith in the synagogue, remarks upon the tendency which showed itself to push the duty of faith (for faith was conceived in the synagogue as a duty, and therefore as a work) to extremes. The Jerusalem Targum on Gen. 40 : 23 blames Joseph for asking the chief butler to remember him; he should have depended on God's grace alone. Any one who, having food for to-day, asks, What am I to eat? fails in faith (*Tanch.*, fol. 29, 4). All means are to be excluded. He then continues (pp. 46 ff.): "Philo blames the employment of a physician as lack of faith; if anything against their will befalls doubters, they flee, because they do not believe in a helping God, to the sources of help which the occurrence suggests—to physicians, simples, physics, correct diet; to all the aids offered to a dying race; and, if any one suggests to them, Flee in your miseries to the sole physician of the ills of the soul, and leave the aids falsely so-called to the creature subjected to suffering, they laugh, and scoff, and say, Good Morrow! —and are unwilling to flee to God if they can find anything to protect them from the coming evil; to be sure, if nothing that man does suffices but everything, even the most highly esteemed, shows itself injurious, then they renounce in their perplexity the help of others, and flee, compelled, the cowards, late and with difficulty, to God, the sole Saviour (*De Sacrifici Abel*, Mang., I, 176, 23 ff.). In this Philo does not express an idea peculiar to himself; the Son of Sirach, xxxviii, 1 ff., shows that in the Palestinian Synagogue also, from of old, the question was discussed, whether the help of a physician was to be sought in sickness: 'The Lord has created medicines out of the earth, and he that is wise will not abhor them; was not the water made sweet with a word that the virtue thereof might

be known? . . . My son, in thy sickness be not negligent; but pray unto the Lord and He will make thee whole. Leave off from sin and order thy hands aright, and cleanse thy heart from all wickedness; give a sweet savor and a memorial of fine flour, and make a fat offering, as not being. Then give place to the physician, for the Lord has created Him; let him not go from thee, for thou hast need of him. There is a time when in their hands there is good success, for they shall also pray unto the Lord, that He would prosper that which they give, for ease and remedy to prolong life' (38 : 4 f., 9 ff.). Sickness, as a judicial intrusion of God into the life of man, presupposes sin and calls therefore the sick to repentance and sacrifice; nevertheless, for the cool intellect of the Son of Sirach, this does not exclude the use of a physician; but the way in which he expressly places medical help in connection with God's working, and also calls the Scriptures to witness for it, shows that he had before his eyes religious doubts against it, thoughts, as Philo expresses them, that a stronger faith would turn only to God."

6. P. 193.

7. Jellett, *Efficacy of Prayer*, p. 41.

8. P. 193.

9. *Op. cit.*, p. 303.

10. *Medicine and the Church*, edited by Geoffrey Rhodes, 1910, pp. 209 ff.

11. *Inaugural Address*, 1891, ed. 2, p. 37.

12. That our Lord's miracles of healing were certainly not faith-cures, as it has become fashionable among the "Modernists" to represent, has been solidly shown by Doctor R. J. Ryle, "The Neurotic Theory of the Miracles of Healing," *The Hibbert Journal*, April, 1907, vol. V, pp. 572 ff.

13. See p. 41.

14. *Loc. cit.*, p. 68.

15. Of course this implication of the passage is not neglected by interested parties. We find for example C. H. Lea in his *A Plea for . . . Christian Science*, 1915, pp. 57–58, writing, on the supposition of the genuineness of this passage quite justly: "All Christendom believes that He gave His followers—not only those of His own time but of all succeeding time—the injunction to preach the Gospel and *to heal the sick*. Now, the giving of the injunction clearly and definitely implies . . . that the mark of one's being a Christian is that he has, or should have, this knowledge and the corresponding power to heal."

16. See above, p. 22.

17. *Op. cit.*, pp. 22 ff.

18. Pp. 52 ff.

19. I have briefly stated the evidence for the spuriousness of the passage in *An Introduction to the Textual Criticism of the New Testament*, 1886, pp. 199 ff. But see especially F. J. A. Hort, *The New Testament in the Original Greek*, Introduction, Appendix, 1881, pp. 28 ff. of the Appendix.

20. The passages between inverted commas may be found in Gordon, *op. cit.*, pp. 29, 31, 33, 34.

21. *Science et Réligion*, p. 189.

22. We say two; for a third, suggested as a possible alternative by John Lightfoot (*Works*, 8 vols. ed., vol. III, p. 316), does not appear to us possible, viz., that the reference is to a common Jewish custom of anointing, in connection with the use of charms, to heal the sick. Lightfoot quotes the Jerusalem Talmud (*Shab.*, fol. 14, col. 3): "A man that one charmeth, he putteth oil upon his head and charmeth." His comment is: "Now, this being a common, wretched custom, to anoint some that were sick, and to use charming with the anointing—this apostle, seeing anointing was an ordinary and good physic, and the good use of it not to be extinguished for that abuse—directs them better: namely, to get the elders or ministers of the church to come to the sick and to add to the medicinal anointing of him their godly and fervent prayers for him, far more available and comfortable than all charming and enchanting, as well as far more warrantable and Christian."

23. Oil was a remedy in constant use, notably for wounds (Isaiah 1 : 6; Luke 10 : 34), but also for the most extended variety of diseases. Its medicinal qualities are commended by Philo (*Somn.* M., I, 666), Pliny (*N. H.*, 23 : 34-50), and Galen (*Med. Temp.*, Bk. II). Compare the note of J. B. Mayor, *The Epistle of James*,[1] 1892, p. 158. John Lightfoot gives (vol. III, p. 315) some apposite passages from the Talmud. His comment seems to be thoroughly justified (p. 316): "Now if we take the apostle's counsel to be referring to this medicinal practice, we may construe it that he would have this physical administration to be improved to the best advantage; namely that, whereas 'anointing with oil' was ordinarily used to the sick, by way of physic—he adviseth that they should send for the elders of the church to do it; not that the anointing was any more in their hands than in another's, as to the thing itself, for it was still but a physical application—but that they with the applying of this corporeal physic, might also pray with and for the patient, and supply the spiritual physic of good admonition and comforts to him. Which is much the same as if in our nation, where this physical anointing is not so in use, a sick person should send

for the minister at taking of any physic, that he might pray with him, and counsel and comfort him."

24. The sacrament of extreme unction, grounded on this text on the understanding that the anointing was intended in a ceremonial sense, has oddly enough (since the primary promise of the text is bodily healing) become in the church of Rome, the sacrament of the dying. According to the Council of Trent (14th session) it is to be esteemed as totius Christianæ vitæ consummativum; according to Thomas Aquinas, it is the ultimum et quodammodo consummativum totius spiritualis curationis (*Cont. Gent.*, 14, c. 73). It is according to the Council of Trent to be given especially to those who seem to be in peril of death, unde et sacramentum exeuntium nuncupatur. Its effects are described (reversing the implications of the passage in James) as primarily spiritual healing, and only secondarily and solely in subordination to the spiritual healing, bodily healing. Bodily healing, therefore, only very occasionally results from it. As J. B. Heinrich explains (*Dogmatische Theologie*, X, 1904, p. 225): "Since it is generally more profitable, and more in accordance with the divine dispositions, for Christians *in articulo* or *periculo mortis* to take the last step, than to resume the battle of life again for a time, there ordinarily follows no healing." See in general the exposition of the doctrine by Heinrich as cited, pp. 197 ff. The popular expositions follow the scientific, but often with some ameliorations. "Extreme Unction," we read in one of the most widely used manuals for the instruction of English Catholics, "was instituted by our Lord to strengthen the dying, in their passage out of this world into another" (*A Manual of Instructions in Christian Doctrine*, published by the St. Anselm's Society, London, and having the imprimatur of Cardinals Wiseman and Manning, p. 363). Even in this *Manual*, however, the provision of the passage in St. James is not wholly forgotten. We read (p. 365): "If God sees it expedient, this sacrament restores bodily health. . . . Some persons are anxious to put off the reception of Extreme Unction to the last moment, because they seem to regard it as a prelude to certain death; while in truth, if it had been received earlier it might have led to their recovery. It cannot be doubted that miraculous cures are sometimes effected by Extreme Unction; but the beneficial effects which it generally exercises on bodily health are produced in an indirect way. The grace of the sacrament soothes the soul, lessens the fear of death, and brings on such calm and peace of mind as often to lead to the restoration of health. If God be pleased to work a direct miracle it is never too late for Him to do so; but if the sacra-

ment is to act as a natural remedy, indirectly restoring health in the way just explained, it must be received in due time, otherwise, like ordinary remedies, it will not produce its effects." In a similar spirit Deharbe's Catechism (*A Full Catechism of the Catholic Religion*, translated from the German of the Reverend Joseph Deharbe, S. J., . . . revised, enlarged, and edited by the Right Reverend P. N. Lynch, D.D., bishop of Charleston, 1891, pp. 296, 297), after declaring that Extreme Unction "often relieves the pains of the sick person, and sometimes restores him even to health, if it be expedient for the salvation of his soul," asks: "Is it not unreasonable for a person, from fear of death, to defer, or even neglect, the receiving of Extreme Unction until he is moribund?" and replies: "Certainly; for (1) Extreme Unction has been instituted even for the health of the body; (2) The sick person will recover more probably, if he employs in time the remedy ordained by God, than if he waits until he cannot recover except by a miracle; and (3) If his sickness be mortal what should he wish for more earnestly than to die happy, which this holy sacrament gives him grace to do?" "As many of those sick persons who were anointed by the Apostles were healed," we read in *The Catechumen*[3] by J. G. Wenham, 1892, p. 358, "so this is often the effect of this sacrament now—that those that receive it obtain fresh force and vigor, and recover from their illness." Although, therefore, Extreme Unction is "given to us in preparation for death," it is ordinarily explained, in deference to its biblical foundation-passage, as (as Bellarmine puts it, following the language of the Council of Trent) "also assisting in the recovery of bodily health, if that should be useful to the health of the soul." Father W. Humphrey, S.J., *The One Mediator*, ed. 2, 1894, chap. VII, explains the matter more strictly in accordance with the authoritative declaration of Trent thus: "Hence one end, and that the *principal* end, of this sacrament is to *strengthen* and to *comfort* the dying man. . . . Another and a *secondary end* of the Sacrament of Extreme Unction is proximately to *dispose* and *prepare* the parting soul for the new life in which it is about to enter. . . . There is a third and a *contingent end* of Extreme Unction, and that is the *bodily healing* of the sick man under *certain conditions*." On the origin of this teaching and the history of the rite of Extreme Unction, see Father F. W. Puller, *The Anointing of the Sick in Scripture and Tradition*, London, Society for the Promotion of Christian Knowledge, 1904; and *cf.* Percy Dearmer, *Body and Soul*,[9] 1912, pp. 217 ff.

The movement forming nowadays in the Anglican churches, with a view to "the restoration to the Church of the Scriptural Practice of Divine Healing," also bases the "office" of anointing, which it proposes, on James 5 : 14, 15. See, for example, F. W. Puller, *Anointing of the Sick*, 1904, chap. IX; Percy Dearmer, *Body and Soul*,[9] 1912, esp. chap. XXIX, with Appendix III; Henry B. Wilson, B.D., *The Revival of the Gift of Healing*, Milwaukee, The Young Churchman Company, 1914. Mr. Wilson is the director of the "Society of the Nazarene," and writes in its interest, printing also suitable prayers and an office for the anointing of the sick. His contention is that the gift of healing was never withdrawn from the church, and that the church must recover "her therapeutic ministry" by means of this formal ritual act. See also Mr. Wilson's later book, *Does Christ Still Heal?* New York, E. P. Dutton & Co., 1917.

25. It is sometimes suggested that a miraculous healing is promised indeed, but that this promise applied only to those miraculous days, and is no longer to be claimed. Even J. B. Mayor, *The Epistle of St. James*,[1] 1892, p. 218, appears to lean to this view; and it seems to have never been without advocates among leading Protestants. Luther writes to the Elector of Brandenburg, December 4, 1539 (Miss Currie's translation of *Luther's Letters*, p. 378): "For Christ did not make anointing with oil a Sacrament, nor do St. James's words apply to the present day. For in those days the sick were often cured through a miracle and the earnest prayer of faith, as we see in James and Mark 6." Thorndike (*Works*, vol. VI, p. 65, Oxford edition) writes: "This is laid aside in all the reformed churches upon presumption of common sense, that the reason is no longer in force, being ordained, as you see, to restore health by the grace of miracles that no more exist." J. A. Hessey (*Sunday*, 1860, p. 42) agrees with Thorndike. Nevertheless the view will scarcely approve itself.

26. *Op. cit.*, p. 277. This is the way the common sense of Martin Luther met the question of the use of remedies in disease: "Our burgomaster asked me whether it was against God's will to use medicine, for Carlstadt publicly preached that the sick should not use drugs, but should only pray to God that His will be done. In reply I asked the burgomaster if he ate when he was hungry, and when he answered in the affirmative, I said, 'You may then use medicine, which is God's creature as much as food, drink, and other bodily necessities.'"—(*The Life and Letters of Martin Luther*. By Preserved Smith, Ph.D., 1911, pp. 327–328.)

27. "Je le pansay et Dieu le guarit," quoted by A. T. Schofield, *The Force of Mind*, 1908, p. 176.

28. *The New Church Review*, vol. XV, 1908, pp. 415 f.

29. For example Percy Dearmer, *Body and Soul*,[9] 1912, pp. 174 f.,

calmly sets the "nature miracles" aside as "quite exceptional occurrences," and declares that it may be safely assumed that "it was not to such exceptional occurrences that Christ was here referring." On the basis of Mark 6 : 7; Luke 9 : 1, 10 : 1, and the nature of the miracles recorded in Acts, he asserts that "it must have been clearly understood that Christ did not commission His disciples to exercise authority over the powers of nature." Meanwhile, on his own showing, the greatest "works" which Christ did were these "nature miracles"; and it remains inexplicable how Faith-Healings in His disciples can have been declared by Him to be greater than they.

30. So, for example, Luthardt, Godet, Westcott and Milligan and Moulton; see especially the discussion in W. Milligan, *The Ascension and Heavenly High-Priesthood of Our Lord*, 1892, pp. 250 ff.

31. *Op. cit.*, pp. 16 ff.

32. P. 163.

33. As cited.

34. A very little consideration will suffice to show that these attempts so to state the doctrine of the atonement as to obtain from it a basis on which a doctrine of Faith-Healing can be erected, betray us into a long series of serious errors. They imply, for example, that, Christ having borne our sicknesses as our substitute, Christians are not to bear them, and accordingly all sickness should be banished from the Christian world; Christians are not to be cured of sickness, but ought not to get sick. They imply further, that, this being so, the presence of sickness is not only a proof of sin, but argues the absence of the faith which unites us to Christ, our Substitute, that is saving faith; so that no sick person can be a saved man. They imply still further that, as sickness and inward corruption are alike effects of sin, and we must contend that sickness, because it is an effect of sin, is removed completely and immediately by the atoning act of Christ, taking away sin, so must also inward corruption be wholly and at once removed; no Christian can be a sinner. Thus we have full-blown "Perfectionism." Stanton writes: "In so far as the soul may be delivered from sin during life, the body may be delivered from sickness and disease, the fruit of sin"; "in short, if the full deliverance of the soul from sin may be at any time reached on this side of death, so may the body be freed from disease." Perfectionism and Faith-Healing, on this ground, stand or fall together. We wonder why, in his reasoning, Stanton leaves believers subject to death. The reasoning which proves so much too much, proves, of course, nothing at all.

35. Gordon remarks: "It is obvious that our Redeemer cannot forgive and eradicate sin without in the same act disentangling the roots which sin has struck into our mortal bodies." Are these three terms synonymous: forgive sin, eradicate sin, disentangle the roots of sin? And are the forgiveness of sin, the disentangling of the roots of sin, the eradication of sin, all accomplished in one "act"? There is through all this reasoning a hopeless confusion of the steps of the process of salvation and of the relations of the several steps to one another. If we lay down the proposition that our salvation is completed in a single act, in all its relations—why, then, of course, we are not in process of salvation, but we are already wholly saved.

36. Gordon, *op. cit.*, p. 18.

37. *The New Church Review*, vol. XV, 1908, p. 414.

38. Here is, however, one illustration. Doctor Alfred T. Schofield (*A Study of Faith-Healing*, 1872, p. 38) relates the following incident. "Knowing a Christian doctor, favorable to faith-healing, I asked him if he could tell me any genuine cures of organic disease. But he only shook his head. . . . The principal case at the faith-healing centre near him was that of a woman who was really dying and had continual fits, and who, the doctor said, was indubitably cured by faith. Here, then, was an authenticated case at last of some sort. This woman gave great testimony as to her cure at various meetings, but as she had been my friend's patient, he was able to tell me the secret of it. God had cured her by saving her soul, and thus delivering her from the love and constant excessive use of strong drink that had been the sole cause of her illness and fits, and that the doctor had told her would end her life!" The annals of faith-healing are rich in such instances. Doctor Schofield records a touching instance (p. 42) of a young woman who, by trusting in the Lord, was freed from a nervous terror of the sea, and gradually from other disabilities.

39. *Literature and Dogma*, chap. v. Arnold bases really on the notion that all illness is due to sin and that the proper method of attacking it is, therefore, by "moral therapeutics." Christ as the source of happiness and calm cured diseases by eliminating their moral cause; hence what we call His miracles, which were, of course, no miracles but the most natural effects in the world; "miracles do not happen."

40. P. 62.

41. P. 192.

42. *Cf.* W. W. Patton, *Prayer and Its Remarkable Answers; Being a Statement of Facts in the Light of Reason and Revelation*, ed.

20, 1885, pp. 214 ff., drawing on the booklet, *Dorothea Trüdel, or the Prayer of Faith*, 1865, and (pp. 237 ff.) Doctor Charles Cullis's report of a visit to Mannedorf.

43. Doctor A. T. Schofield, *op. cit.*, pp. 23 ff., who gives an interesting account of a visit which he made to Zeller's House at Mannedorf. He found that very many came there for rest and quiet, and many grew no better while there, but rather worse. He could not, on inquiry at the House or from the physicians in the town, assure himself of the cure there of any truly organic disease; and came away with the conviction that "the bulk at any rate of the cases benefited are clearly mental, nervous, and hysterical" (p. 28).

44. *Christian Thought*, February, 1890, p. 289. Another eminent physician, J. M. Charcot (*The New Review*, 1893, vol. VIII, p. 19), writes: "On the other hand, the domain of faith-healing is limited; to produce its effects it must be applied to those cases which demand for their cure no intervention beyond the power which the mind has over the body—cases which Hack Tuke (*Illustrations of the Influence of the Mind upon the Body in Health and Disease, designed to elucidate the Action of the Imagination*, London: Churchill, 1872) has analyzed so admirably in his remarkable work. No intervention can make it pass these bounds, for we are powerless against natural laws. For example, no instance can be found amongst the records sacred to so-called miraculous cures where the faith-cure has availed to restore an amputated limb. On the other hand, there are hundreds of recorded cases of the cure of paralysis, but I think these have all partaken of the nature of those which Professor Russell Reynolds has classified under the heading of paralysis 'dependent on idea' ('Remarks on Paralysis and other Disorders of Motion and Sensation Dependent on Idea . . .' in *British Medical Journal*, November, 1869)."

45. They are sufficiently illustrated by J. M. Buckley, *Faith-Healing, Christian Science, and Kindred Phenomena*, 1892. To the account of Faith-Healing by the Mormons, which he gives on pp. 35 ff., add what is said of this practice among the Mormons by Florence A. Merriam, *My Summer in a Mormon Village*, pp. 115 ff.: "To an outsider, one of the most appalling features of Mormonism is the rooted opposition of the people to Medical Science, their distrust of skilled physicians, and their faith in the Biblical ceremonial of anointing or laying on of hands. . . ." She gives some instructive instances. *Cf.* also W. A. Hammond, *Spiritualism and Kindred Phenomena*.

46. Buckley, as cited, p. 3; *The Century Magazine*, vol. X, p. 222.

47. Buckley, *op. cit.*, p. 27; *The Century Magazine,* vol. X, p. 230.

48. Buckley, *Faith-Healing*, p. 25; *The Century Magazine,* vol. X, p. 229.

49. *Op. cit.*, p. 25.

50. Buckley, *op. cit.*, p. 9. *Cf.* A. T. Schofield, *The Force of Mind*, 1908, pp. 256 ff. "Phantom Tumors," says Doctor J. R. Gasquet (*The Dublin Review*, October, 1894, pp. 355, 356), "deceive even the elect." See also Doctor Fowler's paper, "Neurotic Tumors of the Breast," read before the New York Neurological Society, Tuesday, January 7, 1890, in the *Medical Record*, February 19, 1890, p. 179, and *cf.* Charcot's remarks on it, *op. cit.*, p. 29. Doctor Fowler's tumors were actual, not "phantom," neurotic tumors, and yet, on being subjected to a course of treatment, "in which, so to speak, the psychical element was made the chief point, vanished as if by magic."

51. Reynolds, *op. cit.*, pp. 325–326.

52. "Doctor Cabot's figures," derived from a comparison of a test series of instances of clinical diagnoses with post-mortem findings, have become famous. In this test "the average percentage of correctness of these diagnoses in these cases, taken as a whole, was 47.3. In 1913 the Committee of Inquiry into the Department of Health, Charities and Bellevue and Allied Hospitals in the City of New York compared the autopsy findings in Bellevue Hospital with the clinical diagnoses, and the comparison revealed the fact that clinical diagnoses were confirmed in only 52.3 per cent of the cases." *Cf.* the remarks of Doctor Schofield, *op. cit.*, pp. 39–40, on the difficulties which come to physicians in connection with cases of alleged faith-cure. In examining into a case of reputed tumor healed at once on faith, he wrote to the physicians who had charge of the case and learned that it never was of much importance, and that it had not disappeared after its alleged cure. But one of the physicians added: "I am sorry I am not able to answer your question more satisfactorily. As a Christian, I am greatly interested in 'faith-healing,' but have come to the conclusion that it is wiser for me not to examine patients, or pronounce on their condition, when they state that the Lord has healed them, for I feel it too solemn a thing to shake a person's faith by too critical pathological knowledge."

53. *Op. cit.*, p. 158.

54. Buckley, *op. cit.*, pp. 54–55; *The Century Magazine,* vol. XI, p. 784.

55. These citations are taken from L. T. Townsend, *Faith Work,*

Christian Science and Other Cures, pp. 160 ff., where the matter is discussed at large.

56. P. 196.

57. Pp. 197–198.

58. *Cf.* G. M. Pachtler, *Biographische Notizen über . . . Prinzen Alexander*, Augsburg, 1850; S. Brunner, *Aus dem Nachlässe des Fürsten . . . Hohenlohe*, Regensburg, 1851; F. N. Baur, *A Short and Faithful Description of the Remarkable Occurrences and Benevolent Holy Conduct of . . . Prince Alexander of Hohenlohe . . . during his residence of Twenty-five Days in the City of Würzburg . . .*, London, 1822; John Badeley, *Authentic Narrative of the Extraordinary Cure performed by Prince Hohenlohe*, London, n. d.; James Doyle, *Miracles said to have been wrought by Prince Hohenlohe on Miss Lalor in Ireland*, London, 1823.

59. *Cf.* J. F. Maguire, *Father Matthew*, 1864.

60. *The Varieties of Religious Experience*, p. 113, note; Blumhardt is spoken of by James as a "singularly pure, simple and non-fanatical character," who "in this part of his work followed no previous example." His life was written by F. Zündel, *Pfarrer J. C. Blumhardt*, 1887; see a short notice with Bibliography, in *The New Schaff-Herzog Encyclopedia of Religious Knowledge*, sub. nom. (II, 206).

61. See *The New Schaff-Herzog*, sub. nom., and sub. voc., "Christian and Missionary Alliance."

62. See C. W. Heisler, "Denver's Messiah Craze," in *The Independent*, October 3, 1895; Henry Kingman, "Franz Schlatter and his Power over Disease," in *The Congregationalist*, November 1, 1895. The New York daily press for the late summer and early autumn of 1916 (*e. g.*, *The Evening Sun* for September 28) tells of the sordid final stages of Schlatter's "practice."

63. There are articles on Dowie and on the Christian Catholic Apostolic Church in Zion in *The New Schaff-Herzog Encyclopedia*, to the latter of which a full Bibliography is attached. To this Bibliography we may add Annie L. Muzzie, "One Man's Mission. True or False?" in *The Independent*, September 17, 1896; "New Sects and Old," chap. XII of "Religious Life in America," by E. H. Abbott, *Outlook*, September 15, 1902, and afterwards published in book form; James Orr, "Dowie and Mrs. Eddy," *London Quarterly Review*, April, 1904.

64. See an analysis of Dowie's healing work in *American Journal of Psychology*, X, pp. 442, 465.

65. The literature of Faith-Healing is very extensive. We mention only, along with Doctor Gordon's *Ministry of Healing*,

among its advocates: George Morris, *Our Lord's Permanent Healing Office in His Church;* W. E. Boardman, *The Great Physician; The Lord That Healeth Thee,* 1881; and *Faith Work under Doctor Cullis in Boston;* A. B. Simpson, *The Gospel of Healing,* 1884; *The Holy Spirit or Power from on High,* 1899; and *Discovery of Divine Healing,* 1902. The doctrines involved are discussed by A. A. Hodge, *Popular Lectures on Theological Themes,* 1887, pp. 107–116; *cf.* also A. F. Schauffler, *The Century Magazine,* December, 1885, pp. 274 ff. The whole question is admirably canvassed in L. T. Townsend, *Faith Work, Christian Science and Other Cures,* 1885; J. M. Buckley, *Faith-Healing, Christian Science and Kindred Phenomena,* 1892; A. T. Schofield, *A Study of Faith-Healing,* 1892; W. S. Plummer Bryan, *Prayer and the Healing of Disease,* 1896; W. R. Hall, "Divine Healing or Faith-cure," *Lutheran Quarterly,* New Series, vol. XXVII (1897), pp. 263–276. The literatures attached to the articles, "Faith-healing," in Hastings's *Encyclopedia of Religion and Ethics,* and "Psychotherapy," in *The New Schaff-Herzog Encyclopedia of Religious Knowledge,* will suggest the works on the action of the mind on the body. P. Dearmer's *Body and Soul. An Inquiry into the effects of Religion upon Health, with a Description of Christian Work of Healing from the New Testament to the Present Day,* 1909 (9th ed., 1912), deserves perhaps special mention, as presenting the matter from a high Anglican standpoint, and on the basis of pantheizing theories of being which leave no room for real miracles, whether in the records of the New Testament or in the healings of subsequent times. See also J. M. Charcot, "The Faith-cure," in *The New Review,* VIII (1893), pp. 18–31, which discusses the matter, however, with Lourdes particularly in mind.

NOTES TO LECTURE VI

MIND-CURE

1. Intermediate positions are, of course, possible in the abstract, in which the cure is ascribed both to faith and to God acting reinforcingly or supplementarily. But these possible abstract points of view may be safely left out of account.

2. Ecclus. 38 : 1 ff.

3. This is, of course, the common representation. Thus, for example: H. H. Goddard, *The American Journal of Psychology,* vol. X, 1898–1899, p. 432: "As a matter of fact the principle is as old as human history"; H. R. Marshall, *The Hibbert Journal,* vol. VII, 1909, p. 293: "Were the complete history of medical science written,

it would without doubt appear that the treatment of disease through what seems to be mental influences has prevailed in one form or another ever since man began to realize that certain illnesses are curable."

4. How little they can be ascribed to it has been shown by R. J. Ryle, in an article entitled "The Neurotic Theory of the Miracles of Healing," in *The Hibbert Journal*, vol. V, April, 1907, pp. 572–586.

5. Sir William Osler, *The Treatment of Disease*, 1909, speaks of the necessity in all cases of "suggestion in one of its varied forms —whether the negation of disease and pain, the simple trust in Christ of the Peculiar People, or the sweet reasonableness of the psychotherapist." *Cf.* especially William James, *The Varieties of Religious Experience*,[21] 1911, pp. 712 ff.; Stephen Paget, *The Faith and Works of Christian Science*, 1909, pp. 204 ff.; Henry H. Goddard, *The American Journal of Psychology*, vol. X, 1898–1899, p. 481. That this is not the account given by the practitioners themselves lies in the nature of the case. Consult, *e. g.*, C. H. Lea, *A Plea for . . . Christian Science*,[2] 1915, pp. xv, 70 ff., who appeals to "an ever-operative principle of good, or spiritual law, underlying all life which is here and now available for all mankind." For that matter consult Elwood Worcester, *Religion and Medicine*, p. 72; on pp. 67 ff. Worcester speaks quite in the spirit of the Spiritual Healers spoken of above.

6. Samuel McComb, *The Christian Religion as a Healing Power*, 1909, p. 117: "It does not believe that its cures are due to any miraculous agency . . ."; *Religion and Medicine*, 1908, p. 311: "We dare not pray to God to work a miracle, that is, to violate one of those general laws by which He rules the physical world."

7. *Religion and Medicine*, p. 14, note; *The Christian Religion as a Healing Power*, p. 99.

8. *The Christian Religion as a Healing Power*, p. 39. The remedy which Wesley proposed, however, was not that the minister should turn physician, but that the physician should become Christian: "It follows," he writes, "that no man can be a thorough physician without being an experienced Christian."

9. McComb says expressly, *The Christian Religion as a Healing Power*, p. 92: "In many instances it does not matter what the object of the faith may be; it is not the object but the faith that heals." The matter is more fully stated in *Religion and Medicine*, p. 293: "Faith simply as a psychical process, or mental attitude . . . has healing virtue"; "Faith as a mere mental state has this power"—in accordance with Feuchterleben's saying, "Confidence

acts like a real force." Elwood Worcester, p. 57, agrees with his colleague. Of course it is allowed that if we are seeking moral as well as physical effects it is better that the faith employed should have God rather than Mumbo-jumbo for its object. The plane on which McComb's chapter on "Prayer and Its Therapeutic Value" (*Religion and Medicine*, pp. 302–319) moves is the same. The therapeutic value of prayer resides in its subjective effects. As it is clearly stated in a leading article in the *British Medical Journal* for June 18, 1910: "Prayer inspired by a living faith is a force acting within the patient, which places him in the most favorable condition for the stirring of the pool of hope that lies, still and hidden it may be, in the depths of human nature." McComb does not utterly exclude the prayer of desire or deny that it has an effect on God; even, if it be a desire in behalf of others, an effect on them. We are organically related to God, he says: "We exist in Him spiritually somewhat as thoughts exist in the mind," and "a strong desire in our soul communicates itself to Him and engages His attention just as a thought in our soul engages ours." God may resist this desire of ours, thus entering His consciousness; but "the stronger the thought, the more frequently it returns, the more likely it is to be acted upon." If now we have a desire in behalf of others, "our soul not only acts on that soul," telepathically we suppose, "but our prayer arising to the mind of God directs His will more powerfully and more constantly to the soul for which we pray." This is very ingenious and very depressing. We hope there is no truth in it.

10. *The Christian Religion as a Healing Power*, p. 10. The leaders of the Emmanuel Movement are very insistent that the Christianity which they employ is that of the "critical interpretation" of the New Testament.

11. It seems almost as difficult for clerics to recognize frankly the limits of their functions as spiritual guides with respect to medicine, as with respect to the state. They repeatedly show a tendency not only to intrude into but to seek to dominate the one alien sphere as the other. Andrew D. White, *A History of the Warfare of Science with Theology in Christendom*, 1896, II, p. 37, recounts how the mediæval church sought to secure that physicians should always practise their art in conjunction with ecclesiastics. Pius V ordered "that all physicians before administering treatment should call in 'a physician of the soul,' on the ground, as he declares, that 'bodily infirmity frequently arises from sin.'" Clear differentiation of functions—"division of labor" the economists call it—lies in the line of advance.

12. *The Christian Religion as a Healing Power*, p. 99. See above, note 7.

13. These citations are derived from *Medicine and the Church*, edited by Geoffrey Rhodes, 1910, pp. 35, 64, 73. *Cf.* what Stephen Paget says on the general question in *The Faith and Works of Christian Science*, 1909, pp. 180–190.

14. The primary literature on the Emmanuel Movement is comprised in the two books by its founders: Elwood Worcester, Samuel McComb, Isador H. Coriat, *Religion and Medicine, the Moral Control of Nervous Disorders*, 1908; and Elwood Worcester, Samuel McComb, *The Christian Religion as a Healing Power: A Defense and Exposition of the Emmanuel Movement*, 1909. See also Robert MacDonald, *Mind, Religion and Health*, with an *Appreciation of the Emmanuel Movement*, 1909; C. R. Brown, *Faith and Health*, 1910. A very good criticism of the movement will be found in the article by Doctor Henry Rutgers Marshall, on "Psycho-therapeutics and Religion," in *The Hibbert Journal*, January, 1909, vol. III, pp. 295–313. The most recent literature includes: Loring W. Batten, *The Relief of Pain by Mental Suggestion*, 1917; Isador H. Coriat, *What is Psychoanalysis?* 1917.

15. Hastings's *Encyclopedia of Religion and Ethics*, vol. V, p. 700b. He has explained himself more at large in his book *Spiritual Healing*, London, 1914, and quite in this sense. But a certain amount of ambiguity in this matter is not unnatural, and may be met with in many writers. Elwood Worcester, for example, gives expression occasionally to a mystical theory which assimilates him to the theory of spiritual healing described by Cobb (*e. g.*, *Religion and Medicine*, pp. 67 ff.). On the other hand, Percy Dearmer (*Body and Soul*,[9] 1912, p. 318), who also holds to a mystical theory of the universe, must be classed distinctly as an advocate of "Mind-cure"; although he lays all the stress on religion, and refers everything to God as the ultimate actor, he yet is thoroughly naturalistic in his analysis. "All power is of God," he says, "—whether it be electricity or neurokym, or grace; and to him who does not believe in God, all power must be left unexplained. On the other hand, the high power of religion can quite fairly be called mental; no one would be less ready to deny this than the Christian for whom, as I have said, the very operations of the Spirit of God, his gifts and his fruits, are mental phenomena which are habitually obtained in a lower form without the special aid of religion. There is no ultimate barrier then between what is sacred and what is secular, since all things come of God and of his own do we give him; the difference is one of degree and not of kind."

16. Two other important movements, tracing their impulse back to P. P. Quimby, deserve mention here—the "Mind-cure Movement," the best representative of which is probably Warren F. Evans; and the "New Thought Movement," the best representative of which is probably Horatio W. Dresser. William James, *The Varieties of Religious Experience*,[21] 1911, pp. 94 ff., gives an adequate account of the "New Thought Movement"; a good brief account of both streams of development will be found in Frank Podmore, *Mesmerism and Christian Science*, 1909, pp. 255 ff. Some details of W. F. Evans's career may be found in *McClure's Magazine*, vol. XXX, pp. 390 ff. A useful bibliography of out-of-the-way books on "New Thought" is given in *The New Schaff-Herzog Encyclopedia*, vol. VIII, p. 148, but the best books are missed. See, especially, Horatio W. Dresser, *Handbook of New Thought*, 1917.

17. "The truth, therefore, about Christian Science," says W. F. Cobb (*Mysticism and the Creed*, 1914, p. 316), "seems to be that the power displayed in the cures which it indubitably performs is not peculiar to it, that is, is not Christian Science at all, but that which is its peculiar glory is the bad philosophy by which it seeks to set forth the power which comes from the Spirit, and is under the guardianship of religion."

18. "Many imagine," she says, *Science and Health*, 161st ed., 1899, p. xi, "that the phenomena of physical healing in Christian Science only present a phase of the action of the human mind, which, in some unexplained way, results in the cure of sickness." This, she declares, is by no means the case. She condemns the several books "on mental healing" which have come under her notice as wrong and misleading, precisely because "they regard the human mind as a healing agent, whereas this mind is not a factor in the Principle of Christian Science" (p. x). The phrase "human mind" in passages like this probably is to be read as equivalent to "mortal mind," a cant phrase in the system, as, for example, on p. 303: "History teaches that the popular and false notions about the Divine Being and character have originated in the human mind. As there really is no mortal mind, this wrong notion about God must have originated in a false supposition, not in immortal Mind." This "mortal mind," we are told (p. 45), "claims to govern every organ of the mortal body," but the claim is false; "the Divine Mind" is the true governor. There "really is no mortal mind." Of course this distinction between mind-cure and Mind-cure is not maintained, and endless confusion results. Thus the Christian Science writer quoted in the *American Journal of Psychology*, X, p. 433, in the same breath repudiates the ascription of their healings

to a "material, mental or bodily cause," and affirms that "the only agency ever effective in curing diseases is some faculty of mind."

19. *Science and Health*, 1899, p. xi; *cf.* p. 5: "Christian Science is natural but not physical. The true Science of God and man is no more supernatural than is the science of numbers"; p. 249: "Miracles are impossible in Science." Even the resurrection of Christ was not supernatural: "Can it be called supernatural for the God of nature to sustain Jesus, in his proof of man's truly derived power? It was a method of surgery beyond material art, but it was not a supernatural act. On the contrary, it was a distinctly natural act . . ." (p. 349). "Mary Baker Eddy," says a writer in the *Christian Science Journal* for April, 1889, "has worked out before us as on a blackboard every point in the temptations and demonstrations—or so-called Miracles—of Jesus, showing us how to meet and overcome the one, and how to perform the other." All is natural in Mrs. Eddy's universe.

20. *The Christian Religion as a Healing Power*, p. 19.

21. *Christian Thought*, February, 1890.

22. On "the pedigree of Christian Science," see the admirable article under that title by Frank Podmore in *The Contemporary Review* for January, 1909, vol. XCV, pp. 37–49; and, of course, more at large, Frank Podmore, *Mesmerism and Christian Science : a Short History of Mental Healing*, 1909.

23. Mrs. Eddy herself speaks with contempt of Faith-Healing as "one belief casting out another—a belief in the unknown casting out a belief in disease." "It is not Truth itself which does this," she declares; "nor is it the human understanding of the divine healing Principle" (*Science and Health*, 1899, p. 317).

24. These admissions are greatly modified in *Science and Health*, 1899, p. 397. Here it is taught, as the Index puts it, that faith-cure "often soothes but only changes the form of the ailment." "Faith removes bodily ailments for a season; or else it changes those ills into new and more difficult forms of disease, until at length the Science of Mind comes to the rescue and works a radical cure."

25. *Christian Science Healing, its Principles and Practice*, 1888, p. 102.

26. *Retrospection and Introspection*,[17] 1900, p. 38 (first printed in 1891).

27. *Ibid.* In *Science and Health*, 1899, p. 107, she writes: "In the year 1866 I discovered the Christ Science or divine laws of Life, Truth and Love, and named my discovery Christian Science. God had been graciously preparing me during many years for the re-

ception of this final revelation of the absolute divine Principle of scientific mental healing."

28. Mrs. Eddy's relations to P. P. Quimby have been made quite clear and placed on a firm basis by Georgine Milmine in a series of articles published in *McClure's Magazine* for 1907–1908, and afterward in book form, *The Life of Mary Baker G. Eddy and the History of Christian Science*, 1909; and by Lyman P. Powell, *Christian Science, the Faith and its Founder*, 1907; see also Frank Podmore, *Mesmerism and Christian Science*, 1909, chap. XIV, "The Rise of Mental Healing," and Annetta Gertrude Dresser, *The Philosophy of P. P. Quimby*, 1895. Quimby's fundamental principle is summed up in his conviction that the cause and cure of disease lie in mental states. His practice was to talk with his patients about their diseases, to explain to them that disease is an error, and to "establish the truth in its place, which, if done, was the cure." "I give no medicines," he says, "I simply sit by the patient's side and explain to him what he thinks is his disease, and my explanation is the cure; . . . the truth is the cure." "My way of curing," he writes in 1862, the year in which Mrs. Eddy went to him as a patient, "convinces him (the patient) that he has been deceived; and, if I succeed, the patient is cured." The Pantheistic background appears to have been less prominently thrust forward by Quimby than by Mrs. Eddy, and it would seem that her "discovery" consists wholly in this possible change of emphasis.

29. This is sufficiently characteristic to deserve emphasis. Mrs. Eddy (who describes herself as "the tireless toiler for the truth's new birth") ever assumed the rôle of thinker and teacher rather than of healer; the healing she delegated to her pupils. "I have never made a specialty of treating disease," she writes, "but healing has accompanied all my efforts to introduce Christian Science." By taking the course she did, she understood herself to be assuming the more difficult task: "Healing," she said, "is easier than teaching, if the teaching is faithfully done" (*Science and Health*, 1899, p. 372). She was accustomed to print at the end of the preface to *Science and Health* this: "Note.—The author takes no patients and declines medical consultation." Nevertheless, in a by-law of 1903, she declares "healing better than teaching" (*McClure's Magazine*, May, 1908, p. 28).

30. The Christian Scientist writer quoted in the *American Journal of Psychology*, vol. X, p. 436, declares with great emphasis: "The only text-book of genuine, unadulterated Christian Science is *Science and Health, with Key to the Scriptures*, by Rev. Mary Baker Eddy." Mr. Bailey, editor of the *Christian Science Journal*,

wrote that he considered "the Bible and *Science and Health* as one book—the sacred Scriptures."

31. *Science and Health*, 1899, p. 4.

32. *Christian Science Journal*, January, 1901: *cf. Miscellaneous Writings*, p. 311: "The words I have written on Christian Science contain absolute Truth. . . . I was a scribe under orders, and who can refrain from transcribing what God indites?"

33. In the *Christian Science Journal*, April, 1895, Mrs. Eddy abolished preaching and ordained that the service should be as here described. "In 1895," she says, "I ordained the Bible and *Science and Health, with Key to the Scriptures*, as the Pastor, on this planet, of all the churches of the Christian Science denomination" (*McClure's Magazine*, May, 1908, p. 25).

34. This was not the original order, but was subsequently introduced.

35. Mrs. Eddy says in the *Christian Science Journal* for March, 1897: "The Bible, *Science and Health, with Key to the Scriptures*, and my other published works are the only proper instructions for this hour. It shall be the duty of all Christian Scientists to circulate and to sell as many of these books as they can."

36. G. C. Mars, *The Interpretation of Life, in which is shown the relation of Modern Culture and Christian Science*, 1908. It is related that Mrs. Eddy herself, with, no doubt, a rare display of humor, said once that Bronson Alcott, on reading *Science and Health*, pronounced that no one but a woman or a fool could have written it (*McClure's Magazine*, August, 1897, p. 47).

37. *The Dublin Review*, July, 1908, vol. CXLIII, p. 62.

38. P. N. F. Young, *The Interpreter*, October, 1908, vol. V, p. 91.

39. So say many of the readers of the book with serio-comic emphasis; see three such expositions of the effect of trying to read it given in Stephen Paget's *The Faith and Works of Christian Science*, pp. 205 ff.

40. *McClure's Magazine* for October, 1907, p. 699.

41. God, says Mrs. Eddy, in *Science and Health*, ed. 1875, "is Principle, not Person"; God, she says, in ed. 1881, I, p. 167; II, p. 97, "is not a person, God is Principle"; God, she says still in *No and Yes*, 1906, "is Love, and Love is Principle, not person." In later editions of *Science and Health* the asperity of the assertion is somewhat softened without any change of meaning, *e. g.*, ed. 1899, p. 10: "If the term *personality* applied to God means *infinite personality*, then God *is* personal Being—in this sense, but not in the lowest sense," *i. e.*, in the sense of individuality (*cf.* what is said on the supposition that God should be spoken of as person on p.

510). The entry in the Index referring to this passage (p. 10) is phrased simply, "Person, God is not"; and throughout the text God is represented not as "Person" but as "Principle." To approach God in the prayer of petition is to "humanize" Him. "Prayer addressed to a person prevents our letting go of personality for the impersonal Spirit to whom all things are possible" (ed. 1875). The whole foundation of Mrs. Eddy's theory and practice alike was denial of the personality of God; see the curious deposition printed in *McClure's Magazine*, 1907, p. 103, bearing that this denial was made by Mrs. Eddy the condition of entrance into her classes. "There is really nothing to understand in *Science and Health*," says Wiggin truly, "except that *God is all*." That is the beginning and middle and end of Mrs. Eddy's philosophy. Accordingly, the writer in the *Christian Science Sentinel* for September 25, 1907, p. 57, quoted by Powell, *Christian Science*, p. 242, is quite right when she declares: "principle and not personality is the only foundation upon which we can build safely."

42.   Ed. 1875; in ed. 1899, p. 3: "the divine Mind and idea"; *cf*. p. 8: "In Science Mind is one—including noumena and phenomena, God and His thoughts," *i. e.*, everything. Accordingly, C. H. Lea, *A Plea for . . . Christian Science*, p. 23, says: "The individual man is a part of God, in the sense that a ray of light is a part of the sun."

43.   Ed. 1905, p. 331.

44.   Ed. 1899, p. 7.

45.   *Op. cit.*, p. 23.

46.   P. 74.

47.   P. 81

48.   P. 412.

49.   It is these "cross currents," we are told, which form the chief difficulty in the way of Christian Science practice. Mrs. Carrie Snider even reports in *The Journal of Christian Science* (*McClure's Magazine*, 1907, pp. 692–693) the case of her husband, who, being "under the treatment of two healers, whose minds were not in accord," was caught in this cross current and died, or, as Mrs. Eddy would express it, "showed the manifestation of the death symptoms" ("symptoms" themselves being "shadows of belief"). "The thought from the one," explains Miss Milmine, "confused thought from the other, leaving him to die in the cross-fire." The interested reader will find the precepts of Elwood Worcester on "Suggestion" (*Religion and Medicine*, p. 64) running very closely parallel to Mrs. Eddy's on all such matters: "It is necessary as far as possible to guard against counter-suggestions";

"suggestions . . . contained in books are often of great curative value"; "in order to avoid the danger of opposition and counter-suggestion some practitioners prefer to treat the patient silently."

50. *Medicine and the Church*, edited by Geoffrey Rhodes, 1910, p. 293.

51. Sin is, of course, in Mrs. Eddy's system, like disease, an illusion; there is no such thing. "The belief" of it is in the beginning "an unconscious error" (ed. 1899, p. 81), it "exists only so long as the material illusion remains" (p. 207), and what "must die" is "not the sinful soul" but "the sense of sin" (*ibid.*). It is amusing to observe as we read *Science and Health*, how often, in the preoccupation with sickness as the thing from which we look to Christian Science for relief, sin comes in as an afterthought. The book itself, it is to be noticed, is a treatise on "Science and *Health*"; and what the author professes to have discovered is "the adaptation of Truth to *the treatment of disease*"—to which is added, plainly as an afterthought, "as well as of sin." "The question of What is Truth," she adds in the next paragraph, "is answered by demonstration—*by healing disease*"—"and sin" she adds again as an afterthought. Consequently she goes on to say, "This shows that Christian *healing* confers the most health," "and," she adds weakly, "makes the best men." This preoccupation with sickness rather than sin is grounded, no doubt, in part, in the historical genesis of the system and of the book in which it is presented. It was not as a religious leader but as a healer that Mrs. Eddy came forward, treading in the footsteps of Quimby, who was not a religious leader but a healer. Her theories were religious only because, pushing Quimby's suggestions into express declarations, she found his "all is mind" completing itself in "all mind is God." Her religion, in other words, existed for its healing value, and her interest in it was as a curative agent. Sickness and healing were the foci around which the ellipse of her thought was thrown. Christian Scientists, therefore, teach that there is no such thing as sin; and sin, like disease, is to be treated by denial. C. H. Lea, *A Plea for . . . Christian Science*,[2] 1915, p. 29, says that God, being perfect, all His creations must also be perfect; "consequently that He did not and could not create a sinful man, or even a man that could become sinful." We can never be separated from God; "the apparent separation of man from God is, according to Christian Science teaching, due to the false human consciousness or mortal's sense of sin" (p. 39).

52. One gains the impression that Mrs. Eddy was even exceptionally troubled by sickness. In the *Christian Science Journal* for

June, 1902 (*McClure's Magazine*, February, 1908, p. 399), a contributor very sensibly writes: "Do not Scientists make a mistake in conveying the impression, or, what is the same thing, letting an impression go uncorrected, that those in Science are never sick, that they never have any ailments or troubles to contend with? There is no Scientist who at all times is wholly exempt from aches and pains or from trials of some kind." The "Scientists," of course, are between the two horns of a dilemma, for how can they "deny" sickness without "denying" it! A physician gives this account of an experience of his own with this stoicism of denial (*The New Church Review*, 1908, vol. XV, p. 419): "I was called to a Christian Scientist who was supposed to be sick. I found her hard at work in the kitchen, for she was a boarding-house keeper. I asked her where she felt sick, and she said 'nowhere.' I asked her if she had any pain, and she replied, 'none,' and that she felt as well as usual. I found her carrying a high fever and both lungs becoming solid with pneumonia. I called her husband aside and told him she was probably nearly through, but that she ought to go to bed and be cared for. She insisted upon remaining up and making some biscuit for supper, and did so. She soon lapsed into unconsciousness, and passed away. Just before her consciousness left her, she told me she did have pains and did feel sick, but was taught not to say so, and what was more, to persuade herself it was not so, and that her disease was only an illusion." And then this physician adds: "I speak frankly, as the need is, but I have seen those of this belief with heart disease, saying they were well, yet suffering week after week, till death released them. I have seen them with malignant growths becoming steadily worse, but as I inquired about them I was told they were getting better, and the growth was disappearing; but only for the undertaker to inform me a little later of their loathsome condition. I have seen children . . . hurried down to an untimely grave with appendicitis, while being told practically that there was nothing the matter with them."

53. Observe the case of permitting a baby to die, reprinted in *McClure's Magazine*, October, 1907, pp. 693 ff., from the *Christian Science Journal* of March, 1889, p. 637; but most people will be satisfied if they will but glance over the sixty-eight cases of Christian Science treatments collected by Stephen Paget in pp. 151–180 of his *The Faith and Works of Christian Science*. He closes with a scathing arraignment based on what he, as a physician, finds in them (p. 180): "Of course, to see the full iniquity of these cases, the reader should be a doctor, or should go over them with a doctor. But everybody, doctor or not, can feel the cruelty, born of

fear of pain, in some of these Scientists—the downright madness threatening not a few of them—and the appalling self-will. They bully dying women, and let babies die in pain; let cases of paralysis tumble about and hurt themselves; rob the epileptic of their bromide, the syphilitic of their iodide, the angina cases of their amyl-nitrate, the heart cases of their digitalis; let appendicitis go on to septic peritonitis, gastric ulcer to perforation of the stomach, nephritis to uræmic convulsions, and strangulated hernia to the *miserere mei* of gangrene; watch day after day, while a man or a woman slowly bleeds to death; compel them who should be kept still to take exercise; and withhold from all cases of cancer all hope of cure. To these works of the devil they bring their one gift, wilful and complete ignorance; and their 'nursing' would be a farce if it were not a tragedy. Such is the way of Christian Science, face to face, as she loves to be, with bad cases of organic disease." For the legal questions involved, see William A. Purrington, *Christian Science, an Exposition of Mrs. Eddy's wonderful Discovery, including the Legal Aspects: a Plea for Children and other helpless Sick*, 1900.

54. Ed. 1906, p. 12.

55. Ed. 1899, p. 34.

56. *American Journal of Psychology*, X, 1908–1909, p. 435.

57. See *McClure's Magazine*, May, 1907, p. 103, cited above, note 41.

58. Ed. 1899, p. 443.

59. *Ibid.*

60. Ed. 1899, pp. 49–51.

61. P. 70.

62. Marcus Aurelius says: "Do not suppose you are hurt and your complaint ceases. Cease your complaint and you are not hurt."

63. *Mesmerism and Christian Science*, p. 282.

64. *McClure's Magazine*, June, 1908, p. 184.

65. Ed. 1899, p. 118.

66. Ed. 1881, I, p. 269.

67. Ed. 1899, p. 411.

68. Ed. 1903, p. 174.

69. *McClure's Magazine*, June, 1908, p. 184; *cf. Science and Health*, ed. 1906, pp. 382–383; ed. 1899, p. 381.

70. *Miscellaneous Writings*, p. 288.

71. P. 289.

72. *Science and Health*, ed. 1891, p. 529, and subsequent editions up to and including 1906.

73. Ed. 1881, II, p. 152: "Until the spiritual creation is dis-

cerned and the union of male and female apprehended in its soul sense, this rite should continue"; ed. 1899, p. 274: "Until it is learned that generation rests on no sexual basis, let marriage continue."

74. On this whole subject, see especially Powell, *op. cit.*, chap. VIII; Podmore, *op. cit.*, pp. 294 ff.; Paget, *op. cit.*, pp. 18 ff. When it is declared in the later editions of *Science and Health, e. g.*, 1907, p. 68, that Mrs. Eddy does not believe in "agamogenesis," that must be understood as consistent with teaching asexual generation, or else taken merely for "the present distress"; in these same editions she teaches asexual generation for the better time to come. *Cf.* the commentators already mentioned.

75. The materiality of Mrs. Eddy's golden age seems to be made very clear from the teaching that not sin and disease merely but death itself is non-existent, and will finally cease on due "demonstration." When Miss Milmine says that "a sensationless body" is, according to Mrs. Eddy, the ultimate hope of Christian Science (*McClure's Magazine*, June, 1908, p. 184), she apparently accurately expresses the fact. It seems that we are never to be without a body. It is, though illusion, nevertheless projected with inevitable certainty by "mortal mind." But it is to be a perfect body in the end, free from all the defects with which it is unfortunately now projected. The excitement which Mrs. Eddy manifested, and her manner of speech at Mr. Eddy's death, show her point of view very clearly. "My husband," she wrote to the Boston *Post*, June 5, 1882 (*McClure's Magazine*, September, 1907, p. 570), "never spoke of death as something we are to meet, but only as a phase of mortal being."

76. As quoted by Powell, *op. cit.*, p. 127.

77. *Op. cit.*, p. 106.

78. Ed. 1899, p. 387.

79. This is the conventional mode of speech among Christian Scientists, and may be read afresh any day. Thus Margaret Wright, answering some inquiries in the New York *Evening Sun* of October 17, 1916, quite simply writes: "As to eating, if one feels hungry and can get good food, the sensible thing to do is eat. If they did not do so Christian Scientists would be thought sillier than they already are. Also, if one can't see without eyeglasses one must have them until one's understanding of truth enables one to dispense with them. That is practical, and Christian Scientists are a practical people, or should be." *Cf.* note 85 on p. 325.

80. See particularly, Richard C. Cabot, M.D., "One Hundred Christian Science Cures," in *McClure's Magazine*, August, 1908, pp.

472–476, in which a hundred consecutive "testimonies" published in the *Christian Science Journal* are analyzed from the physician's point of view; and Stephen Paget, *The Faith and Works of Christian Science*, 1909, pp. 99–129, in which two hundred consecutive "testimonies" are brought together; also A. T. and F. W. H. Myers, "Mind-Cure, Faith-Cure and the Miracles of Lourdes," in the *Proceedings of the Society of Psychical Research*, vol. IX (1893), pp. 160–176.

81. Luther T. Townsend, *Faith Work, Christian Science and Other Cures*, p. 56.

82. Ed. 1899, p. 400.

83. Powell, *op. cit.*, p. 174.

84. Powell, *op. cit.*, pp. 174–175, and notes 6 and 7, p. 246; Paget, *op. cit.*, pp. 70 and 231–232; both going back to W. H. Muldoon, *Christian Science Claims Unscientific and Non-Christian*, 1901, pp. 30–31, who cites Mrs. Eddy herself, in Boston *Herald*, December, 1900 (*cf. Literary Digest*, December 29, 1900).

85. The natural embarrassment of Mrs. Eddy in the presence of physical need is equally amusingly illustrated by a story told by Miss Milmine of the days of her earlier teaching in Boston (1878). "Occasionally," she says (*McClure's Magazine*, August, 1907, p. 456), "a visitor would ask Mrs. Eddy why she used glasses instead of overcoming the defect in her eyesight by mind. The question usually annoyed her, and on one occasion she replied sharply that she 'wore glasses because of the sins of the world,' probably meaning that the belief in failing eyesight (due to age) had become so firmly established throughout the ages, that she could not at once overcome it." This, too, was concession to "mortal mind." Compare note 79, p. 324.

86. *The Treatment of Disease*, 1909, quoted by H. G. G. Mackensie, in *Medicine and the Church*, edited by Geoffrey Rhodes, 1910, p. 122.

87. Charlotte Lilias Ramsay, who writes the article "Christian Science," in Hastings's *Encyclopedia of Religion and Ethics*, vol. III, pp. 576–579, in lieu of adding the ordinary "Literature" to the article, informs us that "there is no authorized Christian Science literature except that which issues from the Christian Science Publishing House in Boston, Mass." "The Student of Christian Science," she adds, "must be warned not to accept any other as genuine." Nevertheless, she gives us, here, this brief sketch. Lewis Clinton Strang gives us a similar one in *The New Schaff-Herzog Encyclopedia of Religious Knowledge*, vol. X, pp. 288–291, which would appear to be even more authoritative, as bearing at its head this "Note,"

signed by Mrs. Eddy: "I have examined this article, edited it, and now approve it." The *New Schaff-Herzog* article is rendered more valuable by the adjunction to it of two others, a "Judicial Estimate of the System," by Lyman P. Powell, and a "Critical View of the Doctrines," by J. F. Carson—the whole closing with an extensive bibliography. There is nevertheless added at vol. XII, p. 550, as a "Statement from the Christian Science Committee on Publication of the First Church, Boston," a biographical article on Mrs. Eddy, signed by Eugene R. Cox. Mrs. Eddy's *Science and Health, with Key to the Scriptures*, is, of course, the source-book for the system of teaching. First issued in 1875 (pp. 564) it has gone through innumerable editions; the first edition of the text revised by J. H. Wiggin was published in 1885; but the book has undergone much minor revision since. According to the trust-deed by which the site of "the Mother Church" in Boston is held, all the editions, since at least the seventy-first, are equally authoritative. We have used chiefly the one hundred and sixty-first (1899, pp. 663). Besides the suggestions given by C. Lilias Ramsay, a list of Mrs. Eddy's writings and of the "Publications of the Christian Science Publishing Society" may be found in Appendix H to C. H. Lea's *A Plea for the Thorough and Unbiased Investigation of Christian Science, and a Challenge to its Critics*, second edition, 1915. A good classified bibliography is prefixed to Lyman P. Powell's *Christian Science: the Faith and its Founder*, 1907. The authorized life of Mrs. Eddy is Sibyl Wilbur's *Life of Mary Baker Eddy*, 1908. Georgine Milmine's *Life of Mary Baker Eddy and History of Christian Science*, first published in *McClure's Magazine* for 1907–1908, was issued in book form in 1909; it gives the ascertained facts, and forms the foundation for a critical study of the movement. The books which, along with it, we have found, on the whole, most useful, are Powell's, Podmore's, and Paget's; but the literature is very extensive and there are many excellent guides to the study of the system. Even fiction has been utilized. Clara Louise Burnham's *The Right Princess* (Boston, Houghton Mifflin Co., 1902), for example, is a very attractive plea for Christian Science; and Edward Eggleston's *The Faith Doctor* (a story of New York), 1891, is a strong presentation of the social situation created by it. An interesting episode in the history of Christian Science may be studied in two books published through G. P. Putnam's Sons, New York, by Augusta E. Stetson, entitled respectively: *Reminiscences, Sermons, and Correspondence Proving Adherence to the Principles of Christian Science as Taught by Mary Baker Eddy*, and *Vital Issues in Christian Science, a Record, etc.* A good recent discussion of the inner meaning of Christian Science will be found in the article by L. W. Snell, entitled "Method of Christian Science," in *The Hibbert Journal* for April, 1915, pp. 620–629. Walter S. Harris, *Christian Science and the Ordinary Man*, 1917, seeks to argue afresh the fundamental question. Among the most recent books, see also: George M. Searle (a Paulist Father), *The Truth about Christian Science*, 1916; and W. McA. Goodwin (a "Christian Science Practitioner, Teacher, and Lecturer"), *A Lecture entitled The Christian Science Church*, 1916.